FORBIDDEN FRUIT

FORBIDDEN FRUIT

The Golden Age of the Exploitation Film

**by Felicia Feaster
and
Bret Wood**

**Midnight Marquee Press, Inc.
Baltimore, Maryland**

Front Cover:
Cover Design: A.S. Miller

Copyright © 1999 by Felicia Feaster and Bret Wood
Without limiting the rights under copyright reserved above, no part of this publication may be reproduced, stored in or introduced into a retrieval system, or transmitted, in any form, or by any means (electronic, mechanical, photocopying, recording, or otherwise), without the prior written permission of the copyright owners or the publishers of the book.

ISBN 1-887664-24-6
Library of Congress Catalog Card Number 99-70128
Manufactured in the United States of America
Printed by Kirby Lithographic Company, Arlington, VA
First Printing by Midnight Marquee Press, Inc., April, 1999

Acknowledgments: Ronald V. Borst/Hollywood Movie Posters, Betty Cavanaugh, Photofest, Michael H. Price, Wayne Shipley, Linda J. Walter

**Dedication
To the memory of Will Hays,
for making it all possible.**

Table of Contents

- 8   **Introduction**
- 12   **Chapter 1:** The Exploitation Phenomenon
- 41   **Chapter 2:** In the Beginning
- 55   **Chapter 3:** Survival in the Shadows
- 73   **Chapter 4:** Social Climate
- 96   **Chapter 5:** The Show on the Road
- 124 **Chapter 6:** Sideshows and Skinshows
- 144 **Chapter 7:** No More Make Believe
- 173 **Chapter 8:** Soft-Core and Hard-Sell
- 190 **Chapter 9:** Our Secret History
- 198 **Notes**
- 202 **Filmography**
- 217 **Index**

INTRODUCTION

Just as the storybook Hollywood film preaches romantic couplings and happy endings, many histories of the medium offer an idyllic, if inaccurate, view of an era of cinema dreamily referred to as the Golden Age. Commemorating the biggest and the best while offering lower-profile films and filmmakers little more than disdain, traditional film history has often denied the fact that motion pictures began as a lowbrow entertainment for the uneducated masses.

In elaborate theaters such as S.L. Rothafel's New York Roxy (self-proclaimed "Cathedral of the Motion Picture") and Sid Grauman's Chinese Theatre in Hollywood, armies of dapper ushers may have escorted patrons across red carpets and along marble balustrades, but most American movie houses at that time more closely resembled the Lyric Theatre of Tuckahoe, New York, as described by journalist Art Seidenbaum:

> A squat of plaster between a drugstore and a shoe store... The architecture was forgettable, a rectangle of four walls, slightly curved to suggest aspirations of art moderne. No balcony. No center aisle. No sculpture, no cherubs or open skies on the ceiling.[1]

While a few of the more fortunate movie palaces have been saved from the wrecking ball by historical societies and ambitious chambers of commerce, the small-town, single-screen Main Street theaters continue to quietly succumb to the destructive forces of economic progress, pulled to the ground without fanfare or remorse to make room for parking lots to service new shopping malls that cancerously expand, spawning franchise video rental stores and shoe-box multiplexes. As these modest emblems of a bygone era vanish into oblivion, the complex secrets disappear that these sturdy sentinels once contained. It's a history of the American movies that doesn't jibe with the accepted, idealistic view; a story of brash, vulgar films and a cine-subculture driven by unmitigated greed and the puckish desire to flaunt authority, populated by figures who have long since faded into obscurity.

Cataracts of nostalgia and historical ignorance fog our view of the movie past, obscuring the disreputable pictures that often stained the screens of middle America. Photographs and reenactments of jolly children storming the matinee box office or smartly dressed couples munching popcorn in the reassuring glow of the projected image deny the existence of a mysterious breed of film that was occasionally unspooled in these same picture houses. The crowds that queued up along the sidewalks to see *these* films more closely resembled the throngs of jobless men or women in the breadlines of Depression-stricken New York. Like the shaggier, worn-at-the-elbows crowds they attracted, these films weren't the luminous fantasies sent down from a Hollywood on-high. Their images were generally poorly composed and photographed, the prints were battered and coated in scratches, resisting the technical basics of focus and coherent sound. But the greatest difference between these lowly films and their reputable cousins wasn't so much form as content.

The crowds who trudged to these utilitarian Main Street theaters sought a break from Hollywood make-believe. They came seeking reality in undiluted doses. What they actually found was a bizarre mixture of the two: saccharine morality tales interrupted by moments of raw, ugly truth that studio films would never dare broach.

Behind its innocuous title, the 1944 film *Mom and Dad* (the slick, big-budget *Gone With the Wind* of the exploitation cinema) contained a cargo of bodily trauma. The film regaled crowds of anxious men and women with graphic shots of human bodies covered with ugly raw blisters and chancres. A mouth is opened wide to permit a closer view of a gaping hole in the palate. Detailed closeups showcase flesh rotting away from swollen, discolored eye-sockets. The ravages of venereal disease are shown in remarkable, painful detail. Men and women with their faces hidden, move their bodies, turning arms and legs, opening mouths and reveal their pocked genitalia to allow healthy Americans an intimate look at its worst nightmare, an affront to the national virtue.

Exploring not only the most sordid consequence of sexual intercourse, but also the most sublime, *Mom and Dad* also exposed the gruesome beauty of childbirth at a time when it was more of a mystery to the average American than ever before. Heralding a new age in American health care, deliveries were now performed, not at home by family members and midwives, but in sterilized surgical theaters from which relatives were prohibited. A new taboo surrounding the pregnant woman's body cloaked the grisly reality of childbirth, which *Mom and Dad* was all too happy to reveal. While the respectable citizenry euphemistically referred to pregnancy as "being in a family way" or "expecting," *Mom and Dad* adopted the less gleeful phrase "in trouble," which characterized child-bearing as more of a curse than a blessing.

A portion of *Mom and Dad* consists of a sex hygiene lecture illustrated by an instructional film delivered to a classroom of students (mirroring those in the movie house receiving an education of their own). *The Story of Birth*, as the movie-within-the-movie is called, presents animated drawings of the reproductive system, documenting the biological melodrama that has unfurled in countless health classes across the nation, of the movement of spermatozoa into the uterus, and the subsequent growth of the fetus within the womb. The climax of the film, however, is a live-action jolt after the quaintly oblique diagrams; a graphic motion picture image of a woman, barely visible and cloaked in an expanse of white sheets, giving birth. A doctor's hands lure a baby's head from her vagina. Blood gushes from her body. In the triumphant moment, the entire wriggling newborn is outstretched in a fluid tableaux against his anonymous mother's headless body, kicking against the cold air. His mouth is open but no sound issues forth. And the film's *pièce de résistance*? The childbirth equivalent of a rabbit pulled from a magician's hat: a bold encore in which a second baby is drawn not from between a woman's legs but directly through her stomach via a cesarean incision.

Dozens of such films were exhibited in the big-city and small-town theaters of America, motion pictures later christened "exploitation films" for capitalizing on such delicate issues as venereal disease, childbirth, drug abuse, abortion, prostitution, polygamy, nudism and a host of other thrillingly unwholesome topics. Of these films, *Mom and Dad*, "a lighthouse in the dismal darkness of human ignorance" as its producer cooed in typically florid fashion, was the most popular, reputed to have grossed over $100 million during its life span. A spectacle of flesh and finger-wagging caution-

Looking more like a Depression-era breadline than festive moviegoers, these sex education-starved women circle the block for a segregated screening of Dwain Esper's *Modern Motherhood*, complete with "Dynamic Sex Lecture."

ary tale, *Mom and Dad* stands out as the film which best represents the many bizarre and compelling facets of this seldom-discussed genre.

Prior to the advent of television and home video, the commercial life of a Hollywood picture was measured in weeks. *Mom and Dad*, on the other hand, had a "screen life" of more than 20 years, steadily criss-crossing the nation in an erratic route more akin to the carnival's perennial course than the limited shelf-life of the film distribution loop.

Though it boasted an "All Star Cast," this enticement seemed part of the hopeful deception that fueled exploitation; few of the faces in the film were recognizable. But exploitation's strongest selling point was not the "who" but the *what*, and the glorious spectacle of blood and flesh anticipated like the sickening lurch of a roller coaster plunging down its iron tracks. Oftentimes a film was given a greater novelty value and the magic of a one-of-a-kind performance by the presence of a live lecturer who traveled with the film and introduced it to the local audience, often with the help of several assistants.

The question one inevitably faces when exploring the exploitation film is "why bother?" Is there anything of merit in these crudely produced movies shamelessly engineered to separate an undiscerning public from its hard-earned greenbacks? In a postmodern culture enamored with ironic distance, exploitation films have become yet another relic of an assumedly kitschy past, a diversionary giggle for fans of the outré to plug into VCRs between Russ Meyer and John Waters videos.

Can we learn anything about the art and industry of cinema in its first 100 years from these lowbrow features that received little national attention and were forgotten a few years after they were made? The answer is an unqualified yes. A bounty of insight into the history of the cinema and, also the culture of the 1930s and '40s, can be gleaned from the exploitation film... if one only looks beyond their often hackneyed and amateurish surface. Just as the visual arts have come to embrace the folk art of unschooled, "primitive" artists, exploitation should be seen in a similar light: a cinematic naif art as revealing and sublime as the more polished work of establishment filmmakers.

Exploitation is cinema in the raw. It delivers its visceral charge without the polish and pretense that characterize the critics' darlings: the studio mega-productions and cultish low-budget art films. And as much as the respectable cinema would like to ignore this bastard sibling—laughing it off as camp, schlock or golden turkeys—it lingers resolutely about the fringe, an unwelcome reminder of what, beneath all the multi-million-dollar dressings, the American cinema has always been and continues to be about. Stare into the face of cinema. Strip away the pomp and glory, the high literary subjects and chintzy gold-plated statuettes and you will see, not the lofty ideals of visionary artists, but weary bodies slapping against one another in love and in anger, overwrought melodramas, unabashed carnality, hollow morality, low comedy and carnivalesque theatricality. Within cavernous, sweltering soundstages, actors and technicians struggle madly at their trade, watched over and motivated not by some common muse but by a bottom-line Philistine, rubbing his palms together in anxious anticipation of a film's opening grosses. Both the exploitation hack and his highbrow Hollywood cousin may dream occasionally of laurels; but they lust for the sum total of all the dimes, quarters and dollars that can be wrested from the fingers of a fickle public. Modern-day movie advertising, with its high concepts and its trumpeting of critical accolades (which proclaim *every* movie the best of its kind), are only "tasteful" imitations of the gaudy lobby displays and sensational posters offering timeless queries like "What Makes a Husband Untrue?" and "What Causes Frigid Wives?" and feverish promises to fulfill every dream and reveal every secret.

At the heart of every film—highbrow or low—is a promise of solace or excitement, one of the endless catalog of vicarious pleasures absent from ordinary life. The desire for escape or revelation which drew exploitation moviegoers into the grubby palaces of education and bottom-feeding vice are only less refined versions of the same desires felt by a 1930s shop girl attending an Astaire and Rogers musical, a '50s family of four slurping Cokes at the Miracle Mile drive-in, a '70s film student in a crowded classroom seeking vicarious flight from the encroaching responsibilities of adulthood.

During its most prolific, definitive, two-decade reign, the exploitation film thrived in America, tearing away the trappings of respectability and allowing the public to revel in all its crude, bare-bones majesty. Along the way, these strange little films irrevocably altered the course of film history with a cultural sucker-punch that will continue to be felt on movie screens for many years. Looking upon the exploitation film's remnants, like leaves in a teacup in a midway palmistry hut, we can discern far more about the cinema than its creators ever imagined their quickly assembled audience flytraps were capable of revealing.

Chapter One

THE EXPLOITATION PHENOMENON

> When people lived by the land the facts of life came in a natural way. Modern complex city life has made it necessary for each individual to gain his knowledge through scholastic education, parental instructions, or through reading and study, supplemented by observation and experience.
>
> Sex knowledge is vitally important to persons of every age and station in life, and is essential for happiness and wellbeing.
>
> —Hildagarde Esper, *Your Sex Questions Answered... What Every Modern Mother and Father Should Know*

Before sex education invaded secondary school curricula and Hollywood dared expose the bronzed flesh of its icons to the prying eyes of lowly ticket-buyers, there were few sources of sexual information and titillation. Stolen glances at medical encyclopedias, *National Geographic*s and bathing relatives were all the education some were allowed, while the more adventurous might glimpse the wonders of copulation in Tijuana Bibles, the vulgar, pocket-sized eight-page comics where unlicensed effigies of Popeye and Moon Mullins waved two-foot penises beneath the jaded, unimpressed eyes of Betty Boop or Mae West.

In the prevailing darkness and uncertainty of the Great Depression, the exploitation film positioned itself as the forum where this widely shared, desperate hunger for carnal enlightenment was satisfied.

In myriad small towns across America, the independent theater was akin to the biblical tree of knowledge. Beguiled by serpents in black suits distributing colorful handbills, unschooled Adams and Eves approached the tree, nervously passed a quarter through the semicircular archway cut in the box office glass, then slinked inside to sit in the ice-cooled shade of the theater's velvet and gilt boughs. With darkness' descent came luminous revelation of society's most tantalizing forbidden fruit.

The implications of tasting this tainted apple were unclear. One could never be sure whether exploitation filmmakers were more concerned with imparting a life-enriching moral lesson or just gaily (and graphically) depicting a character's moral plunge into depravity. Sure, Ann Dixon's 11th-hour plea for her parents' forgiveness puts a sweet family-values closure on *Road to Ruin*. But it's a wan, watery finale to a film more interested in the gross and sordid tale of two bad, bad girls learning a hard lesson about the clap, wily playboys and backroom abortions. The film's last-minute "message" has all the sincerity of a Catholic schoolgirl repenting in morning confession for her previous night's sins even as she plots her next evening's adventures.

The illuminating message that each exploitation film offered as a matter of course was little more than a standard, half-hearted effort to placate public officials who might attempt to censor the film and to accommodate the viewer who needed the pretense of education to allow herself to indulge in such prurient displays.

The secret to endurance in the field of exploitation was an ability to maintain a pretense of serving a high moral purpose no matter how iniquitous one's films. Dwain and Hildagarde Esper, a husband and wife director and screenwriter of exploitation classics such as *How to Undress, Narcotic, Modern Motherhood* and *Marihuana: Weed With Roots in Hell* and two of the genre's most notorious figures, were careful not to call their work "sex pictures," "drug movies" or "exploitation films." Instead, the couple referred rather euphemistically to their films as "sensational pictures," a socially acceptable term that disguised the carnality of their film collaborations. The fact that the Espers devoted significant creative energy to at least two films investigating the important anthropological topic of native women mating with gorillas (*Forbidden Adventure* and *Bo-ru the Ape Boy*) should arouse a healthy dose of skepticism toward the nobility of their crusade.

As this 14" x 22" window card illustrates, marijuana was only one of many vices exploited in Dwain Esper's 1936 feature.

The viewer had no way of knowing in advance how ripe—or just plain rotting on the vine—the fruit being served to them would be, since virtually all exploitation films were promoted at the same pitch of demented sensationalism. While revelations of the secrets of humankind's degeneration were promised with every poster, handbill and print ad, the film itself might deliver anything from a cranky dowager's tedious lecture on the errors of today's youth, to the fascinating image of a fetus being violently forcepped from a glistening womb. Those precious seconds in which unclothed skin was at last exposed to the lens might offer up the nubile breasts of giggling skinny-dippers or a syphilitic penis being fondled with black rubber gloves to expose the areas of greatest decay. Like a game of three-card monte, you could either win big, or walk away with the sickening feeling of a concave-chested lad after his first dance with a crafty B-girl,

Kisses were always slightly bitter in the sin-infested world of exploitation, as shown in this still from *What Price Innocence?* **(Photofest)**

of being magnificently had. The mystery that surrounded each screening was part of the serpentine charm the exploitation film offered its anxious viewer. If it was, as roadshowman David Friedman has suggested, curiosity that drew crowds to exploitation, it was the paradoxical narcotic of fascination and revulsion also found in horror and pornography that kept them glued to their seats. Or in some cases, passed out under them; grown men were often reduced to swooning maidens by the sight of a gory C-section. Not ones to waste any scrap of scandal, exploiteers would then have these faint victims transported to cots in the theater lobby to highlight the unique thrills of that night's screening. And exhibitors seemed pleased with the results of such garish showmanship. As a theater owner showing 1933's sex education picture about a girl rendered pregnant out-of-wedlock, who drowns herself in shame in *What Price Innocence?* was happy to attest in one of the typically breathless dispatches from the motion picture frontier:

> Put forth an extra effort on this picture and was amply rewarded. It's one of these program picture [sic] that come along once in a while that brings you out of the red caused by last high priced so-called special played.
> Your patrons will walk out satisfied.

That is, when their wobbly knees could carry them.

Exploitation films often appeared to be the tarnished, lowborn remedy for rural and small-town box offices crippled by the Hollywood practice of block-booking, who fought back with the seemingly sure-fire money-making antidote of exploitation. Nudism films proved especially fortuitous crowd-pleasers. A Pilot Point, Texas theater owner who played *Elysia* to an over-16 crowd trying "to take care of some of my losses on the lemons I have been getting," found that "business was good," adding of the exploiteer's classic bait-and-switch strategy he employed:

> Though it really is in the nude, it is a lot cleaner picture than a lot of the ones I have been showing. It will get the money if you advertise it as hot and that they shouldn't see it, etc., but after they have seen it they will tell you that it wasn't so hot. [2]

The title and subject of a film were never clear indicators of what would ultimately appear on screen, though salivation-triggering words like "Suicide," "Vice," "Slaves" and "Sex" suggested it wasn't going to be a ladies tea. Exploiteers, sensation size-queens, often veered madly from their educational itinerary as if driven by the same intractable, libidinal urges that led their naive protagonists to ruin, so that a film such as *They Must Be Told* (aka *Sex Madness*, 1938)— ostensibly made as a treatise on the 20th century's venereal plague of syphilis—dramatized not just ordinary premarital sex but prostitution, lesbianism and child molestation. Of all exploiteers, Esper seemed the least apt to be constrained by a single topic. His biblical phantasmagoria *The Seventh Commandment* (1932), dramatizing the consequences of adultery, also treated viewers to glimpses of strip poker, transvestitism, lesbianism, syphilis, a cesarean birth and, should this catalog of depravity fail to tantalize, a grisly facelift operation—all in a scant 65 minutes. For its sins, Esper's film was formally condemned as "indecent, obscene, immoral." It was also condemned because it would "tend to corrupt morals."

Original one-sheet poster from Dwain Esper's first film, *The Seventh Commandment*, of which only a small fragment survives today.

This window card from one of many reissues of Louis Gasnier's *Reefer Madness* demonstrates the "title switch" (the film was previously released as *Tell Your Children*), as well as the practice of plagiarizing poster art (see photo 189). The film was also released as *The Burning Question*.

Exploitation films are frequently dismissed for their rabid responses to such harmless threats as marijuana—rendering wholesome kids homicidal maniacs in three puffs. The most famous exploitation film of all time, *Reefer Madness* was offered to modern audiences as a joke, thereby setting the tone for later reception of exploitation. The National Organization for the Reform of Marijuana Laws (NORML) stumbled upon a print of the film and began screening it in 1971 as a means of mocking the government's demonization of the mild narcotic. Soon thereafter, indie distributor New Line Cinema began exhibiting the film to midnight movie audiences who guffawed at its campy cluelessness and added *Sex Madness* and *Cocaine Fiends* as two other rusty souvenirs from a dumber age. Many exploitation films are badly dated and quite campy in their treatment of American vice—and naturally enjoyable for the laughter they sometimes induce. As one of *Reefer Madness*' own performers, Thelma White (who played the vampy Mae, whose apartment is the setting for wild reefer parties) affirmed, exploitation filmmakers did their utmost to produce films that would provoke a visceral response in audiences. "The director wanted us to 'hoke' it up. He wanted us to show the 'madness.'" But unlike actor Timothy Farrell, who seemed to take some of exploitation's incompetence in stride, White was less pleased by her brief stint in its ranks. An RKO contract player loaned out by the studio to make *Reefer Madness*, White saw the film as an embarrassing footnote to her small-scale career, though it was ultimately her most lasting and famous role. She remarked: "I'm ashamed to say that it's the only one of my films that's become a classic."[3]

But the hysteria surrounding marijuana in the 1930s was no less rabid than the Juvenile Delinquency scare of the 1950s, the LSD paranoia of the 1960s or the crack-phobia of the 1980s. Like many drug wars it was a veiled campaign to regulate private behavior. Exploitation capitalized on misinformation and ignorance to ostensibly save gullible youth from the temptations of narcotics, in a manner no less fanatical than the government authorities and supposedly educated sources fanning the same fires of hophead hysteria.

Exploitation filmmakers were hardly goodwill ambassadors duped by the government into fighting a war on drugs. Rather than the hayseeds contemporary audiences (many of whom actually believed the government's claims that reefer was a short road to insanity) often take them for, exploiteers were crafty business people who found a way to profit from society's widespread ignorance and insatiable curiosity. And the more that we learn about the men and women who made such films, the more it appears that they approached the subject matter with tongue planted firmly in cheek, skillfully exploiting America's fears, playfully exaggerating the dangers of vice and, in the end, pocketing the millions of dollars in dimes and quarters offered by a confused populace in search of enlightenment and titillation.

As late as 1972, Dwain Esper was able to convince an Arizona Supreme Court jury that his films (including *Reefer Madness*, a film the notoriously wily Esper did not even direct) were sponsored by the U.S. Government. Shan Sayles, who was engaged in the lawsuit, recalls:

> "He testified under oath in court that that film had been made by him at the request of the United States government and he convinced a jury of that, which was absolutely a blatant lie. And it was absolutely amaz-

ing how he was able to manipulate this jury—not only through his story but through his manner and his dress, what have you, of being a good ole boy."[4]

Just as the exploiteer's primary concern was not liberating his customers from the catacombs of ignorance, moviegoers also turned to exploitation for something beyond moral betterment. The explorations of vice promised vivid displays of human shame and debauchery, and it was for this dramatization that tickets were purchased. The resurgent camp interest in films like *Reefer Madness* often presumes cinema has evolved into a more enlightened, knowing medium, far more sophisticated than creaky, amateurish exploitation. But in reality, current film is only more practiced at hiding its replaying of old conventions.

The "camp" or "kitsch" response to exploitation assumes contemporary viewers are somehow more "in the know" than the exploiteers who were themselves a crew of lowbrow pranksters, charlatans, hucksters and rebels living outside middlebrow notions of good taste and earning an honest living—committed to making a sawbuck off the public thirst for flesh parades.

Another gullible teen falls prey to the temptation of marijuana in a scene from *Reefer Madness* (1936). Clockwise from top left: Carleton Young as Jack, Dave O'Brien as Ralph, Thelma White as Mae, Kenneth Craig as Bill and Lillian Miles as Blanche.

A young college student spends a fateful night with a fast woman, only to face the venereal consequences years later in *Because of Eve*.

Obviously the exploitation cinema's role as a legitimate educational tool was as spurious as the pedophilic scoutmaster professing to teach his young charges the merits of good citizenship and knot tying. The filmmakers' underlying, ultimate apathy and comprehension of drug or reproductive issues all affected these films and the degree of truth, conjecture or outright bad advice they gave their audiences. It is too late now to assess what effect these mixed messages preached within a context of greater sexual repression had upon yesteryear's youth. One can only look back at this distant era and wonder.

As with any genre, from film noir to melodrama, there is no absolute formula for defining which films belong in the fold. However, it is possible to assemble a very reliable model of the typical exploitation film by examining the genre's distinctive features. Exploitation (as in "the act of exploiting") has always been and will undoubtedly remain a central facet of the motion picture industry as a whole. The specific exploitation movement chronicled in this book, however, is of a particular style, practiced in its most representative phase in an era that coincides with Hollywood's most repressive censorship. The Production Code instituted in 1934 and outmoded by the mid-1950s defined the parameters of exploitation's most prolific decades and allowed exploitation to flourish as an alternative to its strictures. The exploitation films of these years were characterized by a kind of tabloid sensationalism, devoting thousands of feet of celluloid to topics unsuitable for dinner-table discussion. In flagrantly bogus crusades of public betterment, filmmakers used these issues as a license to indulge in every imaginable vice.

Often there was an effort to maintain a certain dignity and sensitivity when addressing these delicate subjects, but more often the "problem" was dramatized, hyperbolized and demonized to such gross extremes that it hardly constitutes a serious investigation of social ills.

If defined according to the moral pitfalls depicted on screen, the exploitation film can be divided into five general categories: drug scare, sex education, wayward women, documentary and social problem film.

Audiences were invited to experience Dwain Esper's *Narcotic* as not only a drug expose, but as a voyeuristic glimpse of sexual depravity.

DRUG SCARE. Probably the best known exploitation film is *Tell Your Children*, re-introduced in typically tongue-in-cheek, comical fashion to the midnight movie circuit in the 1970s under the title *Reefer Madness* by New Line Cinema. This picture of teenagers turned into sex maniacs and killers by marijuana may have looked outrageously campy to a savvier, post-1960s audience taught that harder drugs like LSD and Angel Dust were the *real* menace. But *Reefer Madness* is at times a genuinely disturbing look at the Dr. Jekyll and Mr. Hyde transformation drugs can inspire; no less troubling a glimpse into the unfettered human psyche than Robert Louis Stevenson's classic novel. Dramatizing the physical and moral decay brought on by a few "harmless" puffs of marijuana, the drug scare film was sure to prominently feature an element of sex, capped off with harsh retribution for the curious drug user. Other titles in this subgenre include *Marihuana: Weed With Roots in Hell, Wild Weed* (aka *She Shoulda Said 'No'!*), *Assassin of Youth, Narcotic, The Pace That Kills* (aka *Cocaine Fiends*), *The Devil's Harvest* and *The Devil's Sleep* (aka *Hopped Up*).

SEX EDUCATION. Depicting the process by which naive couples are schooled in the perils and pleasures of sexual activity, marital advice films constituted a considerable portion of the exploitation genre. Usually involving the stern warnings and warm wishes of a paternal family doctor (who always seemed to have a 16mm projector and a few reels of syphilis footage handy to freak out his young patients), the sex-ed films ushered the ignorant pupils (be they on screen or in the theater) into a bright future of monogamy and sexual well-being. Titles include *Damaged Lives, Damaged Goods, Because of Eve, The Story of Bob and Sally*, and *Mom and Dad*. One film, *Mated* (sometimes referred to as *Mismated*), dispensed with the narrative format altogether, and functioned as a direct feature-length illustrated lecture covering virtually every aspect of reproductive health and disease. Unfortunately, *Mated* offered none of the wit and charm that makes the exploitation drama so endearing and so ripe for parody, as in the 1975 exploitation film send-up *The Rocky Horror Picture Show*, with its clash of

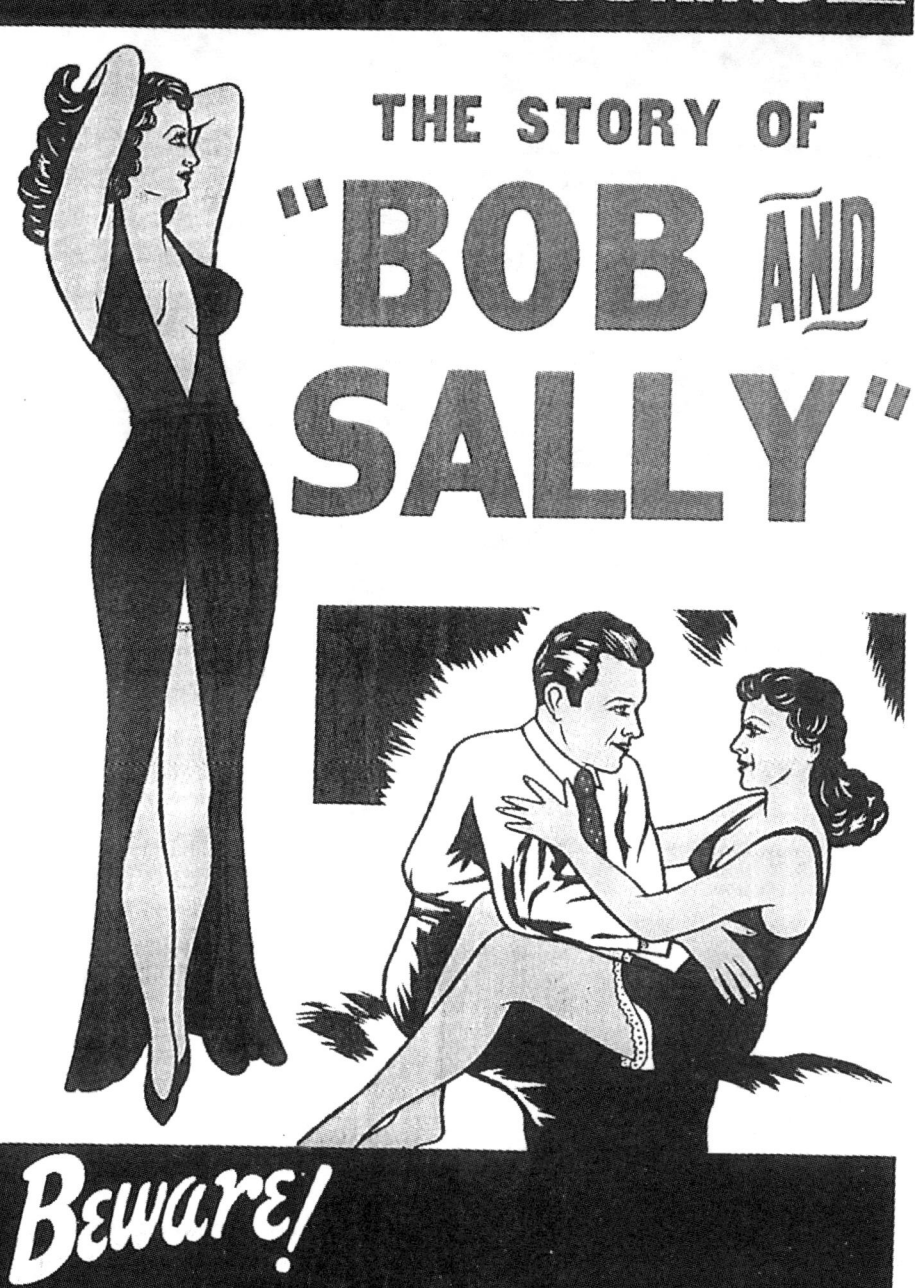

While not as elegant as the typical Hollywood movie poster, this crude placard for *The Story of Bob and Sally* **has a beauty all its own, oddly befitting the exploitation film's aesthetic spareness.**

sparkling innocence and deforming sexuality. When lecturers toured with a film, it was almost always the sex-ed picture, though resourceful speakers could tailor a spiel to any topic.

Another innocent youth is led down the path of destruction in Willis Kent's *The Wages of Sin*, starring Constance Worth (right) as good-girl-gone-bad Marjorie.

WAYWARD WOMEN. Similar to the sex-ed/marital advice film is the exploitation saga of the wayward woman. Cinematic renditions of parental warnings against female independence and sexual experimentation the wayward women film originated in the 19th-century melodramas of fallen women such as Thomas Hardy's *Tess of the D'Urbervilles* (1891), Gustave Flaubert's *Madame Bovary* (1857) and Alexandre Dumas' play *La Dame aux camelias* (1852). In a definitively 20th-century continuation of such cautionary tales and tragedies, exploitation films revealed the dire consequences of parking, petting and curfew-breaking more effectively than any maternal lecture or Sunday sermon... although most mothers and ministers would not have devoted quite so much lascivious attention to the girls' tumble from grace as the exploitation films did. By film's end, the once-innocent girl inevitably found herself a victim of white slavery, pregnant and unmarried, syphilitic or having narrowly escaped one of these ever-present threats to high school virtue. *The Road to Ruin, Wages of Sin, Slaves in Bondage, Reckless Decision, They Must Be Told, Enlighten Thy Daughter* and *Mad Youth* exemplify the wayward women phenomenon.

DOCUMENTARY. Explored in detail in chapter seven, the exploitation documentary used a mingling of authentic and fraudulent footage to expose the horrors and thrills of a schizophrenic range of subjects, from American crime to the sexual lawlessness of exotic African jungles, backed by typically sensational ad campaigns, overbearing voice-over narration and the requisite injection of exploitation's contradictory mire of titillating and revolting imagery.

SOCIAL PROBLEM. Endeavoring to broaden the exploitation boundaries of sex and drugs, many filmmakers developed projects around other controversies of the day, taking sensitive issues and splashing them like tabloid newspaper headlines across theater marquees. Quite often the filmmakers avoided taking a stand on either side of the issue in a mimicry of journalistic objectivity or else freakishly contradicted themselves by arguing both sides of the case in adherence to the exploitation tradition of never completely grasping the mechanics of the controversy in the first place (as in the examination of forced sterilization in *Tomorrow's Children*). These exploitation films tackled the topics of abortion (*Race Suicide*), child marriage (*Child Bride*), nudism (*Elysia, Unashamed*), the Ku Klux Klan (*Nation Aflame*) and polygamy (*Polygamy*). Religion even found itself the subject of several exploitation films. Knowing better than to point their critical lens at any widely shared belief, the exploiteers targeted scripture-twisting fanatics whom even the most devout worshiper would shun as in *The Lash of the Penitentes*, about a rogue religious group founded by Franciscan friars traveling with Spain's conquistadors, whose repertoire of worship is a Bettie Page/Catholicism hybrid of flagellation, crucifixion and torture. Instead of ideological mavericks unleashing their twisted, anti-establishment vision on their audiences, exploitation's makers were often just as conservative, moralistic, sexist or racist as Hollywood though they exhibited a far more populist, flavorful and hysterical streak.

In addition to matters of content, exploitation is characterized by distinctive methods of production, distribution and exhibition, as well as unique narrative structures and idiosyncratic visual devices. Such films are *always* low-budget independent productions and *not* the well-financed product of any of the major studios of the day. In fact, true exploitation films were a rung or two below the economic and respectability levels of not only the minor studios (such as Columbia and Republic) but also the so-called Poverty Row producers (Monogram, Educational, PRC and Mascot), into whose soundstages some exploitation producers scrambled after hours, leasing the studio's equipment and tailoring their scripts to take proper advantage of any standing sets at their disposal. If properly organized, a typical feature could be shot in a single week though a glossier production like *Reefer Madness* might take a luxurious three weeks to wrap.

The Lash of the Penitentes **proved that even religious fanaticism in the form of a New Mexican cult could be profitable if marketed with a little sex appeal.**

23

Main Street Girl was most likely an alternate title for J.D. Kendis' *Street Corner* (1950).

Exploitation films were produced not with studio money but usually from the investments of the same few self-made moguls—men such as J.D. Kendis, Kroger Babb, Louis Sonney, Dwain Esper and Willis Kent—who booked the films into theaters and in some cases traveled the byways of America to preside over the screenings firsthand. No fancy logos opened their films; the companies that they headed were short-lived concerns (Jay Dee Kay, Hygienic Productions, Roadshow Attractions, Hollywood Producers and Distributors and Real Life Productions, respectively) that have long since vanished from the corporate registry. A small crew, a sketchy script, an unrehearsed cast and a few thousand dollars were all that was needed to gain entry into the exploitation fold.

The beauty of the exploitation business was that success did not depend upon being born into a certain class or professionally established family. It required no formal training, just some hustle, bravado and an imagination both fertile and devious. A few good ideas and a driving determination to profit from breaking social taboos turned unsophisticated Everymen into prosperous film executives. The size of one's hometown seemed inversely proportionate to the size of one's success in the field. Exploitation's high priests came from the most brackish of backwater towns and exacted a kind of poetic vengeance upon their humble origins by plowing headlong into precisely the big-city vice they were warned of in their hayseed boyhood. Lees Creek, Ohio incubated the wily spirit of Kroger Babb; while Anniston, Alabama yielded Dave Friedman; Snohomish, Washington produced Dwain Esper. Previous occupations were likewise no indication of a future exploiteer's success. Babb was a professional sports referee, Esper a building contractor, J.D. Kendis a jeweler and Louis Sonney a policeman in Centralia, Washington.

They were men who translated their hardscrabble backgrounds, many of them cutting their teeth on the deprivations of the Great Depression, into a brass tacks work ethic of making the most from the least.

Exploitation actor Timothy Farrell, whose brilliantined hair, meticulously groomed sardine moustache and monotonal delivery make him exploitation's cut-rate Clark Gable, recalled the filmmaking process under producer George Weiss (Screen Classics) in the late 1940s and early '50s. When playing a central role, Farrell typically worked:

"three days of the five days' shooting, making the magnificent sum of $300 for the movie. It was a little over SAG minimum... We used the Jack Miles Studios in Larchmont, but mostly Quality Pictures on Santa Monica Boulevard, which was owned or leased by Merle Connell. And Merle, I think he did a lot of the set work, just like Jack Miles at his studio, building the sets, etc."[5]

In addition to the regular Poverty Row studios whose stages were always available for a price, there were several facilities that catered to the ultra-low-budget exploiteer. Foremost among these was the EVI Complex ("Capital of the Exploitation-Film Industry" its ads proudly proclaimed), built by Louis Sonney circa 1948. Located in Los Angeles along Cordova Street (a block removed from the more mainstream Film Row of Vermont Ave. and Washington Blvd.), the complex included office and storage space, leasable production equipment and even an Art Department where the eager exploiteer could start concocting a juicy ad campaign—as important to a film's success as the movie itself, maybe more so. Dwain Esper entered the business first as a landlord, leasing production and post-production space at 843 Seward in Hollywood. Chicago's exploitation filmmakers had their own Film Row on Wabash Avenue, and New York had the Film Center Building at 630 9th Avenue, among other facilities in the outlying boroughs. Willis Kent often staged his moral sagas at the ragtag sounding "Ralph Like's International Studios."

Production was carried out by unemployed technicians, free-lancers, aspiring artists and former studio professionals whose careers had been dashed by an unshakable propensity for drink. A number of Babb's exploitation classics were directed by once-notable filmmaker William Beaudine, who first entered the industry in 1909 under D.W. Griffith, and who later achieved notoriety with a pair of Mary Pickford films (*Little Annie Rooney*, 1926 and *Sparrows*, 1926), but whose battle with the bottle poisoned his career at the major studios. After a period of expatriate filmmaking in England, he returned to America to enjoy a long and prosperous career on filmdom's poverty row, where one's attention span need only last as long as

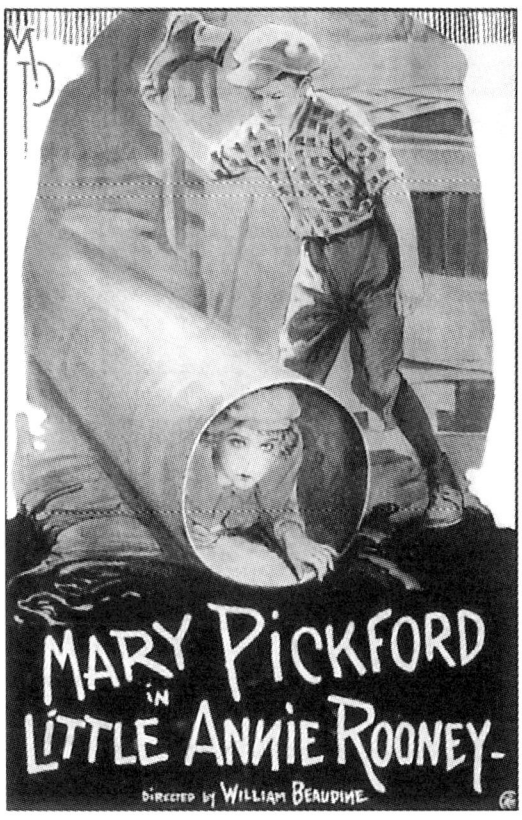

Before contributing his directorial talents to *Mom and Dad*, **William Beaudine made a series of high-profile silent films, including** *Little Annie Rooney* **(1925).**

25

a day's shoot. In 1944, the year in which he directed *Mom and Dad*, the movie marketplace saw the release of an astonishing 10 Beaudine opuses.

Big-studio veteran Erle C. Kenton also began his career in silents (under Mack Sennett) and had directed an Abbott and Costello film, *Island of Lost Souls* and dozens of other obscure and significant Hollywood films before helming *One Too Many* and *The Story of Bob and Sally*. After making these exploitation titles, he took another professional step down and became a popular television director.

J.D. Kendis engaged as his veteran director Elmer Clifton, who, before directing dozens of routine melodramas in the 1910s and '20s, was prominently featured as an actor in D.W. Griffith's *The Birth of a Nation* and *Intolerance*. Cinematographer Ernest Laszlo was one of the few contributors whose career actually improved in the wake of his exploitation work, the kind of work generally considered a career's death rattle. Having shot Willis Kent's *The Pace That Kills*, he achieved renown as the director of photography on such films as *Stalag 17*, *The Big Knife* and *It's a Mad Mad Mad Mad World*. Actress Betty Grable also found fame after appearing in the "lite" exploitation film *Probation* as wayward 17-year-old Ruth Jarrett, involved with an aristocratic playboy engaged to be married.

At one time a prominent actor—starring in D.W. Griffith's *Intolerance*—Elmer Clifton later became an exploitation auteur under producer J.D. Kendis.

Farrell described the camaraderie and chaos that characterized the typical exploitation production.

> Most of these features were shot by William Thompson. Bill Thompson was the oldest active cinematographer at the time... He started with Edison back in New York... There was a fellow who was George Tallis' first assistant camera operator and Art Lasky, the ex-prize fighter was the second assistant. Well Art was legitimately blind in one eye from fighting and couldn't see very well out of the other one. Bill Thompson wore fairly thick glasses. So did the first assistant, who was sort of a drinker... That was the Three Stooges out there, setting up this stuff at night without a lot of light. Bill tripped over the curb once or twice, he

couldn't see where he was going! It was a kick! To see those three guys. I really thought that first night we were going to have problems. I really thought they weren't going to get anything the way they were going. But apparently it all came out.[6]

The aesthetics of the exploitation film were understandably erratic as a result, but deliciously so, carrying the viewer on a bumpy ride through its pot-holed, back-alley narrative in a welcome departure from the slickly staged Hollywood production, which tended to present life in a high-gloss vacuum.

While exploiteers cobbled together a film from a haphazard jumble of previously established conventions, found footage and skimpy budgets, Hollywood was adopting a militaristic approach to filmmaking, striving to factor the messy, uncontrollably human element out. Back at the feudal gates of the major studios, producers were following the lead of boy genius Irving Thalberg, the taskmaster who shaped the M-G-M of the 1930s into the acme of movie glamour and prestige with his combination of artistic insight and shark-like business tactics. In an effort to develop a uniform product, M-G-M instituted a mode of factory-style film production in which projects moved steadily through a series of Fordian assembly lines without any one person devoting too much attention to any particular task. Where once a close-knit team of artists collaborated on a project from beginning to end, usually working together on a series of films, Thalberg's new "producer-unit" system put them under the pencil of a central producer, who supervised the production of several pictures simultaneously and in rapid succession. With all the precision and artistic acumen of a shipping clerk, he broke apart crews and rearranged the parts to meet stringent production deadlines, keeping each individual busy at all times performing his or her clearly defined duties, with very little awareness of the project's evolution outside of their narrow focus. The pur-

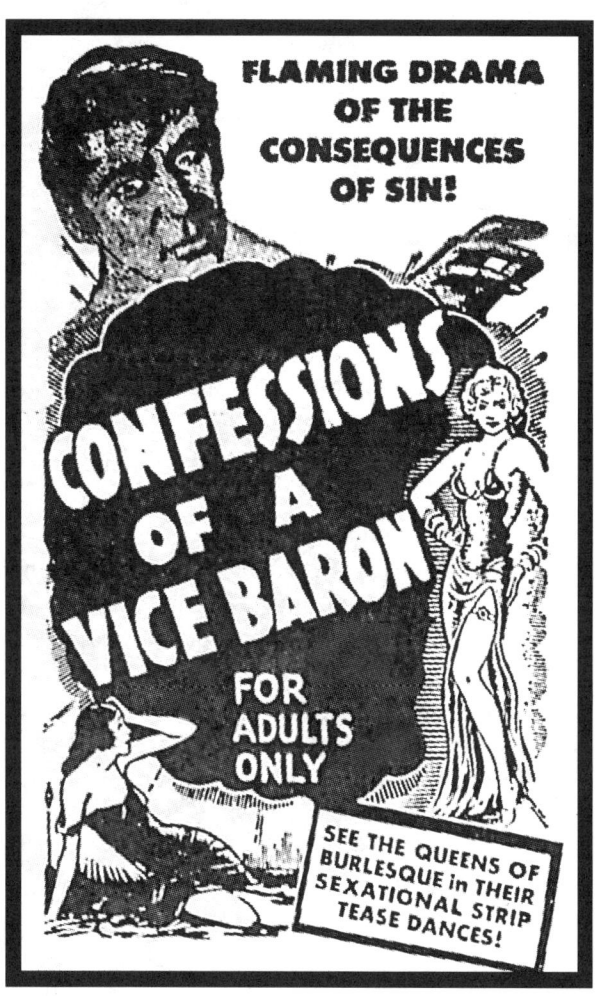

Shunning the high-art pretense of the typical major-studio release, films such as *Confessions of a Vice Baron* **(aka** *Smashing the Vice Trust***) sold sex in the raw... but with just a trace of moral enlightenment.**

This stiffly posed still from 1944's *Delinquent Daughters*, a relatively high-end exploitation film, demonstrates the sex appeal and sales potential of a good old-fashioned catfight. (Photofest)

pose was not only to maximize the rate of production but to avoid fluctuation in the quality of output, so that the artist whose signature was represented in the finished product was not the director's or screenwriter's or actor's, but the studio's.

Not too surprisingly, this method diminished the positive influence an individual artist might have on a film if allowed to involve him or herself in its construction on more than one clearly demarcated stage. Films in the '30s, '40s and much of the '50s took on a uniform appearance because of this methodical, profit-based approach to creativity: crisply photographed, clearly recorded, skillfully acted, directed and edited in accordance with well-established rules of cinematic storytelling. This quality became known as "invisible style," and is one of the defining features of the Classical Hollywood Cinema, as the era was later christened with a congratulatory air.

The exploitation cinema stands in direct contrast to, and in defiant revolt against, the CHC on multiple levels, aesthetics foremost. The exploitation pictures' minimalist production values, stilted dialogue, maladroit performances and fragmented narratives clashed with the films viewers ordinarily watched at first-run theaters. At odds with the fluid design of the streamlined Hollywood production were a succession of films punctuated by jump cuts, overexposed daylight scenes, underexposed interiors and actors incapable of producing tears (and often lines of dialogue) on cue. In an expository rhythm as familiar to exploitation aficionados as the conventions of a fairy tale are to a six-year-old, the films set up prototypical storylines which were freely embellished at the whim of their directors.

A concerned social worker (Luana Walters, left) attempts to save confused teen Adele Pearce from a life of sin and shame in *No Greater Sin*. **(Photofest)**

The basic exploitation formula is well illustrated by 1941's *No Greater Sin*, a paradigmatic venereal disease tract directed by Hollywood veteran William Nigh for University Film Productions. In a town hall meeting, an assembly of women's group representatives, newspapermen and health officials debate the future of their fair 'burg, thus establishing the pious status quo... soon to be tainted. Lurking in the shadow of the upstanding citizenry is a contingent of troublemakers, often endowed with suspiciously swarthy good looks and sinister ethnic names, like *No Greater Sin*'s silver-haired varmint,

29

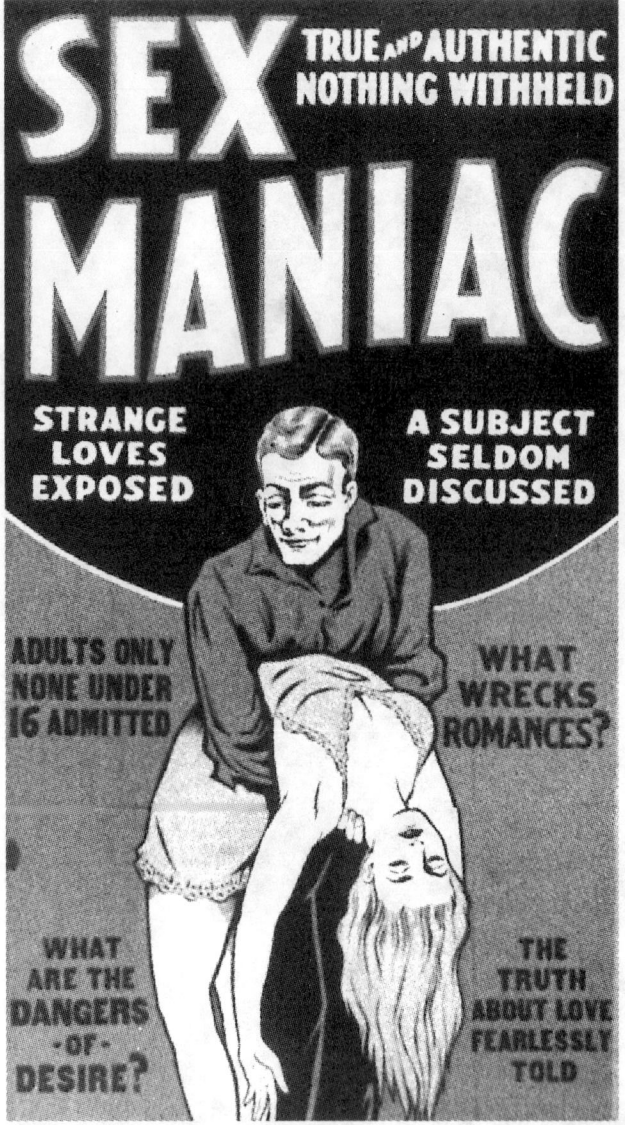

When it proved less-than-sensational at the box office, Dwain Esper's *Maniac*, a hyperbolic treatise on mental illness, was retitled and sold as a sex film, pure and simple.

Nick Scitorro. Mastermind of a prostitution ring based out of the local roadhouse, the Owl's Nest, Nick hides his corrupt traffic in souls behind the seemingly innocent jitter-bugging and free-flowing soda pop that attract the local teens. This unsavory menace is challenged by a crusading health commissioner, whose pitch for public education "I want to place posters all over this city telling people what to watch out for—what they're up against," sounds distinctly like the roadshowman who brings enlightenment to Anytown, U.S.A. But first, the health commissioner, high school teacher, newspaperman or woman must counter community ignorance, most often represented by the antediluvian, self-righteous women's group, sketched as a bridge-playing clique of sexless battle-axes more often motivated by jealousy and snobbery than a desire to protect others' virtue. And in between this establishment of conflict and then, resolution, is the soy in exploitation's hamburger: the requisite scenes of hedonistic jitterbugging, an often saucy musical or dance number performed at the roadhouse and oftentimes a climactic courtroom showdown between the forces of good and evil.

Yet, the exploitation film—not in spite of, but because of such formulaic, technically handicapped productions—often yielded moments of sublime beauty and poetic ugliness superbly matched to the outlandish subject matter. Though a shining example of exploitation at its most incoherent and ludicrous, Dwain Esper's *Maniac* also contained moments of visceral creepiness and glimpses of the kind of mental squalor and economic despair writer Michael Lesy treated in his picture book of middle-American turn-of-the-century social decay, *Wisconsin Death Trip*. A cult favorite for its frenzied, non sequitur storyline, *Maniac* is a sensational horror saga in which a mad doctor Meirschultz experiments with re-animation before his crazed assistant Maxwell takes over his demonic practice. In *Maniac* (1934) a shot of a man squirming through a crawlspace is sped up to hurry his progress, resulting in a remarkable *image juste*, transforming the mortuary-robbing Maxwell into a skittering human cockroach navigating the darkened cavities of civilization. In *The Devil's Sleep* (1949), about a "pep" pill racket at a health spa, the actor playing "Bob" (the exploitation film being notoriously unclear in identifying its cast), well beyond the age of puberty, dons v-neck sweater and what appears to be a horrendous blonde pompadour wig in order to portray a gullible high-schooler, producing a hilarious, monstrous but apropos representation of adolescence at its most awkward.

The makers of *Highway Hell* (aka *Honky Tonk Girl, Going My Way, Mr.?, Hitchhike to Hell*, Dir: Patrick Carlyle, D.P: J. Rey Palmer), a sordid tale of hitchhiking prostitutes, were seemingly unfamiliar with the key lighting methods of the major studios. They positioned their lamps erratically, so that at times they cast vividly expressionistic shadows behind the emotionally troubled bartender "Pop," a moral vigilante who seems to derive his greatest joy in condemning others' sins. Other scenes replicate stark crime scene photography, as when a surreptitious snapshot—for purposes of blackmail—is taken of two drugged teens posed in a compromising position, a hand reaching into the frame and brutally pulling the girl's panties from the shadowy recesses of her hiked skirt and down her pale, fleshy hips (a stark, disturbing image the New York State Censor Board in 1954 demanded be removed before lifting its 13-year ban on the film). Something in the sudden, unpolished choreography of this gesture gives an element of eerie veracity to this brutal violation. Many of the exploitation cinema's inky nighttime shots have the same grubby, polluted veneer of Weegee's tabloid photography, intensifying the genre's associations with squalid hyper-realism.

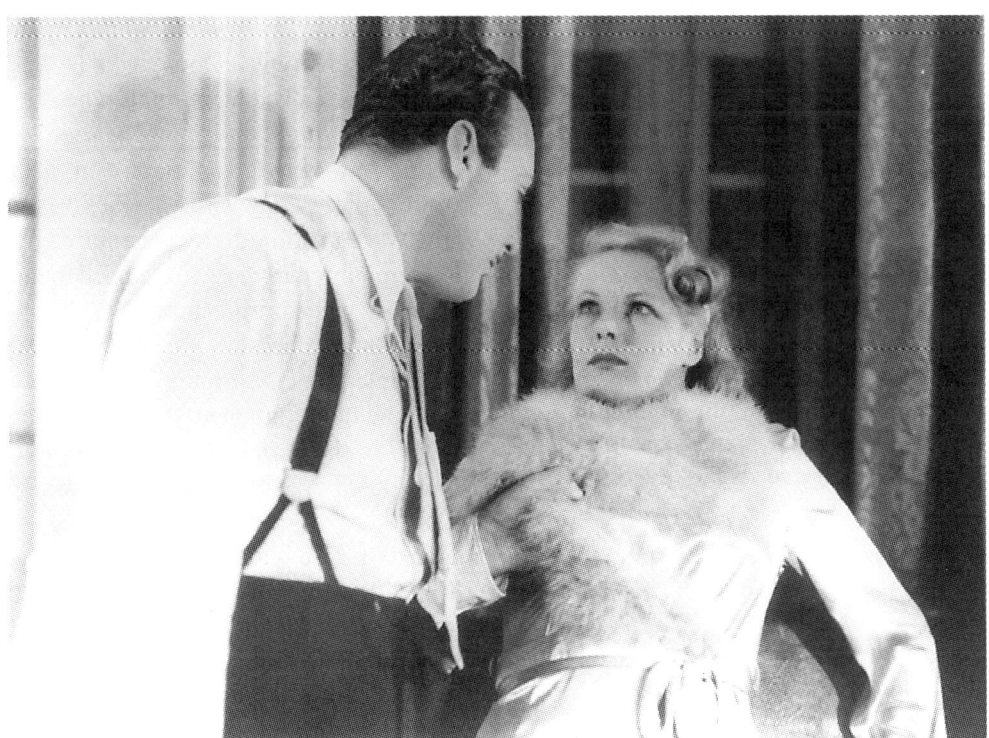

Stark love: Willis Kent's *The Wages of Sin* features Willy Castello as a brutal pimp and Constance Worth as his unwilling victim. (Photofest)

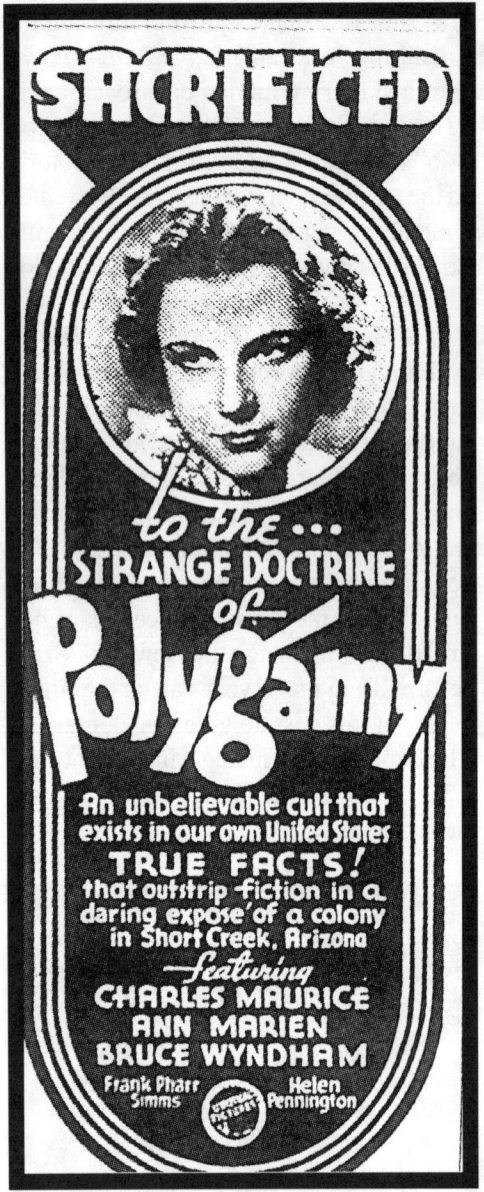

Though one would hardly call it an art film, Patrick Carlyle's 1936 *Polygamy* (aka *Illegal Wives*), inspired by the prosecution of Short Creek, AZ polygamists, features moments of unexpected visual force.

Also directed by Carlyle, with cinematographer Irving Akers, A.S.C., *Polygamy* (1936) features a startlingly effective shot in which a villainous bigamist climbs shadow-bisected stairs to greet his virgin bride, bringing to mind the expressionistic staircases and fatal wedding night in Charles Laughton's similar story of sexual menace, *The Night of the Hunter* (1955), photographed by Stanley Cortez.

Already well documented in Rudolph Grey's *Nightmare of Ecstasy* and Tim Burton's biopic *Ed Wood* (1994) are the clumsy aesthetics of Edward D. Wood, Jr., whose heartfelt, very personal treatise on cross-dressing, *Glen or Glenda?* (1953), was an intoxicating symphony of stock footage, stilted dialogue and budget-necessitated improvisation wed into a surprisingly pained-and-provocative whole.

The major studios sought their own brand of homogenized perfection not only in the visual design of its scenery but in their cast as well. Their spotlight shone only on model specimens of youth, beauty, criminality, parental authority or whatever stereotypical figure or value was being pimped. The individuals who dotted the exploitation firmament seemed slightly flawed by comparison—in face, body or voice—wayward branches on the family tree banned from penetrating Hollywood's pearly gates. Damned to the purgatory of bad production values, low wages, short schedules, poor scripts and erratic releasing, these humble understudies to the never attained status of "star" labored in the pariah company of others who would never escape the exploitation gulag.

Occasionally in an exploitation film one might spot a recognizable character actor such as Pedro de Cordoba (*Damaged Goods*, 1937), Sterling Holloway (*Tomorrow's Children*, 1934), Lyle Talbot (*Glen or Glenda?*) or Angelo Rossitto (*Child Bride*, 1942), but any truly famous figure appeared only after all professional bridges to Tinseltown had been reduced to ash. It was only after she had extracted all the money and publicity she could from her well-publicized divorce from John Barrymore that Elaine Barrie fired her parting shot in the tawdry instructional film *How to Undress* (1937, opposite one-time burlesque queen Trixie Friganza, then aged, overweight and reduced to comic relief) in which she revealed to an audience of strangers all the feminine attributes only her husband had formerly been privy to. Lita Grey Chaplin (*The Devil's Sleep*) was another Hollywood ex-wife who gulped her last breath of celebrity on a Poverty Row soundstage, which also provided final stabs at fame to silent movie veterans Wheeler Oakman, Betty Compson, Lila Lee, Marceline Day, Clara Kimball Young and Francis Ford (older brother of director John Ford, in whose films he occasionally continued to appear).

Having briefly shared the spotlight with Robert Mitchum following their infamous marijuana bust on August 31, 1948, aspiring starlet Lila Leeds left the lockup to find that her acting opportunities had evaporated, except for an offer made by a clever exploiteer who capitalized on her notoriety and featured her in a melodrama on the pitfalls of pot: *Wild Weed* (aka *She Shoulda Said 'No'!*, 1949). Mitchum's brother John also served a stint in exploitation (as a doctor in *The Devil's Sleep*), his thick, cardboard demeanor perfectly suited to the two-dimensional morality picture. And the glories of *Citizen Kane* (1940) and *Dracula* (1931) were only faded clippings in a scrapbook when Ruth Warrick and Bela Lugosi made their respective appearances in *One Too Many* (1951) and *Glen or Glenda?*

The "stars" of the exploitation film—reliable actors whose faces become familiar as one journeys through its seamy archives—never achieved more than marginal success. An actor with the charisma and good looks that somehow never carried him up and out of the exploitation racket, Timothy Farrell (*Test Tube Babies* [1948], *The Devil's Sleep*) reached his professional zenith with a bit part as a bailiff in *A Star Is Born* (1954).

But sometimes the most recognizable face in an exploitation film was not an actor but a familiar snippet of celluloid. Stock footage, as dependable a narrative filler as a roadhouse acrobatic act or torch song, was an oft-employed tool in the exploitation trade. However incongruous they may have been, these uncopyrighted trimmings of unknown origin were integrated into virtually every exploitation film as an inexpensive means of patching holes in a poorly filmed continuity, adding production values to a cheap picture or padding the length to reach the requisite 60 minutes. Most common are the passage-of-time shots—clocks ticking, seasons changing and calendars gliding past the camera—closely followed by sequences of roaring newspaper presses, churning out thousands of five-star finals whose headlines invariably mismatch that of the customized front page thrown into closeup to illustrate the magnitude of the marijuana menace. A squadron of police cars and motorcycles roaring into action with sirens wailing is another sequence that recurs with surprising frequency in the exploitation cinema. Generic shots of crowded metropolises serve to establish urban settings. Stock shots of lightning could either indicate inclement weather (*Child Bride*), the wrath of God (*Because of Eve*, 1948) or a character's turbulent state of mind (*Glen or Glenda?*).

Applied sparingly, stock footage could nicely enhance an inexpensive production, but subtlety was a concept embraced by few exploiteers, who instead pasted in as much footage as possible. Such errors in aesthetic judgment were hilariously exemplified in *The Wages of Sin* (1938), in which nine o'clock is signified by a closeup of a cuckoo-clock sounding the full nine times, followed by an uninterrupted 10 chirps to illustrate the passage of an hour. In *They Must Be Told*, a character's train journey is illustrated by numerous shots of a locomotive (heading in various directions, blithely violating the

Adventurous teen Eve (Nell O'Day) prepares to taste the forbidden fruit that will eventually transform her into a syphilitic sex delinquent in *The Road to Ruin*. (Photofest)

CHC's laws of spatial continuity), including one gratuitous closeup of the boiler being stoked, lest one question the origin of said locomotion. Shots of telephone wires and busy operators occasionally enhanced an otherwise ho-hum phone call sequence, for no discernible reason other than an almost overcompensatory need to make oneself understood at any cost.

A related shortcut was the recycling of footage from other exploitation films. *Teenage* (1941) featured scenes borrowed from *Gambling with Souls* (1936) and *Slaves in Bondage* (1937), while the "Introduction to *Forbidden Desire*" (1944) is illustrated with clips from *The Road to Ruin* (1933), *The Wages of Sin, The Pace That Kills* (1936), *Mad Youth* (1939) and *Guilty Parents* (1934), among others.

One unique application of stock footage was the exploiteer's frequent use of reels of surgical films, shockingly graphic views of the human body purloined from medical colleges and educational film houses which they not-so-neatly spliced into their own narratives. It was generally possible to find actresses willing to shed their dresses before the cameras, but photographing the birth of a baby or finding someone willing to demonstrate the grotesque physical effects of syphilis was more of a challenge. Medical supply houses, who sold such reels to educational institutions and doctors who wanted a motion picture of certain procedures, were a handy source in attaining such thrilling fare. Footage of bodies racked by venereal diseases, as well as images of natural and cesarean birth were the most popular, though resourceful filmmakers found ways to integrate other, less conventional reels (such as Dwain Esper's use of a face-lift operation in *Modern Motherhood*).

Generally, these pieces of found footage were cut into the narrative as films-within-the-film, though occasionally the medical reels were meant to be a part of the story—as in the gratuitous cesarean birth which saves the child of a woman killed in a unwarranted car accident (more stock footage) in *Narcotic*.

One of the most effective integrations of a medical reel into an exploitation narrative occurs in Edgar G. Ulmer's *Damaged Lives*. A doctor takes a young husband on a tour of the long row of doors—like some game show nightmare—that comprise his V-D ward. He opens a door, the young man looks in, and we see a snippet of medical verite, of a body covered with lesions. Another door: a man blinded by syphilis. Another door: a woman crippled by syphilis. Another door: a woman who has given birth to seven "defective" children. The doctor opens another door and, before we can look inside, out steps the young man's wife. The effect is devastating. For it is as though the wife has stepped out of—not an exam room, but—a medical reel of venereal disease victims: not the domain of actors and imagination, but of the genuinely afflicted. The severity of the characters' predicament is made chillingly clear.

Such moments of creative inspiration recur in exploitation films in spite of their technical limitations. Poorly miked sets with creaking stairs, vocal reverberations in hollow rooms and noisy props thumping against tables and walls nevertheless more accurately represented natural sound.

Just as the CHC visuals were designed to unscroll before the customer's view without disturbing the ideal dream state of passive, unthinking enjoyment, sound was also orchestrated to enhance and subtly reinforce (never running contrary to) the tone of the picture. Each second of screen time was programmed to coordinate with dialogue, stock sound effects and, of course, lushly orchestrated, narcotic melodies.

The quickly, cheaply, sometimes amateurishly packaged exploitation fable neglected this cinematic ingredient more than any other, perhaps because of its invisibility and the high cost and skill involved in synchronizing sound to image. During the 1930s, the aural quality of the exploitation film was especially crude since multi-track sound technology was still rather complicated. At the majors, sound departments had ingeniously conquered many of the obstacles inherent in the clumsy mechanics, while the neophyte exploiteer struggled for mere intelligibility.

In exploitation, music was never composed to fit the scene. Instead, a scene was edited and a disc of generic library music (without copyright or unionized musicians' strings attached) was laid over it, often indelicately balanced so it drowned out much of the dialogue, before being abruptly chopped off in a psychologically discordant screech of a needle yanked off a turning record at the close of a scene. Usually, though, the story progressed without benefit of music and the hurried speech of poorly coached actors was separated by imposing gulfs of pregnant stillness—the theater was silent except for the crisp whisper of dust and scratches being pulled past the glowing beam of the projector's optical-sound exciter lamp.

These niggling technical seams in the exploitation film—like a white tag curling out from beneath a vamp's black brassiere—anchor the exploitation experience in quotidian reality, acting as effective reminders of the difference between its gritty and true shadow world and the pristine fantasy concocted by its more prosperous siblings. A wonderful example of such a pleasantly disruptive moment occurs in the otherwise well-produced Willis Kent production *Mad Youth*. When an old lady hunches over to turn on a lamp in a darkened room, we hear a metallic clang as the switch of a theatrical spotlight is thrown just off-screen, providing the illumination for the small on-screen prop.

Not all the exploitation films were riddled with imperfections, and not all the flaws of the afflicted are so endearing. At a glance, the films of Kroger Babb might hold their own, technically at least, alongside the typical B picture. The same higher standard is also seen in such reasonably well-made exploitation films as *Damaged Goods* (aka *Forbidden Desire*), *Tomorrow's Children, Assassin of Youth* (1937) and *Road to Ruin*, whose telltale seams have been effectively concealed.

At the opposite extreme, some films buckle beneath the double burden of lack of imagination and technical crudity. *Reckless Decision* (aka *Suspicious Mothers*, 1933), patched together under the laughable aegis of High-Art Pictures Corp., consists of a not-very-exploitive good-girl-going-wrong film (*Protect Your Daughter*, purchased or pirated from another producer by John Noble), padded—or yoked, one should say—with an excruciatingly static framing device of parents worrying over their own potentially wayward daughter. The framing was a lengthy sequence of poorly recorded dialogue filmed on a single minuscule set. Such disappointments, however, are easily forgotten upon the discovery of a film which brazenly violates screen convention in a manner that is original, intriguing and, by design or by accident, purely vanguard (e.g., the films of Dwain Esper, Ed Wood, moments of Edgar G. Ulmer's *Damaged Lives* and, occasionally, Patrick Carlyle).

One of the more technically polished exploitation films, *Escort Girl* might have passed for a Monogram or PRC picture, if it weren't for its licentious subject matter and the "Adults Only" tag, which functioned as a magnet for the carnally curious.

It could be argued that the exploitation film is truly more cinematic than its polished Hollywood rival because the viewer is made aware of the mechanics of the film's design, the methods of its construction, drawing the viewer in on a much deeper level by requiring that greater attention be paid to plot and character.

In the realm of subject matter, exploitation held a distinct advantage over the Hollywood picture, as it was not as constrained by the guidelines of taste, having no widespread corporate image to protect. In addition to addressing topics forbidden in legitimate films, the exploitation picture often took a radically different tack in the way it depicted vice.

Hollywood on occasion indulged in scenes of "forced seduction." In the exploitation film girls were raped. While violent sexual advances in big-budget films were depicted in expressive closeups and symbolic gestures, the exploitation film showed physical action. Even the more daring pre-Production Code films could only artfully allude to sex, as in the corn-crib rape in *The Story of Temple Drake* (1933). Presented in facial closeups, the rape is implied by the heroine's face reacting with horror, and her attacker's leering fiendishly in partial shadow as he moves toward her out of frame, followed by a generic scream. A heroine's sexual scramble up the corporate ladder made in *Baby Face* (1933) is similarly implied as the camera zooms out the side of a skyscraper window and climbs higher up the structure as the heroine climbs her way to the executive suite. *Reefer Madness* (1936) gives an ugly vocabulary to Hollywood's artful, expressionist ravishments as a hopped-up marijuana fiend pulls a naive teenage girl into his lap and claws madly at her dress, pulling the back open and yanking her bra straps into disarray while she struggles in resistance.

Exploitation inherited much of its villain/victim design from Victorian literature and the melodramatic stage, but made its formulaic seductions more visceral through seedy production values and low-caliber performances.

The awkward delivery of lines distances these films from the slick invisibility of the CHC, as do the unglamorous appearances of some of the actors. For example, in *Guilty Parents* the typically suave, tuxedoed cad Al (Lynton Brent) pours champagne not into the rouged lips of a frail, soft-focused, well-coifed starlet, but down the gullet of Betty Wagner (Elen Aristi), a plump, awkward girl with poor posture and blunt features. When his hand squeezes her breast she grunts wearily and nauseously, delivering an effect of genuine carnal corruption that C.B. DeMille with his lavishly audacious tableaux of modernist debauchery (e.g., *Madame Satan*, 1930) never equaled. Al later finds Betty passed out fully clothed in a bed and, while the stock-music jazz pumps on in the background, he stirs her into aroused consciousness. Betty later dies of a botched back-room abortion.

The ugly reality denied by Hollywood, but which keeps slipping through the cracks in exploitation, gives

In this publicity photo (which resembles nothing in the film), good-girl-gone-wrong Burma (Harley Wood) appears to beg for one more fix from the dope-dealing Nick in *Marihuana: Weed with Roots in Hell*.

the genre an intoxicating quality—the mesmerizing impression provided by documentary film or news photography, of an actual, arrested sliver of the past. It manifests itself in many ways, large and small, obvious and subtle. It convinces the viewer, in spite of the film's aesthetic ungainliness, that the story is more real than make believe.

Actresses with authentic regional speech patterns instead of the typical faux European dialects with which CHC leading ladies flavor their roles; actresses with shiny faces; actors with beady eyes; the visible imprints of bras and labels beneath sweaters and gowns; ill-fitting costumes; the lack of full composure (authentic hysterics, genuine passion and drunkenness); exterior scenes filmed on actual locations (complete with traffic noise and casual passersby)—are all tiny fragments of a reality that Hollywood attempted to ward off its premises like rats.

Frequently the bitter truths exploiteers offered were not so minute. Though they often teased audiences and failed to live up to their promises, the exploitation film did at times reveal to the public sights that would never stain the studio's screens: the bare breast, the flaccid penis, venereal diseases in all their suppurating, flesh-eroding glory. Had he lived to see *Mom and Dad*, perhaps Will Rogers would have rescinded his maxim about screen lewdness, "You can't make a picture as bad as the ads lead you to believe it is."[7] Homespun cinema-related witticisms, it seems, don't apply to every genre.

Admittedly, most exploitation films failed to live up to their own hype, offering the public a pale semblance of the fully exposed iniquity promised in their advertisements. At best the exploitation film offered the thrill of the carnival strip show—only instead of a middle American Salomé dropping her veils, it was a wayward high school girl raising her skirt in a stocking-baring dance celebrating escape from oppressive parental eyes... a feral outburst fueled by beer and marijuana, a sudden launch into a lifestyle of strip poker, the occasional loin-cooling nocturnal swim and various other exploits resulting from the all-too-common formula of irresponsible parenting, narrow-minded teaching, quack doctors and urban hoods who roam small town and suburb for nubile women to stock their whorehouses and peddle their dope.

The best way to depict a woman's salvation from iniquity, the exploiteers repeatedly asserted, was to depict her tumble from innocence to depravity in thorough detail. By sharing in her misfortune,

Teen revelry in *Mad Youth* climaxes with jitter bugging and a baton-twirling drum major.

serving as silent voyeur-witness to every unrolled stocking, gulp of champagne and puff of marijuana, the viewer was complicit in her downfall and would be better warned of the seductive power wielded by these vices that threaten the well-being of every young man and woman.

Absent from these instructional narratives, however, was any dramatization of a healthy sexual relationship, so that the flashes of flesh hungrily anticipated by the zealous viewer were usually "degenerate" in nature. The possibility of a sound, upstanding relationship hinted at in the quaintly titled *Mom and Dad* was nullified by shocking closeups of male and female genitalia corroded with syphilis, or the unnatural image of a vagina shrouded in white sheets and surrounded by surgical technicians from which a baby appears.

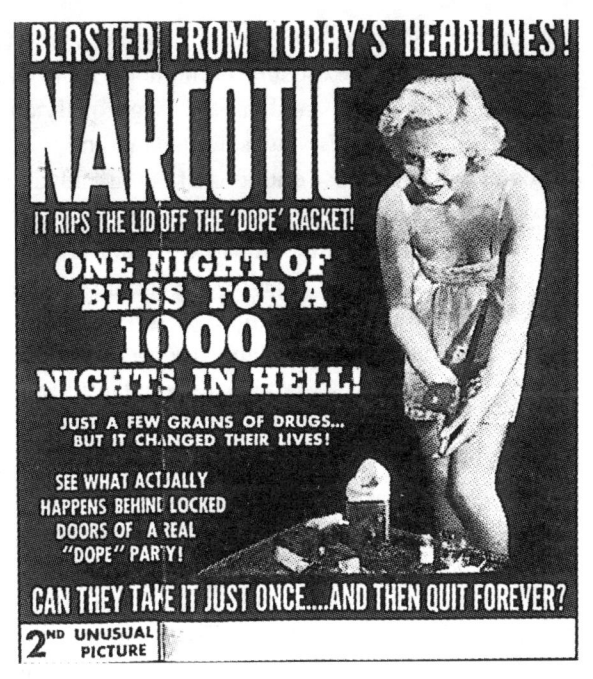

An innovative doctor (who in one scene removes a baby from a dead woman's womb) experiences a sexual downfall—losing a virtuous wife and consorting with skid-row whores—when he becomes addicted to opium in *Narcotic*.

On those rare occasions when sexual representation wasn't associated with moral and physical decay, it was usually without purpose or meaning of any kind. If it couldn't be logically worked into the narrative, exposed flesh would be brought on-screen with little rhyme or reason. Women disrobing for doctors' examinations provided audiences the opportunity to steal glimpses of the verboten female form in *Maniac*, *Race Suicide* (aka *Victims of Passion*, 1937) and *Test Tube Babies* (the medical realm as setting for sexual display is discussed at greater length in Chapter Eight, "Soft Core and Hard Sell"). In *Marihuana*, giggling schoolgirls jiggle into the surf on a weed-induced lark, while a swimming pool is the site for a nocturnal mass baptism into depravity in *Road to Ruin*. A catfight allows the stripping away of garments in *Test Tube Babies*, strip poker in *Mad Youth* and strip craps in *Road to Ruin*. In *Guilty Parents* an initiation into a gang of reckless teenagers forces new female recruits to undress to the jeering savagery of the "gang." In *The Devil's Sleep* a health-minded woman's casual entry into a sauna is the setting for delivery of "the goods." In *Child Bride*, the prepubescent protagonist (Shirley Mills, who had portrayed little Ruth Joad in *The Grapes of Wrath* two years earlier) communes with nature and her dog in a daytime swim without the proper apparel, leaving the male viewer to instinctively steal what glimpses he could and wrestle with his conscience at a later time.

When no legitimate excuse to strip the starlets could be extracted from the narrative, producers had the women disrobe for no reason whatsoever. The need to show women in casual undress instigated a profusion of dialogue scenes set in women's boudoirs and backstage dressing rooms. In *Escort Girl* (1941), a group of women in minimal costuming chat about their customers while filing nails and rouging lips. Such a scene of gratuitous exposure is included in *Maniac*, including a woman casually exposed in a tub of suds and another vigorously and lasciviously shaken by a reducing belt. *Test Tube Babies* stages a husband and wife tête-à-tête at the kitchen table, with the camera placed close enough to take full advantage of the sheer negligee worn by the Mrs.

Reefer Madness illustrates how such crude devices became oddly lyrical in the exploitation film. The steadily advancing narrative is momentarily frozen for a voyeuristic vignette in the bedroom of a female dope peddler dressing for another day's work. All attention is suddenly focused on the hushed spectacle of a leg protruding from a parted robe, a stocking nonchalantly tugged into place on a thigh, forming a sequence somehow as eloquent as it is unnecessary, a stolen moment quickly eradicated by whirling tides of jazz and hard-boiled dialogue that rush back in and hurry the plot on its way.

Other scenes of undress were less eloquent. In *Child Bride*, a self-explanatory yarn about the backwoods custom of children marrying their elders, an impoverished woman is shown in a state of extreme décolletage as she defends herself against an abusive husband. The schoolteacher trying to improve the mountain people's living conditions is tied up and stripped by angry hillbillies in a lurid scene of country versus city, foretelling such mainstream and exploitation hits as *Deliverance* (1972), *The Hills Have Eyes* (1977) and *The Texas Chain Saw Massacre* (1974). It is a raving lunatic who rips the gown from the body of a woman (actually a reanimated corpse) in *Maniac*. Viewers of *Lash of the Penitentes* (1936) saw perhaps the genre's most gruesome instance of sadism, as a woman hanging by her wrists has her bare chest flogged with a whip.

Among the few instances in which flesh was exhibited without moral condemnation were nudist features such as *Elysia* (1934) and *Unashamed* (1938), which preached the message of physical rejuvenation through full solar exposure. Unfortunately, the only way these films could skirt the authorities was by clinging to their sermons, which meant characters were forbidden to sexually interact with one another or even embrace in a way that might cause the flesh of one to rub the flesh of another in a suggestive manner. After half an hour of *Unashamed*, one stops noticing the bared breasts and buttocks and is merely bored by the stale romantic plot in which a woman converts a man to nudism, only to have him stolen away by another. Her only recourse is to leap, still naked, to her death from a craggy peak in melodramatic desperation. Of *Elysia*, one satisfied theater manager of 1934 advised other exhibitors:

> "Though it really is in the nude, it is a lot cleaner picture than a lot of the ones I have been showing. It will get the money if you advertise it as hot and that they shouldn't see it, etc., but after they have seen it they will tell you that it wasn't so hot."[8]

The only consistency in the corporal exposure is that—with rare exception—the body which is bared in the name of science, sermonizing or raw entertainment is female.

Chapter Two

IN THE BEGINNING

Pinpointing the precise moment at which the motion picture was born is an impossible task, simply because the cinema was more the product of evolution than spontaneous creation. But wherever one opts to posit the big bang that spawned the cinematic universe, its genesis also marks the beginning of exploitation. Film history is also exploitation's history, for the two are congenitally joined.

Thomas Edison's kinetoscope is often considered the seed from which the cinema sprouted, though its images were not projected for a mass audience but cycled within a wooden cabinet into which the individual viewer peered. Woodville, Otway and Gray Latham's eidoloscope was the first American invention to spread dancing photographs above the astounded gazes of a communal audience. Although prior to the Lathams' and even Edison's contraptions there was the zoopraxiscope of photographer Eadweard Muybridge, its significance is qualified by the fact that it projected not photographs but transparent paintings on spinning glass discs, akin to the magic lantern shows popular in music halls at the time (some of which were quite elaborate, incorporating movement, color, intertitles and music).

As inventors boldly appropriated, or downright stole, ideas from one another, there evolved a series of highly touted contraptions christened with names of jumbled Greek and Latin: phantascopes, zooscopes, cineographs, animatiographes, cinographoscopes, vitascopes and vitagraphs. The invention of these motion picture apparati was not the birth of cinema. The metamorphosing machines over which visionary men labored were only attempts to harness "cinema," an ethereal phenomenon with which they were truly obsessed—some kind of indefinable quality of which they knew little, except that riches awaited the first to lay claim to it. The entrepreneurial endeavor would climax when, in a crowded music hall or rented storefront, the crank of another mechanism would be turned and the cinematic essence would be unharnessed from the coils of film onto which it had been temporarily imprisoned.

When the swirls of gray shadow were finally thrown onto a reflective sheet to the amazement of the Victorian audience, art was not born. Exploitation was.

Poised behind the charismatic genius of all the Edisons, Lathams, Muybridges, Dicksons, Smiths and Blacktons was a common dream of the pot of gold awaiting the man whose patent was superior to the rest. Cinema was not born of high ideals but ferocious conniving, and it was men (and, in time, women) such as these who, a few short decades later, would constitute the motion picture genre known as exploitation. As it would be half a century later, piracy was rampant in the first decades of cinema, as filmmakers very literally remade the popular films of their competitors, when not laying their hands on a rival picture, cutting on fresh titles and selling it as their own.

Unlike their forebears, however, the exploiteers would be neither praised nor respected for their contributions, only despised and feared. Because while the cinema at large has grown sophisticated, cloaking its crass money-making objectives in the gilt

Even the earliest films bear the imprint of exploitation. For example, *Après le Bal - le Tub* **(1897, Georges Méliès)**

vest of aesthetics, these individuals have not. The exploiteers remained true to the tradition of the men who brought the motion picture into being. In their novelty and lurid charms, exploitation films were true to the spirit of the dancing shadows that first astounded a naive America some 40 years previously.

Many of the pioneer filmmakers who sought their fortunes in this new profession invoked the pretense of scientific innovation. It must have been with a smile of satisfaction that Muybridge (née Edward Muggeridge) tallied his evening's receipts from an exhibition of "photographic representations of animal locomotion," thinking back on the hush that fell over the hundreds of highbrows in the lecture audience as the zoopraxiscope ceased its concentration on camels, elephants and horses and began emitting images of men and women in movement, their nakedness cloaked only in Darwinian theory as they walked, climbed stairs, danced. The stunned, reverent silence of the audience was inevitably broken by thunderous applause which snapped the viewers out of their brief reverie and returned their minds to the extraordinary contributions of the images' ingenious "creator."

But Muybridge's fixation on locomotive nudity was no anomaly in the cinema's infancy. Throughout these early years, technical innovation and taboo were inextricably linked. The latter ensured the popular success of the former, which in turn earned such widespread renown that the coarse substance of its being was legitimized in the name of scientific endeavor.

Not every pioneer exploited the lure of the carnal to advance their inventions. In 1896 France, Auguste and Louis Lumière developed a contraption of their own, the portable and versatile Cinématographe. With it they recorded subtly staged scenes of everyday life, or "actualités": children at play, laborers hard at work, families in repose and wonderfully scenic vistas that the urbanite might never otherwise have the opportunity to behold.

In America, where the competition was more fierce, another impulse was at work, as filmmakers opted to focus their lenses on vistas of an entirely different sort. The working-class clientele would only drop so many nickels into the slot to see trains pulling into a station or inert views of faraway lands, however exquisitely framed.

Rather than an extension of the respectable dramatic stage, early cinema was more a creation of the industrial age. Its poetry was not bound in leather or rimmed in gold, it was wound onto battered metal reels with sharp edges, stacked into greasy cans and wedged into splintery wooden crates.

Annabelle Whitford's Serpentine Dances, one of the earliest performances to be captured for posterity by the lens of Edison's kinetograph, had previously been performed not in the perfumed air of the European ballet theaters, but within the stale-beer-and-cigar-smoke stench of the American music hall.

In addition to the beguiling dances of Annabelle (and a host of anonymous impersonators), audiences enjoyed the theatrics of cockfights, the muscular bare torso of Eugene Sandow and comedic vignettes of a decidedly racist tone (*Dancing Darkies* [1896, Biograph] and *Watermelon Contest* [1896, Edison] to name but two). The very first films turned out by the forefathers of the American cinema were not the whimsical novelties they are often blindly dismissed as, but shockingly frank moving tableaux intended to gratify the eyes of an adult male viewership, the sporting gentleman in particular. *A Windy Corner* (1898, Biograph) is a prelude to *The Seven Year Itch*, as a woman's dress billows up while she stands over a ventilation grate.

An 1895 New York newspaper article reported the debut of the Lathams' eidoloscope:

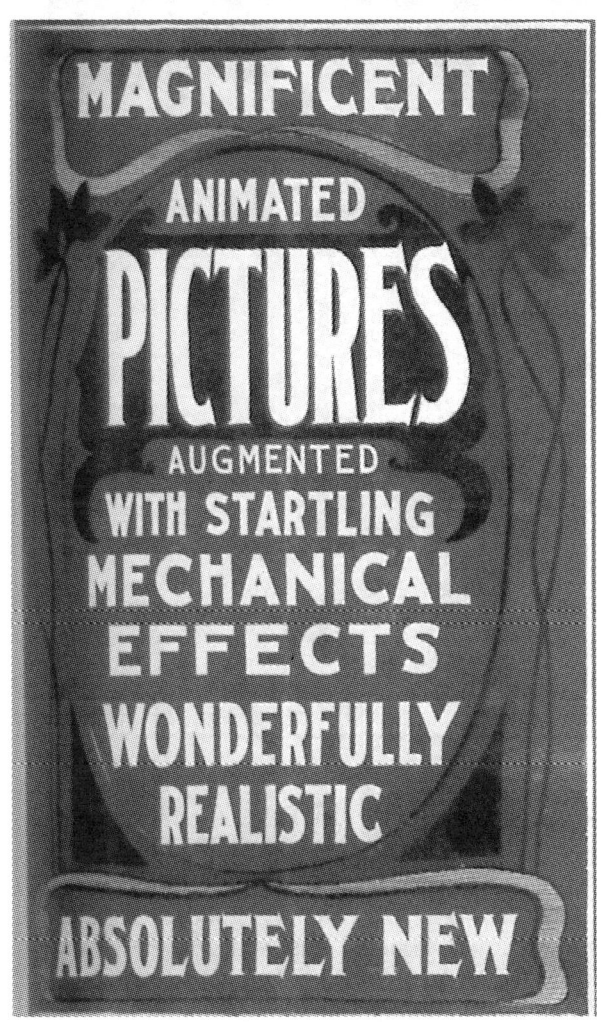

Early cinema advertisement c. 1900.

> You'll sit comfortably and see fighters hammering each other, circuses, suicides, hangings, electrocutions, shipwrecks, scenes on the exchanges, street scenes, horse-races, football games, almost anything, in fact, in which there is action, just as if you were on the spot during the actual events.[1]

TEN NIGHTS IN A BAR-ROOM

KEEP THEM OFF! KEEP THEM OFF! OH HORROR! HORROR!

First adapted to the screen by producer Sigmund Lubin in 1903, Timothy Shay Arthur's temperance novel *Ten Nights in a Bar-Room* would return to the screen in 1931 via exploitation producer Willis Kent.

Prominent among the initial subjects of Muybridge's serial photography were nude women, boxing men, horses and dogs (two of God's creatures especially beloved by bettors). The first film ever released by the American Mutoscope and Biograph Company (later to foster the talents of D.W. Griffith) was *Sparring Contest at Canastoda* (1895), serialized in four segments.

Illegal "blood sports" such as prizefights, bullfights, cockfights and rat-baiting (in which men wagered on how many vermin a fox terrier could kill in an enclosed arena within a certain time limit) were popular cinematic subjects in the latter years of the 19th-century, calling for a great deal of tact on the part of their promoters lest the exhibitor fall prey to forces of reform which had already targeted this new, vulgar sensation.

The newborn medium was hardly an unsightly blemish appearing suddenly on the ivory epidermis of American society. There were already places to be visited and publications to be read by men who sought certain unsanctioned pleasures. The cinema's predecessor, with its seemingly unbridled concentration on lowbrow subjects, was the *National Police Gazette*, a weekly New York tabloid (est. 1845) that catered to the worldly male. In the 1890s, the tabloids primary ingredients were sports (especially boxing and bettors' games), sex (primarily music hall dancing girls not unlike Annabelle) and crime (sparing no detail in describing its performance and punishment), and it frequently featured stories made up of combinations thereof.

Many early motion pictures—especially the Edison shorts which embraced carnal interests more wholeheartedly than other pioneers'—were merely *Police Gazette* stories transferred onto filmstock. Pillow fights in boarding schools were frequently the subject of *Police Gazette* woodcuts (e.g., October 26, 1895) and were later brought to life on film in *Seminary Girls* (1897, Edison). The exploits of artists' models and women who take up arms against one another were also sources of great fascination to both the reading and viewing public of the day (e.g., *Fate of the Artist's Model* 1-5 [1903, Biograph] and the stripping, then dueling, femmes of *An Affair of Honor* [1897, Biograph]).[2] On July 19, 1895, tabloid and cinema were sublimely united when the grapplings of wrestlers Duncan C. Ross, Harry Dunn and Ernest Roeber were captured by the eidoloscope's lens on the roof of the *Police Gazette* building.

Before it became "The Leading Illustrated Sporting Journal in the World," crime and political corruption were the central focus of the *Police Gazette*, which brazenly exposed the misdeeds of New York (organized and random) as well as the names of the people who perpetrated them. When the publication was sold to Richard K. Fox in 1876, the genuinely brave and noble ambitions of its founders, George Wilkes and Enoch Camp, gave way to pure sensationalism as the *Police Gazette* threw its weight upon an axiom of yellow journalism that would become one of the fundamental principles of the exploitation cinema: Any subject, no matter how gruesome or salacious, could be brought to the public if properly cloaked in the guise of moral enlightenment.

This idea was quickly absorbed by the early filmmakers. Thus could the Edison Manufacturing Company in 1901 proudly bring to the screen its (staged) filmic account of the fate of the man who assassinated William McKinley:

> *Panoramic View of Auburn State Prison*; Where LEON CZOLGOSZ was taken after his sentence, and kept until the day of his EXECUTION. The door leading to the DEATH CELL. Taking Czolgosz to the EXECUTION ROOM. Testing electric chair with lamps. Arrival of Czolgosz. He stumbles as he comes to the chair. This was his only faulter (sic). Received 3 SHOCKS OF 18,000 VOLTS and is pronounced dead by the doctors.[3]

Apparently struggling under the burdensome compulsion to warn the general public of the wages of sin, early filmmakers made such enlightening works as *Execution of a Spy* (1902, Biograph), *Execution of the Spanish Spy* (1898, Lubin), *Beheading a Chinese Prisoner* (1900, Lubin), *Execution of Mary, Queen of Scots* (1895, Edison) and, lest the animal kingdom feel exempt from the wages of sin, *Electrocuting an Elephant* (1903, Edison, *not* a reenactment).

In France, Georges Méliès offered a frank examination of world history, highlighted by reenactments of tortures and executions, in *La Civilisation a travers les ages (Civilization Through the Ages*, 1907), also distributed under the title *The History of Human Atrocities*, a fitting title for an early-century exploitation documentary.

Before the end of the first decade of the 20th century, the flimsy veil of scientific advancement and moral edification was moth-eaten and worn thin and filmmakers sought to rejuvenate the earning potential of their films by somehow heightening their potency. The public was willing to accept longer films, and films of greater narrative complexity. Thus the libidinal impulse that was once relieved through unveiled depictions of vice and carnality was channeled with a vengeance into more socially acceptable directions, namely melodrama—for well-crafted melodrama tempered the sting of purely carnal sensationalism.

The carnally minded filmmaker unleashed his or her dark impulses in wildly exaggerated stories of intensified romance, subhuman villainy, ferocious violence and glorified martyrdom, all neatly packaged in a standardized visual style formulated to rip emotional responses from the hearts of its viewers, protected from too much criticism by its separation from reality. These stories, which usually justified their vulgar means with a morally enlightening end, were mere entertainment... harmless... purely imaginary.

The American Vitagraph Company led the way. Film historian Charles Musser writes of their 1906 release *The Automobile Thieves*:

> During the course of the 985-foot, 23-shot drama, the thieves—an attractive young couple—commit a string of holdups and robberies. They are indifferent to the fate of their victims, who are often beaten or shot. They manage to escape a police trap, largely because of the fearless intervention of the woman, but the ensuing chase ends in a shoot-out and the death of the couple. At the conclusion, the dying man staggers to his beloved, kisses her, and dies. (In fact, his actions throughout appear based on sexual obsession, and his periodic sense of guilt is assuaged by alcohol).[4]

A stream of similar films capitalized on the success of *The Automobile Thieves*, each discreetly testing the limits of social acceptance, eventually overburdening the market with the morose and incurring the wrath of Progressive-era activists who launched an all-out attack on the cinematic enterprise, which had grown to such an extent that it could be fairly referred to as an industry. The aggressive reform groups targeted the cinema as both a medium of entertainment and a place where society's dregs could congregate. The storefront theaters were nothing more than incubators of iniquity, where—in the musty-smelling darkness—vulgar images nurtured impure thoughts into full-fledged immorality. One Chicago judge in 1907 wrote, "These theaters cause, indirectly or directly, more juvenile crime coming into my court than all other causes combined," citing as partial causes such films as *Beware, My Husband Comes*, *The Bigamist*, *Gaieties of Divorce*, *Child Robbers* and *Paris Slums*.[5]

As censorship pressure intensified, the blood-and-flesh cinema of the turn of the century was shrewdly reshaped into something more palatable. Even that pioneering purveyor of the abject, Thomas Edison, acknowledged in 1907 the necessity of assimilation, quoted in the trade magazine *Moving Picture World* as saying, "In my opinion, nothing is of greater importance to the success of the motion picture interests than films of good moral tone."[6] The long-term survival of this potentially lucrative technical novelty depended on its respectability. Prurient spectacle could still be the cinema's *raison d'etre* but the only way it could gain a proper foothold in the burgeoning American popular culture industry would be by making itself suitable for mixed-sex audiences of disparate age groups.

True visionaries of the day had even higher aspirations. They sought the long-term profits of immortality, and knew such things were within reach if they could only confer on their merchandise the noble designation of "art."

Immense factories were designed to improve the appearance of the motion pictures. And dank storefront nickelodeons gave way to ornate palaces where even the most vulgar dancing shadows were enshrined, then elevated and, in a matter of time, vindicated. The rising stature of the moving picture was not only the work of the jodhpur-and-beret-wearing director (already designated the paramount *artiste* of the medium) but was as much the result of lesser known craftspersons: the press agents and publicity photographers whose work was not evidenced on screen, but who were just as influential in shaping the way the public perceived the films, differentiating as best they could the formulaic product that was shipped out of the industrious studios with metronomic regularity.

But the veil of art was only so thick. No matter how respectable the cinema became, there remained embedded within it an impulse to embrace all that was forbidden, repressed and ignored in its society—like a tainted gene that cannot be extricated from an otherwise wholesome chromosome. The delinquent impulse toward the abject would not always reveal itself in the celluloid offspring. Some films (bred in a genteel environment) might be healthy in outlook, while others would exhibit only marginal symptoms of genetic corruption.

A quickly produced imitation of *Traffic in Souls*, *The Inside of the White Slave Traffic*—like all good exploitation films—justified its prurient content with the credentials of various public health groups.

Every generation, however, produced a few microcephalic spawn, which (be they films or humans) would generally be grouped together, cast aside, ignored and, if at all possible, forgotten.

Temporarily suppressed, the deviant impulse awaited its chance to reappear, which occurred almost immediately. Perhaps the bloody side of the cinema would have politely allowed itself to be assimilated into the socially acceptable mainstream were it

47

A pair of New York cops save a woman from a life of prostitution in the influential 1913 film *Traffic in Souls*.

not for the well-intentioned actions of its innovator, Thomas Edison. In doing his share of rubbing away the cinema's unsightly tarnish, he involved numerous welfare organizations in the making of special films of moral enlightenment, focusing on such popular issues as the exploitation of child labor (*Suffer Little Children... For of Such Is the Kingdom of Labor*, 1909), unsanitary living conditions (*The Awakening of John Bond*, 1911) and the fight against tuberculosis and other diseases (*The Red Cross Seal*, 1910). Other production companies followed suit and through such noble cinematic efforts, the aberrant cinema again made its way into the movie houses of America—a Trojan horse rolled into theater lobbies in the name of the very reformists who had sought its exile.

Inspired by the social problem dramas then popular on the American stage, these films pursued topics that had been sternly forbidden by the newly founded state censor boards and the National Board of Censorship of Motion Pictures (in 1915, more congenially renamed the National Board of Review), only now they did so in the name of universal health and righteous living.

Among the first and most successful of these salacious social conscience films was George Loane Tucker's *Traffic in Souls* (1913), which was purportedly based on findings of "the John D. Rockefeller White Slavery Report and on the investigation of the Vice Trust by District Attorney Whitman." Among the most effective films of its day—combining a fresh cinematic naturalism with stagy melodrama—*Traffic in Souls* offered a taste of what would soon be delivered in the exploitation film. It was the first feature film released by Universal and was a resounding success (Carl Laemmle's skepticism smashed by reports of a mobbed box office in New York), due partly to the hyperbolic promotion that surrounded its release.

Rockefeller later denied his participation in the film's production but the blow had been struck. A precedent had been established for all studios, writers and directors who sought to profit from life's seamier side. Because of the urgency of their messages, these films transcended mere entertainment and deserved to be above judgment by those who graded ordinary filmic fare, or so their makers suggested. This notion was reinforced by trade ads surrounding the release of the armed service training film about the dangers of venereal disease for our fighting men, *Fit to Win* in 1919:

> The United States Public Health Service asks the co-operation of State and Municipal governments and requests the abrogation or suspension of such censorships as might impede this very essential missionary work.[7]

Discerning the genuine nobility of these politically aware exploiteers is difficult today, since many of the films have vanished like the men and women who made them. But the advancement of exploitation was fostered not only by the socially sacrilegious but by the idealistic as well, who inadvertently laid the groundwork for decades of the less virtuous who would surface in their wake.

One of the most visible and influential activists of the 1910s was Margaret Sanger, whose crusades against reproductive ignorance led her to open the first contraceptive clinic in America in 1916, at a time when in many areas health workers were forbidden by law to discuss birth control with their patients. Inspired by the women she had seen die pregnant and despondent, either of back-room abortions or by their own hands, Sanger wrote and organized the production of a semi-autobiographical film entitled *Birth Control* (1917). Its plot, which serves as a partial blueprint for *Mom and Dad* and its many imitators, involves a sex-ed crusader who is persecuted for daring to reveal the truth of sex hygiene to a suffering patient (and forced to watch the suffering of those she is forbidden to enlighten).

In 1922, the Hays Office was established to curtail the production of films such as *The Unmarried Mother* (c. 1920).

49

More than the soon-to-be-standard plot design that makes *Birth Control* significant, the method in which it was made and released proved critical. Most reformists in the early 1910s sought to ban films with worldly themes because the motion picture audience was deemed largely poor and uneducated (and in reformists' eyes incapable of intelligent moral judgment). Sanger and others like her took the reverse approach, proclaiming the cinema as the ideal means of communicating with the common classes: the illiterate, those who did not attend hygienic lectures, who lacked an intimate, compassionate relationship with a family doctor and those not being reached by the morally superior crusaders. The cinema allowed her to circumvent the postal system (which forbade the distribution of contraceptive literature through its channels) and break through the barriers of class and wealth. No longer was birth control the exclusive property of intellectuals and the well-to-do. The lower classes now had access to information moralists previously denied them.

The distributor's handling of Sanger's film was considerably less virtuous. Concerned more with widespread booking than public awareness of birth control, the B.S. Moss Motion Picture Corporation hyped it in the trades with a coin-jingling fervor that seems more appropriate to the sales ads of the 1930s:

> You don't have to be a film buyer or seller to clean up a quick profit on this. Everyone in the world will want to see it. It's the safest, surest states rights proposition since big film features began, and we'll guarantee you it's law proof and censor proof.[8]

Other similarities to the archetypal exploitation film include the use of an alternate title (*The New World*) and cleaned-up advertising materials in less receptive regions; the employment of states rights distribution; and the upright-sounding name of the production company (Message Feature Film Corporation). The film was generally accompanied by a lecture by Mrs. Sanger herself, since she found it impossible to circulate the film any other way, the opposition to contraception being so intense (even though her delicate handling of the topic earned the approval of the National Board of Censorship).

Birth Control's notoriety opened the floodgates of the exploitation industry, though others were careful to approach their sensational subject matter in less confrontational terms. During the 1910s, through a process of cinematic natural selection, the social problem films steadily developed the features that would later distinguish the exploitation film.

The cinematic/contraceptive crusade was later taken up by Lois Weber, whose forte was a harmonious coalescence of melodrama and social commentary, and who made two birth control films immediately after Sanger's: *Where Are My Children?* and *The Hand That Rocks the Cradle* (both 1917). The former has the notable distinction of being released with a lengthy introductory scroll. *Fit to Win* (1919) was shown to adult audiences only, and segregated by sex. Virtually all the vice films of the 1910s claimed the cooperation of government authorities, including *The Cocaine Traffic* (1914), made "with the assistance and approval of the Director of Public Safety and the Police Department of the City of Philadelphia."

Public opinion of the social hygiene films varied. In 1914, *Variety* stated:

> When one sees the endorsements and reads the press stuff on these "vice films" to "save souls" it is almost laughable, when the self-same pictures are sending more souls to hell at 25 cents each at the box office than were ever captured by all cadets [cadets being an outdated term for pusher or pimp].[9]

Then, the following year, the same publication said of *Damaged Goods*:

> Everyone should be made to see it, for they are to become the American manhood, and the cleaner physically the better.[10]

The hygiene film movement continued to intensify in the 1920s, but with a noted shift from the legitimate uplift film to more insidious exploitation. During World War I, the venereal health of American soldiers was an issue of great concern (since many soldiers were bivouacked within range of prostitutes and non-professionals with less than exemplary sexual hygiene), sparking a propaganda campaign that spread from military outpost to homefront. Training films were an effective tool within the armed forces and following the resolution of the conflict, carried on the fight by invading stateside theaters. *Fit to Win* was actually a modification of *Fit to Fight* (which served as the motto of the American campaign against sexually transmitted diseases), with the VD fable polished up a bit with some fresh studio-produced footage. Other sex hygiene films of the era include *End of the Road* (1918), *The Spreading Evil* (1918), *Open Your Eyes* (1919) and a British remake of *Damaged Goods* (1919).

In time, reaching the downtrodden victim of society's ills became little more than an obvious ruse by which the social problem films could cater more noticeably to the public's lascivious desires. Child labor and tuberculosis were topics of the distant past, as sex-related films dominated the market. Films in the sex-ed boom of the late 1920s include *Wild Oats*, *Are You Fit to Marry?*, *T.N.T.* (*The Naked Truth*), *The Body Beautiful*, *Tell Me Why*, *False Shame*, *Motherhood: Life's Greatest Miracle*, *Streets of Forgotten Women*, and *Enlighten Thy Daughter* (remade in 1934).

This herald, or handbill, was distributed to promote the 1928 exploitation film *Secrets of Life*, one of the first to be shown to sex-segregated audiences.

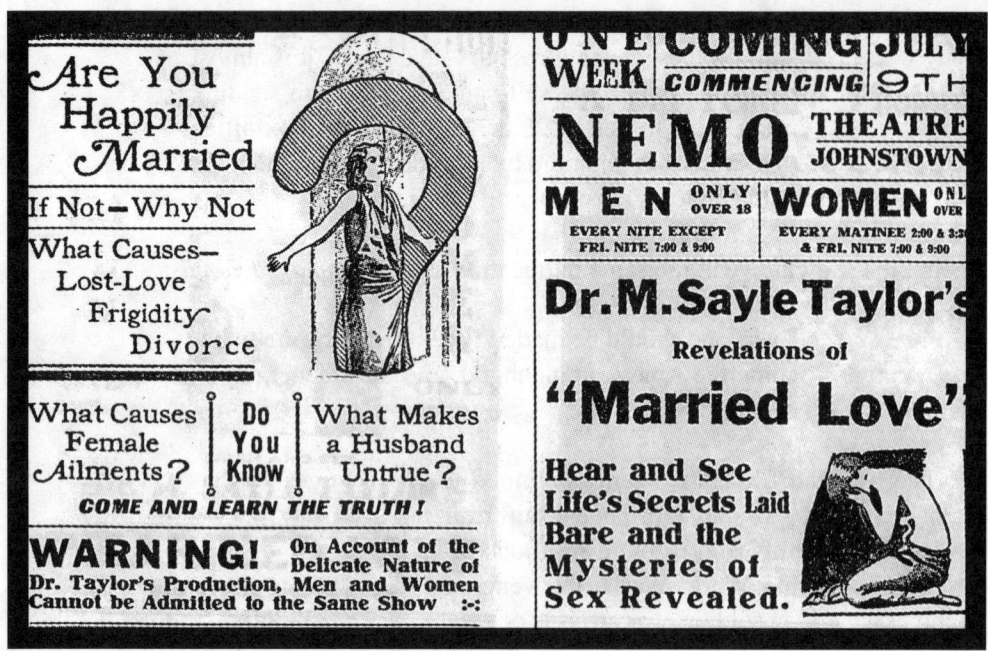

By the late 1920s, the practice of combining exploitation films and live lectures was already common, as shown in this herald for *Married Love*.

And the steady progress of cinematic evolution carried the exploitation film ever closer to maturity. Screenings of *The Pitfalls of Passion* (1927) were accompanied by pitches for sex-ed booklets.[11] *Is Your Daughter Safe?* (1927, aka *The Octopus*, made by S.S. Millard, one of the pioneer roadshowmen of exploitation's golden era) often featured a medical slideshow and lecture, and concluded with a reel showing "the effect of venereal disease on children born of parents afflicted with said disease."[12] And, in a strange premonition of sensational theater lobby displays to come, *Is Your Daughter Safe?* was often ballyhooed by the sidewalk exhibition of a live young woman enclosed in a glass case.

So distressed were the bastions of respectable cinema by this rising tide of cinematic vice that whatever nobility the social hygiene films once possessed was thoroughly eradicated. Appointed head of the Motion Picture Producers and Distributors of America (MPPDA) in 1922 to improve the image of the movie industry, Will Hays' content-controlling manifesto of "Don'ts and Be Carefuls" shooed the major studios away from the morally questionable topic of sex hygiene, leaving the spoils to the independent filmmakers against whom the channels of widespread distribution were securely locked.

Even the once-noble crusaders were now harshly rebuffed. P.S. Harrison, of the virulently pro-censorship publication *Harrison's Reports*, wrote of a Movietone (M-G-M) short featuring Margaret Sanger lecturing on birth control in 1929:

> As I did not hear the lecture, I cannot say whether what Miss Saenger (sic) said was or was not offensive.
>
> Whether the lecture was or was not offensive, however, is not the point at issue, but the fact that a producer controlled theater circuit should have undertaken

Advertisements were formulated to offer enlightenment not only to men but to women, who comprised a considerable portion of the exploitation audience.

to touch on so controversial a subject... it is evident that the showing of such a picture is harmful. Bear in mind that the average picture-goer does not remember where he has seen such a picture; all that he remembers is that he has seen it in a picture theater. As a result he condemns all picture theaters.[13]

As a means of profitably sidestepping organized resistance from the studio-controlled chains and the Motion Picture Theatre Owners of America, exploiteers found an alternate source of big-city exhibition: stageplay theaters, which were still quite popular in the silent era—though the death knells of Movietone and Vitaphone were sounding—and which were traditionally dark between theatrical seasons. The exploiteer would four-wall the auditorium (that is, rent it outright for a flat fee, without obligation to share receipts with the owner), and run a series of exploitation titles over the course of a summer.

Some dramatic touring companies took note of the exploitation film's success (and the controversial popularity of Brieux's *Damaged Goods*) and mounted live productions that were almost identical to their celluloid contemporaries.

By 1928, the stage was completely set for exploitation's golden era. Willis Kent's *The Road to Ruin* ranks among the best of the genre, superior to the 1934 remake and just about anything else that bore the producer's name in the coming decade. In it, a

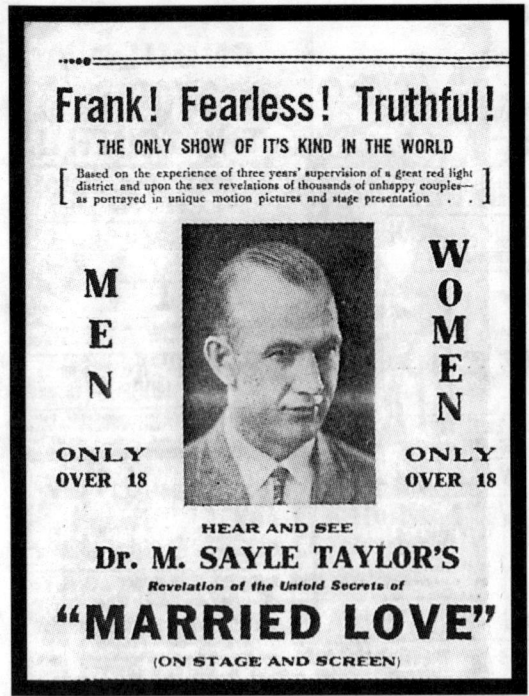

> **Frank! Fearless! Truthful!**
> THE ONLY SHOW OF IT'S KIND IN THE WORLD
>
> [Based on the experience of three years' supervision of a great red light district and upon the sex revelations of thousands of unhappy couples—as portrayed in unique motion pictures and stage presentation.]
>
> **MEN**   **WOMEN**
> ONLY OVER 18   ONLY OVER 18
>
> HEAR AND SEE
> **Dr. M. SAYLE TAYLOR'S**
> Revelation of the Untold Secrets of
> **"MARRIED LOVE"**
> (ON STAGE AND SCREEN)

The ancestor of Elliot Forbes, Alexander Leeds and Curtis Hayes, Dr. M. Sayle Taylor guided silent-movie audiences to the path of knowledge during screenings of *Married Love*.

high school girl named Sally (Helen Foster), the child of an overly trusting mother and an adulterous father, befriends a promiscuous party girl and embarks on a fun-filled trek toward damnation. In addition to a few drinks, a few hands of strip poker and a tour through "The Barn," a seedy roadhouse, Sally becomes pregnant by her boyfriend Don. The only way he can afford an abortion is to whore Sally out to a group of businessmen, one of whom turns out to be Sally's father, who takes his daughter home just in time to watch her die. This climactic scene is one of the most beautifully staged moments in the exploitation world. As the life suddenly drains from the bed-ridden Sally, a heavy shadow falls across her brow and spreads across her body, leaving her grieving parents in darkness at her side.

Oftentimes the quality of sound in exploitation films of the early '30s was so poor that it acted more as a hindrance than an enhancement. Without such technical distractions, this first version of *The Road to Ruin* seems like a far more professional film than its remake, employing painted title cards (a spider web behind the text describing Sally's moral decline) and other more subtle details to depict one girl's fall from grace. The obligatory moralizing is, remarkably, confined to a single, densely worded intertitle—"The object of the police department is not to punish juvenile delinquents but to correct their waywardness. And it is the duty of parents to protect their children by intelligent instructions and advice on the subject of sex."—which barely intrudes upon the genuine drama and shameless sensationalism of the film.

Kent's *The Pace That Kills* is an important cinematic milestone planted at the threshold of the sound era, and as its silent reels unspool before the flame, one senses change in the wind. It begins less like a racy Hollywood thriller than a fable passed down from parent to adolescent child—not so much an original screenplay as a quaint urban legend brought to life. "So many good clean boys leave home and never return," says a mother as her son motors his way from the family farm to the big city.

Because silent exploitation films were technically outmoded as soon as sound production became accessible to the independents, they were quickly dropped from circulation in the 1930s. Since producers could not afford to store prints that would never be shown, and since the films were not made by studios with protective vaults in which to preserve the original negatives, this Cro-Magnon era of the exploitation cinema exists only in a few tattered scraps of celluloid—scraps which stand as exciting harbingers of the revolution that was to come.

Chapter Three
SURVIVAL IN THE SHADOWS

Since venereal disease, drug abuse and cesarean births were not conventional topics for the mainstream cinema of the 1930s and '40s, it was necessary for the exploitation movement to develop alternative means of distribution and exhibition. Without access to the expansive networks of circulation the major studios had established over the years, exploitation films were never able to enjoy coordinated national releases.

Rather than simultaneously dispatching hundreds of prints of a single film to theaters across the nation, exploitation distributors would work with a handful of prints, "bicycling" them from one showplace to the next, in a carefully planned trek through the major cities and rural townships of America.

It was generally within the means of the exploitation distributor to handle only a portion of the nation's theaters. The companies routinely made up the difference by selling rights to other distributors on a regional basis. "States rights" distribution, as this method was known, not only enabled filmmakers to secure (staggered) nationwide exposure but allowed exploiteers without the funds to make pictures of their own to affordably acquire the works of another, gradually expanding their empire to include other territories and eventually allowing for the production of their own films (which could then be parceled out to other states rights distributors). "My dad would buy the states rights, always buying the 13 western states which we worked in," remembers Dan Sonney, son of early roadshow mogul Louis Sonney, a veteran of traveling crime shows and later one of exploitation's primary producers and distributors. "He ran the L.A. office, my brother Edward ran the San Francisco office and I ran the office in Seattle and Portland. That was the whole West Coast."

With ads such as this—as enticing to film exhibitors as to audiences—exploitation producers sold states rights to other distributors outside their own territories.

55

Proving exploitation was not only a man's game, hordes of women elbow their way to a segregated screening of *Street Corner* **(1950). (Photofest)**

Upon the completion of a new film, Sonney would dole out the rights to his regular clients to immediately recoup his investment. "I would go to Chicago and sell to Dave Friedman, and to New York. I had customers there and Texas and so forth."[1]

Exploitation films played in cities and towns of every size and location but their primary venue was the independently owned second- or third-run house. Often referred to as "Main Street" theaters, these houses carried reputations within the industry as being small, poorly maintained, catering to a rough clientele and willing to sacrifice taste in the battle over box office receipts. In a review of Willis Kent's *The Pace That Kills, Variety* smugly wrote:

> Picture will only be patronized in the Main Street houses where they can feature a lobby display of hop cooking utensils. They could give away needles as door prizes.[2]

Bobby Glendon was an usher at Chattanooga, Tennessee's American Theatre (part of J. Solomon's small Independent Theatres chain), located literally on Main Street, and he recalls, "It was a cut-rate theater... in what was becoming a run-down part of town... That's where they showed all the adults-only movies." Glendon recalls a 1950 screening of *Mom and Dad*, "It was practically all men, all in their early 20s and 30s. They showed it at midnight, after the theater had closed. It was pretty much what would be the beer joint crowd at that time. They were very strict about no one under 21 being able to get in."[3]

Many exploitation films deserved to play in nicer venues and many of them did. But the generally low standard of these theaters had less to do with the quality of the films than the narrow field of options available to the exploiteer. The major studios (e.g., MGM/Loew's, 20th Century-Fox, Paramount/Publix, RKO, M-G-M and Warner Bros.) owned and operated their own chains of theaters across the country, so that all stages of filmmaking (production, distribution and exhibition) and thus all the profits were kept within the corporate family. Independent theater owners were forced to comply with the studios' law of "protection," under which high-profile releases were given first to the studio houses, then allowed to trickle down to the smaller chains, several months old and drained of box office value. Because the studios' lavish motion picture cathedrals were privileged to offer the cream of the cinematic crop, it was therefore possible for them to command 75% of all American box office grosses, even though they owned only 16% of the nation's theaters.[4]

In addition to protection, the indies were strong-armed into "block booking," an all-or-nothing process of film distribution in which a theater could only get a handful of A pictures by accepting everything else the studio deigned to ship them, usually a package of 25 to 80 assorted B's, mostly run-of-the-mill filler.

The battle over the major studios' vertical integration and oligopolistic business practices eventually reached Congress, where in 1932, Iowa Senator Smith W. Brookhart angrily remarked, "The competitive methods employed to drive out the independent theaters constitute one of the most shocking chapters in the annals of American business."[5] It wasn't until July 20, 1938 that formal charges were laid against the Big Five studios by the U.S. Department of Justice, but the industry kept their opponents at bay (and their theaters tightly in fist) through a series of postponements, outside-of-court negotiations and assorted stalls, such as their drafting of the self-regulatory Trade Practice Code (which didn't for a moment fool the DOJ, whose Antitrust Division summarily ruled such a Code not only worthless but illegal). America was well into the 1950s when the studios finally began to dismantle their monolithic empires.

The exploitation film prospered like fungus in this shadow of vertical integration and block booking, and many an independent theater vied for a dose of its penicillin to slow the economic disease spread by the majors. When properly promoted in a community, an exploitation film could outdraw the best Hollywood had to offer.

Although the states rights pictures were generally ignored in the trade periodicals, which catered to the major studios, occasionally among the exhibitors' reports the voice of an elated small-town theater owner was heard:

> Don't often book roadshows, but took a shot at this one (*The Road to Ruin*) at a raised admission price, and how they piled in. Folks that never had before been in my theater came.
> —Henry Sparks, Grand Theatre, Cooper, Texas.[6]

Played to capacity shows and broke all midweek records in my theater. People liked the picture and received many favorable comments. Enuf said.
—C.H. Sartorius, Capitol Theatre, Hartley, Iowa.[7]

Advertised 'No Children Under 16 Allowed' and it brought the S.R.O. sign, which hasn't been used for a long time.
—H.M. Johnson, Unique Theatre, Bricelyn, Minn.[8]

I just want to say that I broke a six-months' record with this one (*Back to Nature*). It's a box office plus. They came for 100 miles in every direction to see it... I got the surprise of my life because it beat every big picture I have had in many months... watch your banker smile when you take the deposit down and make a payment on the past due note. It's a box office honey.
—S.H. Rich, Rich Theatre, Montpelier, Idaho.[9]

In cities dominated by studio-run theaters, a smaller house could debut a film with a racy title (and content to match) that the upscale theaters would never allow to soil their screen. And, if an indie was committed to a packed schedule of pedestrian studio product, it could still rake in a basketful of shekels by turning to the friendly exploiteer for a few matinees and midnight shows to boost the ailing gate. Will Hays (the head of the Motion Picture Producers and Distributors of America, or MPPDA) and the majors fought a war against those "wildcatting" theaters who stooped to showing unauthorized pictures—threatening that any house showing independent sex hygiene films would find themselves without any legitimate product[10] —but their stern warnings and lectern-thumping were sounded in vain.

Even when they weren't addressing any identifiable social issue, exploitation films were recognizable as such by their poster artwork. Bryan Foy's *High School Girl*.

The moral law under which Hollywood operated was known as the Production Code, drafted in 1930 by Martin Quigley (who published *Motion Picture Herald* for the film trade) and Daniel A. Lord, a Jesuit priest. It is a deliciously detailed catalogue of the taboo, expanded from the MPPDA's list of "Don'ts and Be Carefuls" of 1927. It also, apparently, served as a blueprint for many exploitation films. When scripting their pictures, exploiteers often seemed to turn to it for inspiration, for among its tenets one finds all the distinguishing features of the traditional sex-hygiene narrative:

> Sex perversion or any inference to it is forbidden... White slavery shall not be treated... Miscegenation (sex relationship between the white and black races) is forbidden... Sex hygiene and venereal diseases are not proper subjects for theatrical motion pictures... Scenes of actual childbirth, in fact or in silhouette, are never to be presented...
>
> Complete nudity is never permitted. This includes nudity in fact or in silhouette, or any licentious notice thereof by other characters in the pictures...
>
> Dances which emphasize indecent movements are to be regarded as obscene...
>
> The following subjects must be treated within the careful limits of good taste: actual hangings or electrocutions as legal punishments for crime. Third degree methods. Brutality and possible gruesomeness. Branding of people or animals. Apparent cruelty to children or animals. The sale of women, or a woman selling her virtue. Surgical operations. [11]

Will Hays, father figure of the MPPDA, was a high-profile bureaucrat left over from an era of empty figureheads and corrupt politics—"a bagman in the Teapot Dome affair," said Depression-era filmmaker Pare Lorentz. "He was postmaster general under Harding and extricated himself from association with the gang by becoming the chief magistrate of the motion picture industry. One assumes he is busy stuffing ballot boxes in hell."[12] Senator Brookhart dismissed Hays as a "'fixer'... not employed to clean up the movies... retained merely as a smoke screen to protect the industry against molestation by public authority."[13]

So ineffectual was Hays that in the early 1930s, the major studios habitually delved into forbidden territory, abiding by the letter of Hays' law while gleefully violating its spirit. Trade paper *Variety* even proclaimed that "Sinful Girls Lead in 1931," reporting that:

> Important ladies of the screen... found smash films the wages of cinematic sin. The Great God Public, formerly considered as a Puritan censor, voiced its ap-

proval with admission fees that fully endorsed the heroines of easy virtue... Public taste switched to glamorous shameful ladies, coddled by limousines, clothed in couturier smartness. [14]

In time, this tasteful bottom-feeding sent shock waves through the civic groups and moral watchdogs (in particular the Catholic Legion of Decency) which had always eyed the cinema with some suspicion. Deathly afraid of losing their hard-earned respectability, the higher powers of Hollywood bowed before Hays in 1934, endowing this sham of a figurehead with actual authority, giving his newly formed Production Code Administration (PCA) the power to veto the releases that failed to meet its moral standards. Gone were the sordid storylines and the ingenious innuendo. "I told them that the dark clouds of a storm were gathering," Hays later wrote:

> But it was occasionally a strain both on diplomacy and Christian charity to deal with those pseudosophisticates in our midst. Had they been allowed to dominate the industry's thinking, they would have put the movies right back into the peep-show class, something fit only for Skid Row theaters and amusement parks. [15]

The first feature film released by Universal Studios, *Traffic in Souls* (1913) exposed New York's white slavery rings in sensational detail.

At Hays' beckoning, the movies took another long stride away from their sordid ancestry. Under penalty of $25,000 per violation, they became wholesome and would remain so for at least two decades to come.

Volatile topics were swept aside as Hollywood purified its image. Popular gangsters and small-time hoods like James Cagney and Edward G. Robinson became charismatic lawmen in films such as *G-Men* and *Bullets or Ballots*, or else gangsters who whimper when they die. Studios abandoned the fallen woman film in favor of sophisticated costume dramas, making greater investments in hopes of greater returns, laying the groundwork for the blockbuster approach to cinema that now dominates the medium.

Into this lucrative void came the exploitation film.

Although the exploiteers were still incapable of meeting the major

What Price Innocence? **(1933) was produced by Columbia Pictures, the studio that came nearest to entering the exploitation marketplace. (Photofest)**

studios' technical standards, the purification and standardization of the projected image was a major victory for the exploiteers, who finally cornered the market for on-screen iniquity. The independent theaters now had something the Loew's (M-G-M) and Publix (Paramount) chains didn't.

The bold salaciousness that surpasses the Hollywood tease is the core of the exploitation film phenomenon. Resorting to depictions of nudity, violence, drug usage and other cinematic taboos was the only way the independent producer, distributor and exhibitor could hope to survive against the monolithic competition, especially during the Great Depression, when capital for new business endeavors was especially scarce.

Though the exploitation cinema never rivaled the larger studios in terms of public respectability and gross box office revenues, the established studios occasionally mimicked their illegitimate cousins in an attempt to apply their profitable stratagems to large-scale motion picture production.

Universal Studios might be credited with having released the first feature-length exploitation film, George Loane Tucker's *Traffic in Souls* (1913), which dramatized the plague of white slavery. The following year, it attempted to recreate the stir caused by Tucker's exposé by producing *The Hand That Rocks the Cradle*, a thinly disguised bio of controversial birth-control educator Margaret Sanger.

Occasionally the B-picture studios plagiarized the exploitation cinema's wayward-woman narrative format (e.g., PRC's tepid *Delinquent Daughters*, which starred *Mom and Dad*'s June Carlson). Such films were without the sexually suggestive and medically explicit footage of the true exploitation feature, but the producers at PRC and the exhibitors who booked the film were banking that the general public wouldn't discover the impotence of the drama until after the tickets had been paid for.

Exploitation producer J.D. Kendis produced similarly tame pseudo-sensational films—*Hoodlum Girls*, *Teenage Jungle* and *Paroled from the Big House*—in an effort to profit from exploitation's salesmanship and identity without undue hassles with the PCA and regional censors.

Before breaking into the majors with Frank Capra's *It Happened One Night* (1934), Columbia Pictures tapped into the exploitation vein in an effort to rejuvenate its lagging grosses. In 1933 they released *What Price Innocence?*, in which a lack of sex education leads a young woman to premarital pregnancy and death by her own hand, and *Damaged Lives*, a venereal disease tract produced in cooperation with the Canadian Social Health Council, a film complete with educational lectures for sex-segregated audiences, but bearing the insignia of Weldon Pictures instead of the Columbia corporate logo.

Five years later, even after Columbia had solidified its respectability, producer Irving Briskin wrote to Joseph Breen of the PCA:

> We have had a desire to do a picture called *Child Bride*, the title itself almost tells you what we want to do. It is our intention to try to portray on the screen the subject that has raised so much controversy in the papers of nine and 10 year old children marrying the "backwoods" adults.
>
> Most naturally we will not go into any of the censorable parts but will tackle the subject from a standpoint of the hill-billies' belief in the subject and oppose it with government investigation. I naturally do not know yet what the story will contain but I am dropping you this line to find out whether the subject itself meets with any resistance on your part.[16]

The response from Breen was predictable.

> The subject of "child brides" has been suggested on numerous occasions, and we have always given as our opinion that the very nature of the subject is such as not to lend itself, properly, to screen dramatization. We feel that the very *suggestion* of a marital association between a nine, or 10, year old child and an adult is shockingly offensive, and we think no matter how the subject is dealt with, it would be almost certain to result in the kind of material, which would give serious offense to all who saw it.
>
> Specifically, we refused, as recently as March 24th, last, to approve a story, somewhat along the lines, suggested in your letter, because the general subject matter is repelling.

> I wish to urge you, as strongly as I can, to dismiss this thought from your mind. [17]

Briskin's reply to Breen was major-studio typical.

> In view of your feeling on this subject, we will for the moment abandon the idea. [18]

A script for a film entitled *Child Wives* had already been submitted that year by Victory Pictures' Sam Katzman, who generally focused his energies on the production of cheap Westerns. Though the story was deemed "sordid and low-toned throughout" and was rejected by the PCA, Breen wrote Katzman he was "willing to consider a further basic revision." [19] Mr. Katzman apparently never followed through with the project.

It wasn't until 1942 that America was enlightened to the dangers of child marriage, in the form of Raymond Friedgen/Harry J. Revier's exploitation classic *Child Bride*.

"The whole subject of child marriage," wrote the PCA in its unusually harsh rejection of the film on August 28, 1943, "is so abhorrent to normal people that any treatment of it inevitably suggests sexual abnormalities on the part of the participants in this story." [20] *Child Bride* was rejected by the New York Censor Board in 1942 (and again upon appeal in '44), and the Pennsylvania board in 1944.

To the PCA, the genre was a blemish on the industry and only with greatest reluctance did they hand over the few seals of approval earned by such films.

C.C. Pettijohn of the Film Boards of Trade seems to have clearly overstepped his authority when he dispatched letters to all the nation's regional Boards of Trade (censorship boards), circa 1937, condemning, "pseudo-social-hygiene-educational pictures" and advising them "not to cooperate in the theatrical distribution of this type of picture." [21] The exploiteers are

The sanctity of marriage (in one of its more unusual forms) was questioned in Patrick Carlyle's *Polygamy*.

63

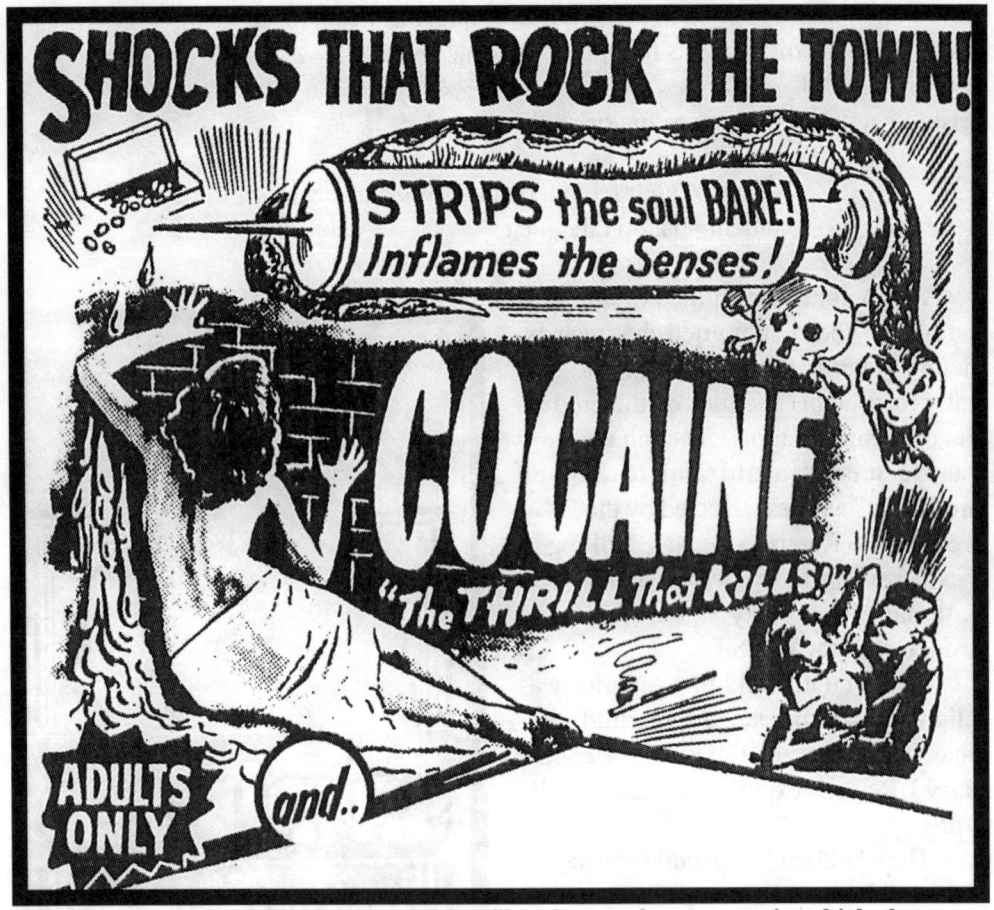

The Production Code applied not only to films but to the manner in which they were advertised.

crudely equated with the Red Menace by Pettijohn's observation, "These pictures are not made by any of the producers regularly engaged in the making of photoplays for the theaters." Pettijohn's dictum amounts to an informal ban on all exploitation films, but fortunately his advice was not widely heeded.

Many exploitation distributors politely complied with PCA and censor board rulings. *Cocaine Fiends*, originally titled *The Pace That Kills* and released in 1936, underwent numerous revisions demanded on a state-by-state basis, with specific lines and scenes cut. *Sex Madness* was rejected by censors in New York, Kansas and Pennsylvania. *Road to Ruin* (Birmingham, Alabama), *Tomorrow's Children* (New York), *The Birth of A Baby* (New York; Lynchburg, Virginia; Cincinnati, Ohio; Omaha, Nebraska), *Mom and Dad* (New York; Chicago, Illinois), *She Shoulda Said 'No'!* (Pennsylvania), *Assassin of Youth* (New York) were all rejected in specific states. A Pennsylvania judge condemned the relatively tame exploitation film *She Shoulda Said 'No'!*, as "moral trash and garbage."[22] And of the sterilization yarn *Tomorrow's Children*, in which a healthy young woman is forbidden to procreate because of her believed genetic defects, the New York courts banned the film along more political lines, because it "publicizes and elucidates sterilization as a means to prevent the conception of children, that it is a form of birth control, contraception without penalty, and that it is 'an immoral means to a desirable end.'"[23] This judgment was offered regardless of the fact that the film itself never delivers an entirely forceful case either for or against sterilization, though the court seemed to find mere mention of the issue a travesty and potential endorsement.

The more wily exploiteers resorted to unorthodox practices to salve the censors' sting and thumb their noses at authority. Sometimes the best way to respond to censorship was to publicize it. Like all good promoters, exploiteers recognized the profitability of good controversy and often played on the public's resentment toward these defenders of public morals. Bryan Foy's pressbook for the nudist film *Elysia* encouraged theater managers to hold a "trial by jury":

Some posters for *Ingagi* made it appear to be an ethnographic adventure...

> Send out invitations in the form of a summons for court jury duty for an advance or preview showing of *Elysia*, scheduled for several days ahead of your opening. Each guest should be provided with a "VERDICT" slip upon which his or her comment on the picture may be written at the close of the showing...[24]

A similar approach was taken during screenings of the 1930 jungle picture *Ingagi*, which was banned by the Hays Office. A.W. Nichols, northwest distributor of the film, devised a short film which was circulated to theaters within his sales jurisdiction. The featurette described Hays' actions, then explained the educational value of the film and asked viewers to vote in the lobby whether or not the theater should book it in spite of Hays' commands. Testament to the short's prejudicial power:

> At the State, Lakota, N.D., out of a paid attendance of 97 there were 67 ayes and only three negatives. At the Grand, Pierre, S.D., 115 of the 160 present voted in favor of seeing the picture and not one against it. There were 91 affirmative votes and no negative ballots at the Lyric, Rubgy, N.D.
>
> As a result of the elections, all three houses have booked the films.[25]

How then could the exploitation films escape the wrath of the PCA? As previously mentioned, it held no legal authority of any kind. Not that the exploiteers were without worries. There were still censor boards in New York, Pennsylvania, Kansas, Ohio and Maryland and numerous individual cities.

Some exploiteers—the more professional ones—submitted films for certificates of approval and made the required cuts for screenings within that territory, while others either avoided these regions entirely (selling films off to states rights distributors there) or circulated prints on the sly. Certain producers, like those at the major studios, dis-

...while other promotional items did more than hint at sensational thrills beneath its pseudo-scientific surface.

cussed projects with the PCA during preproduction, so that a film could be scrapped if the board was firm in its plans to reject it.

This was the case with Willis Kent, who met with Breen and PCA memger Geoffrey Shurlock to discuss "an idea he had to make an 'educational film' dealing with the pervert-criminal, and especially his depredation upon youth." Although Kent did his best to sell the film as an educational picture ("He explained it was his purpose to get hold of one or two outstanding doctors, Mr. J. Edgar Hoover, and a number of others to join their voices in pointing out the dangers which are suggested by the activities of the pervert criminal and thus to warn parents in the interest of their children... He emphasized in his entire talk his desire to do something 'worth while' of an 'educational nature' etc."), Breen refused to entertain the notion of a "sex perversion film" being approved by the PCA. "We left the gentleman with the clear understanding that no such type of film could be approved by us," wrote Breen in his memorandum. The film was nevermade. [26]

Another, more devious approach—akin to the "bait and switch" of the carny racket—is revealed in this memo from Breen to James Wingate in the New York office of the MPPDA:

> With regard to *Scarlet Flower*: Please let me say that the picture, submitted to Dr. Esmond's group (New York Censor Board) is, quite definitely, *not* the picture approved by us. On the contrary, it looks to us to be the picture, which we disapproved and rejected. Mr. Dwain Esper, the gentleman who has the picture in tow, seems to be a gentleman who is not responsible. If you will look at the files, you will see that the very material which Dr. Esmond points out as unacceptable, is the exact stuff, which we insisted to be taken out. [27]

The Scarlet Flower was a sexually frank Swedish drama which Esper dubbed into English and sold as exploitation, often under the title *Man's Way With Women*. Esper submitted the film to the PCA, deferentially made the required excisions, but then circulated the original, uncut version.

Once an exploiteer was caught in the act of swapping prints, his skills as a negotiator (and sometimes as a boldfaced liar) were tested in the offices of the censors. Remarkably, the transcript survives of a meeting between Harry Woodin (partner with Ed Mapel in Denver and Dwain Esper in Los Angeles) and his associate J.F. Freeman, and the New York Censor Board, represented by Director Irwin Esmond, Charles A. Brind Jr., Frank M. Dermody and Mrs. Cherlov. [28] The group convened to discuss the jungle/bestiality picture *Forbidden Adventure*, which had been approved with no less than 22 cuts, then screened in an unauthorized version, in addition to being advertised by posters, photos and banners that "were obscene, indecent and immoral." [29]

> MR. ESMOND: ...in viewing the picture, it was found that in reel five (the narration), "Beyond was another elaborately carved wall depicting monkeys and women—women and monkeys" was in, which we had ordered eliminated.
> MR. WOODIN: Mr. Esmond, that has always been in the picture.
> MR. ESMOND: It should have been out, as we stipulated it out.

Although the PCA objected to the line "See Sex Starved Women Break Their Bonds," it is nevertheless boldly displayed beneath this theater marquee.

MR. WOODIN: We always kept it that way.

MR. ESMOND: In Mr. Dermody's report, he lists other eliminations which were ordered to be cut.

MR. WOODIN: Mr. Esmond, I can recall exactly the conversation relative to those different scenes. In the full print there is very much more footage and closeups which were eliminated, so when the picture was finally passed, there was a lot eliminated. We did take down a couple of stills which showed closeups.

MR. ESMOND: I think we had a discussion in regard to those scenes, and I told you I would not stand for them... I saw the views; they were very offensive to me, and I ordered them out.

MR. WOODIN: Take, for instance, the three girls lying on the ground, there were closeup views of that, which were eliminated at the time it was reviewed; it was cut down to a long shot, and that particular scene is exactly the same as it was the last time it was reviewed. I believe there is a line there—for instance, you take any picture: "Eliminate the sex of the kid running down to the river." The kid is still running down, but it is not as close up as it was before, but it is still in there.

MR. ESMOND: It is either there or it is not. If you have a scene where the sex is visible, it should be out of the picture. We never pass a picture of any kind or description, where the sex is shown...

MR. WOODIN: I have at no time had any complaints made in regard to this picture all through the state of New York.

MR. ESMOND: You had plenty right in New York City.

MR. WOODIN: It is possible.

MR. ESMOND: It is not only possible, but it is so. I have been having telephone calls, when it was playing at the Miami and Gaiety Theatres. I never had such unfavorable comment as I had in connection with that picture. It seemed to me that this has been aggravated, starting in when it played at the Miami Theatre. Now it is starting in again.

MR. DERMODY: Mr. Woodin stated that he was unaware of what happened at the Bronx Theatre. I talked with the Manager, Mr. Zack, and he said that the advertising material was given to him by Mr. Woodin, that Mr. Woodin saw the advertising that he was to use.

MR. WOODIN: I gave it to him. Sometimes I'm there, my wife is there or the checker. I get no money out of this; I'm busy working at something else; I'm working in Jersey at the same time, so I don't know.

MR. DERMODY: You evidently had seen this advertising; then you came up and wanted it back.

MR. WOODIN: I did pick up some material; I didn't know what was playing. I didn't see the lobby at all. I store all my stuff there. I gave him the New York stuff. What he showed, I don't know, because I didn't know what he showed; I wasn't there when the lobby was up.

MR. FREEMAN: If you permit the playing of half a dozen dates, there will not be one scene of an objectionable nature.

MR. WOODIN: When would we expect to hear? The picture is opening tomorrow at the Howard Theatre in Brooklyn; the Manager spent considerable money in advertising, and it would be quite a loss to his business if it were withdrawn. We would like your decision and notice next week, if convenient to you.

In spite of Woodin's polite yet insubstantial defense, the license seals and certificates were revoked.

Harry Cording hits his moral bottom in Dwain Esper's remarkably factual, and heavily censorable, *Narcotic* (1933, frame enlargement).

When all else failed, the exploiteer might be lucky enough to have a trump card tucked away in his sleeve, as Dwain Esper did when he attempted to play *Narcotic* in Boston.

> Screened it for the censors... I paid my fee, sent the film in to be screened and I was out in the hall pacing up and down. Pretty soon out comes some dude, hollered to the guard there, "Where's the man that submitted this picture?" he said, "I want him arrested and I want to confiscate the print. Lewd, indecent, immoral, sacrilegious, tend to corrupt morals, incite to crime."
>
> So I quietly stepped out the side door and I said to some guy there, I says, "Where's the mayor's office?"... I finally got over to the mayor's office and I had a hell of a time getting in... getting a note sent in. Finally I told them, I said "Somebody's going to get fired if they don't take that note and at least tell the mayor

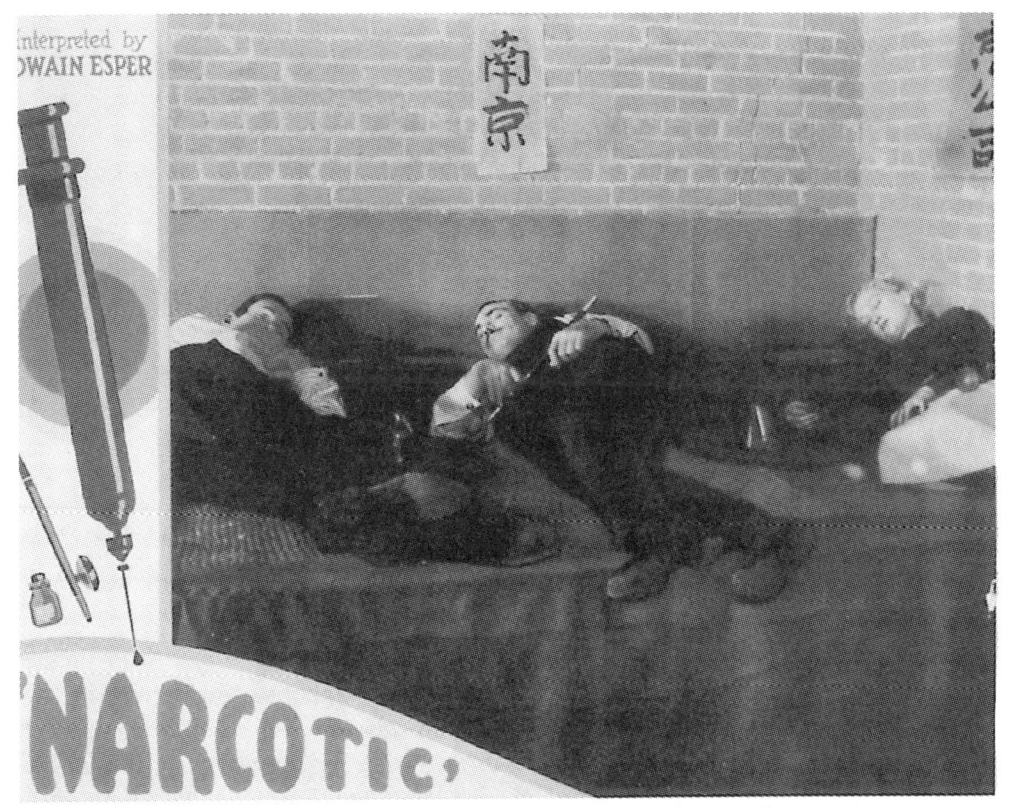

This lobby card for *Narcotic* reveals some of the film's shabby but suitably stark production values. Dwain Esper's bold promotion and headstrong distribution of the film broke many of the barriers that hindered exploitation's growth.

that I was here." I said, "It's been some time since we've seen [sic] but we're old pals together." When the note got in there he come through the side door of his office and said, "Dwain, come on in here." He run everybody out. He pushed a button and out come a circular bar. We started drinking. It was lush... first class. He said to me, he said, "Looks like you've got a little problem." I said, "Yes I have. I don't know whether you can help me or not but I brought a picture called *Narcotic* up here and sent it to the censor board and now they're looking for me and they want to confiscate the print, they want me arrested." He said, "Is that all?" He pushed a button and some guy come in and he says, "Go over to the censor board and get Mr. Esper's print and get a permit."

While the guy was bringing my print over, he said, "You want a date now quick don't you?" He was pretty sharp. I said yeah so he called a friend in the Tremont Theatre, right on the commons, right direct ... and called him and he said, "I got a friend here that's got a picture called *Narcotic*. He's got a seven-day permit and he needs a date quick." He says, "How about Friday?" and I say "Swell." He comes right over and he says... he put it right in and I got the advertising and he had a sign made... oh 50 feet long and about 10 feet high: "NARCOTIC.. From Heaven to Hell with a Hophead. You can take it out of the body but you can't take it out of the mind"... We played 17 or 18 or 20 weeks right there. No bother, no trouble, no nothing. When it was all over, I wanted to give Jim something for his campaign, he said, "No. Friends I don't accept anything from. From bad friends I accept." So we went out to his house for dinner, up the river about twenty minutes. Stayed all night. I stayed for the opening. We did a hell of a business in Massachusetts. First time any sex picture, sensational picture was in Massachusetts.[30]

Even in regions without censor boards exploiteers operated with their wits, on the fly, since virtually every municipality had a sheriff who might be called into action by a concerned civic group. Exploitation films would stay one step ahead of the law by playing very short runs, usually one or two days, as was the norm for any film in the 1930s and '40s. By the time police acted on complaints, the film would have long since vanished (the 20-week Boston run of *Narcotic* was an anomaly... or perhaps a bit of an exaggeration by the 88-year-old Esper).

Because of the intricacies of meeting a tight schedule of playdates while fending off the interference of local government agents (who usually asserted their authority by confiscating offensive prints), exploitation films were often accompanied from town to town by guardian angels who were adept at handling the myriad complexities inherent in releasing independent films of a controversial nature, the wily showmen who made the business of exploitation as sensational and idiosyncratic as its subject matter.

Chapter Four

SOCIAL CLIMATE

"It's no sin to make a profit."[1]
—Kroger Babb

The Progressivist movement born at the turn of the century in some ways parallels the current end-of-the-millennium zeitgeist: the fears of an endangered American family, doubts about the feasibility of social welfare, racial tension and a fear of immigration threatening a native workforce. It was the increased urbanization and a widening, more diverse public opinion which seemed to also call for new policies to address an America entering the chaotic 20th century. In some ways, we are living with the legacy of American Progressivism. Determined to use government to regulate the behavior of urban and immigrant working-class populations, Progressivism was a largely middle-class movement willing to sacrifice—at least for others—personal freedom for the greater benefit of expanded social control. A movement that gained its primary foothold between 1900 and 1920, Progressivism was composed largely of educated, white middle-class men determined to impose a middle-class order in the name of greater efficiency and social control, offering social improvement by governmental action.

The exploitation cinema, and the popular outcry accompanying its arrival in small towns and city centers, was informed by the Progressivist mind-set. Progressivists' attempts to restore social cohesion to a bloated, diverse population were echoed by critics of exploitation, who feared a cinema targeted at and enjoyed by the working class, the uneducated and those perceived as unable or unwilling to submit their base desires to the greater social good.

The climate of the turn-of-the-century affected exploitation on a variety of levels. Progressivism's linkage of degeneracy with the city—a myth still discernible in contemporary fictions like *Hardcore*, Charles Bronson films, *Taxi Driver*, Terry Gilliam's urban nightmares and the cycle of L.A. apocalypse cinema seen in films like *Grand Canyon, Falling Down, The New Age,* and *The Rapture*—echo modern conservatives' cries of pestilent, depraved American metropolises and posit the city as national wasteland, devoid of hope: the last stop on a long spiral to utter ruin for their characters. Films like *Sex Madness*, both versions of *The Pace That Kills* and *Mad Youth* also address this dichotomy between city and country, in addition to other bugaboos of the era: alcoholism, irresponsible reproduction and the effect of popular entertainments on the lower classes, as well as preach the responsibility of the social reformer in restoring the health of the nation. The Progressivists demanded a greater stake for government in the private life of Americans, so that the age of the betrothed, VD tests before marriage and increased scrutiny of who could and could not be married entered the public arena.

Even though exploitation films generally espoused the beliefs of the Progressive movement, the two groups seemed forever at war. Progressivists systematically opposed the genre as the exclusive domain of the ignorant and corrupted, and sought its censure. Exploitation films responded with parody and scorn, capitalizing on and perpetuating the popular opinion of reformists as intrusive busybodies.

Just as the typical exploitation film offsets pious moralizing with brash immorality, so does it perpetuate Progressivist claims while refusing to be associated with the movement. The holier-than-thou moralizing of the Progressivists was lampooned in the exploitation film's suggestion that such meddling in the personal affairs of strangers derived from these do-gooders' own impotence at home.

Mom and Dad typifies the conflicted, often schizophrenic approach of the exploitation film. It indicts an anti-sex woman's group, spearheaded by teenager Joan Blake's puritanical mother, for the very attitudes of prudery and anti-education that result in Joan's unfortunate pregnancy. The ruinous effect for the young and innocent of public agendas which seek to regulate daily life are targeted in *Tomorrow's Children* as sterilization crusaders threaten to neuter a healthy woman for her suspected genetic inferiority.

In his enlightening book *Behind the Mask of Innocence*, Kevin Brownlow traces the history of the "social issue" melodrama to the early silent pictures which presented realistic stories of vice, prostitution and moral corruption. While the educational, headline-informed melodramatic quality of these early social problem films links them with the formative exploitation of the '30s and '40s, the earlier genre never reached the bombastic, hyperbolic and visually explicit levels of the later films. Instead, films like *Traffic in Souls, Damaged Goods, Fit to Win, Human Wreckage* and an entire flourishing genre are the rudimentary skeletons from which exploitation builds it lurid stories, embellishing social crusading with the visual "goods"—the hidden truth of tissue, blood, decay, and sex behind narrative allusions. Exploitation *exploited* the claims made by industry representatives and laypeople for film as an educational vehicle—what a "clubwoman" called their ability to "save our civilization from the destruction which has successively overwhelmed every civilization of the past. They provide what every previous civilization has lacked—namely a means of relief, happiness and mental inspiration to the people at the bottom."[2] During the heyday of exploitation, however, these optimistic turn-of-the-century claims had been deflated by a new trend of condemning these reputedly infecting, corruptive films which appealed to the "bottom" segment of society. The educational potential of the nickelodeon had given way to Progressive claims of the need for uplift from the lower classes' moral degeneracy, principally through stricter control of the images which assaulted their ranks.

As Brownlow observed in D.W. Griffith's 1913 film *The Reformers, or the Lost Art of Minding One's Business*, the attempts of reformers to purify society through censorship of this incipient medium were often critiqued and lampooned by its makers. Like Griffith's tale of upper-crust reformers who can't keep a firm handle on their own domestic dens of iniquity, exploitation films draw from this original give-and-take between the social movement and movies. Films such as *Mom and Dad* and *Enlighten Thy Daughter* stressed the hypocrisy of crusaders whose own children's degeneration flourished as their parents preached to others' sins. The socially prominent Mrs. Morris in *Race Suicide* typifies the finger-pointing hypocrisy of exploitation's good upstanding citizens when she condemns her secretary Florence (*Slave in Bondage*'s Lola Andre) for undergoing an abortion, "I've always kept my house respectable... I won't have [my children] exposed to this contaminating influence," though her manipulative son Charles is the one who knocked poor Florence up in the first place.

The 1930s—the years in which exploitation flourished—were notable for crystallizing Progressivist claims: re-examining morality, redefining social taboos, and contributing to an upheaval in representations of the body. The private and the public merged as issues of entertainment and the family became the definitive terrain of debate over "proper" values. According to historian Frederick Lewis Allen, this new morality could be traced through subtle shifts in the popular press.

> Although the magazines contained more discussions of family and sex problems during 1930 and 1931 than at any time during the preceding years, the tone was on the whole more conservative. In the year 1930 the magazines expressed more approval of marriage and family life, more approval of "comradeship, understanding, affection, sympathy..." than in 1920.[3]

Concerned with mopping up the fallout of the Jazz Age (as the talk of "family values" in the 1980s and '90s attempted to mend the disrepair of '60s and '70s liberalism) and upholding standards of decency and self-control as a response to the Depression, the 1930s were a time of remarkable transition and intense discussion of sexual and moral matters. As critic Arlene Croce observes, "When you don't have money—and in the Depression nobody had any—manners, morals, ethics are coin of the realm."[4]

Thirties America stood on the precipice of modernity, industrialization, standardization and urbanization; issues that threatened to change the nation for good, but not necessarily for the better. While regionalist artists like Grant Wood and Thomas Hart Benton lamented a "waning pioneer farm culture" and the encroaching dominance of the city,[5] exploitation films also expressed an almost quaint fear of the 20th century's mechanized conveyance of vice: the automobile. In *The Pace That Kills* (1928), one

Exploitation films such as *Enlighten Thy Daughter* (1934) often played it both ways, beseeching parents to come, even as it blamed them for the ills befalling Depression-era youth.

75

A Motel room on wheels, the high schooler's jalopy provided privacy for petting and rapid transit to the outlying roadhouse in *The Road to Ruin*. (Photofest)

young man's fall from innocence is set in motion by his decision to leave the family farm (where he is shown pitching hay onto a horse-drawn wagon) for the city, a journey depicted in a dizzying montage of a spinning automobile tire dissolving into a locomotive's steel wheel dissolving into the undercarriage of an urban streetcar. It is as though the succession of spinning wheels mesmerizes the gullible lad, for he cannot match the city's hectic pace and quickly seeks vitality in the unmarked "headache powders" proffered by a co-worker.

The subtext of rural versus industrial America often surfaced in the Luddite concern of exploitation's town elders for the spread of vice, not via the enabler of liquor or loose morals, but the automobile, in the classic exploitation formula, gleaming symbol of youth's folly. Those ramshackle jalopies and polished Packards, exploitation films instruct, lead to a wide variety of modern vice, from necking on deserted country roads and access to out-of-the-way roadhouses (*The Road to Ruin*) and wanton city life to hitchhiking prostitution rings (*Highway Hell*). Ignoring the more immediate means of bacterial transmission, *No Greater Sin* sees the automobiles driven by the loose ladies at the Owl's Nest roadhouse as the conduit between the soldiers stationed in the town and syphilis.

In reaching back to a Victorian code of morality and literary melodramas, exploitation shared the same yearning for the past expressed by artists such as Wood. The

Depression years were a time of great myth-making, and the myth Americans were returning to was a 19th-century ideal of archetypal, sturdy, largely white American values. Writing of Grant Wood's idyllic visions of Iowa farms and peasant stock, art historian James M. Dennis cuts to the heart of the 1930s zeitgeist, "Myth became part of a pictorial search for continuity with the past."[6] But film was uniquely conflicted, for it often favored a conservative, pre-industrial Victorian mindset while representing to many skeptics of progress, the very machinery and industrialization and big-city values that were threatening America.

The sleek, art deco sets of Hollywood melodramas and crime pictures were visual endorsements of modernity expressed in design. While regionalists feared industry, Hollywood's futurists welcomed it, seeing in material progress a chance for the nation to escape the ravages of the Depression. In this cataclysmic age, every aspect of daily life was being thought out and re-evaluated. An entire culture was looking for the germ that started the Depression, the flaw in the American character and how the new, sterile designs in cars, tableware, and architecture of Le Corbusier, Marcel Breuer and Mies van der Rohe could perhaps offer a vaccine. For those looking forward—looking to escape the Depression by changing the way America looked and thought and its backwater regionalism—a vigilant industrial and private sector was vital to inoculating America against another economic devastation.

Modernism, with its love of streamlined, hard surfaces expressed a heroism in simplicity, clean lines and "honesty in materials"[7] that Soviet Constructivism had similarly offered its citizenry in the '20s. The underlying message of the muscled, broad-shouldered working *volk* of Soviet Constructivism was shared by Depression design rhetoric, which similarly stressed health and vigor. To Americans inclined to see salvation via the future rather than the past, exploitation smelled of corrupting, sick regression, of entertainments invested in the past; a past that needed to be escaped.

In 1931 Will Hays, the originator of Hollywood's Production Code set the heady tone of America's segue into a new purer decade, "We have a new generation, now rising from the jazz age, that promises to support clean, high-purposed entertainment."

But the movie business was just one facet of American life being re-envisioned in the rush toward clean-living modernity. Another one of the varied institutions shaped by this rapidly changing, progress-oriented society was the funeral industry, whose reconfiguration symbolized the larger changes America was undergoing. Dr. Stanley B. Burns has shown in his studies of postmortem "memorial" photographs how the issue of death, once an intimate facet in the life of the American family, became the responsibility of medical and funeral professionals with America's move toward increasingly impersonal, standardized industries. By the 1930s the funeral industry had largely replaced the at-home preparation of the corpse and the family's involvement in caring for its dead. With America's tidy, dynamic modernist look came a desire to relegate vestiges of the distasteful and morbid to an industry trained in such matters. Burns demarcates several important transitional moments in this de-evolution of the processes of dealing with death:

> 1930: The funeral parlor becomes the center of care for the dead. "Slumber rooms" replace the home parlor setting. With each decade death continues to become more and more hidden...

> 1933: The concern with "elimination of the fear of death," is a popular topic in early 20th century social literature...
>
> 1940s: Elaborate funeral parlor services become the tradition across the country. Official mourning becomes a very brief event, usually not lasting more than a week. Public displays of grief and mourning are frowned upon. People are expected "to go on with their lives" as if little has happened.[8]

Memorial photographs, once taken as sentimental, final documents of a loved one's presence, became an unwholesome, morbid remnant of an outdated culture. This once necessary representation of the body in death, like many aspects of modern life, was becoming ghettoized in the medical community, where doctors extended life and cared for the sick. A concomitant move was also well established by the 1930s to transfer the family's involvement in the birth process from the home to the hospital. An intimate connection to the body at various life stages was gradually passing from experience and memory. The mythology of America no longer had room for death, birth, decay, if the momentum of progress was to be sustained; and a vast cultural interest in the Real was being obliterated with the rise of a middle-class standard of right and wrong which located displays of the body in the latter camp.

In the realm of film, notions of the distasteful and socially unacceptable were collapsed in the explicitly detailed restrictions of the Production Code which was drafted in 1930:

> Theatrical motion pictures, that is, pictures intended for the theater as distinct from pictures intended for churches, schools, lecture halls, educational movements, social reform movements, etc., are primarily to be regarded as entertainment. Mankind has always recognized the importance of entertainment and its value in rebuilding the bodies and souls of human beings. But it has always recognized that entertainment can be of a character either HELPFUL or HARMFUL to the human race, and in consequence has clearly distinguished between: (a) Entertainment which tends to improve the race, or at least to re-create and rebuild human beings exhausted with the realities of life, and (b) Entertainment which tends to degrade human beings, or to lower their standards of life and living.[9]

The institution of the Production Code also indicated the necessity for the entertainment industry demonstrating a commitment to restraint and "good taste" as an economic weapon. The threat of organized boycotts and public condemnations of immorality on screen cemented a new code with issues of sex and the body excised from film.

Films like *Mom and Dad* and Kroger Babb's other 1943 birth-of-a-baby film *Dust to Dust* were anathema to the iron fist of American Catholicism—the National Legion of Decency. The Legion awarded the latter film a "C" or Condemned rating and had the power, during the critical debates that marked the Depression, to set the aesthetic and moral agenda of the American cinema. Stressing rarefied bourgeois values, the purity crusaders steered the popular cinema toward a sanitized, sanctified society and Hollywood suddenly had the twin forces of religious boycotts and dwindling movie attendance to contend with. By embracing the tenets of decent, upstanding entertainment, Hollywood could protect itself from the wrath of the Legion of Decency while working hand-in-hand on the campaign to return America to moral and, as a result, economic prosperity.

As Olga J. Martin, former secretary to Joseph I. Breen, noted in her 1937 handbook to motion picture writers, "The time was ripe for a moral revolution. Thus 1932 to 1933 marked the era in which the pendulum was to begin to swing back to morality."

The attempts by reformers to purge the exploitation films' immorality from popular culture, whether through outright banning or excision of prurient scenes, reflects a ten-

Kroger Babb's *Mom and Dad* had dozens of promotional "catch lines" and sales angles to make the film a surefire sellout.

dency for self-appointed defenders of morality to monitor and oversee popular consumption as a means of exercising political control.

Certainly exploitation's reliance on body spectacles of disease, pregnancy and female nudity suggested a "wastefulness" of sexuality when it is not steered toward the monogamous, heterosexual family. To the moralist then, the exploitation film, by concentrating more on the wages of sin than the rewards of virtue, encourages an improper channeling of the viewer's desire toward a nonproductive end and is, therefore, politically subversive.

Social theorist Michel Foucault, in studying the varied power relationships implicit in a cultural understanding of sexuality, has suggested the importance of viewing sexuality as a metaphor for the health of society. He writes:

> One also sees it becoming the theme of political operations, economic interventions (through incitements to or curbs on procreation), and ideological campaigns for raising standards of morality and responsibility: it was put forward as the index of a society's strength, revealing of both its political energy and its biological vigor. [10]

Foucault's linkage of the sexual state of affairs with the political, social zeitgeist is significant for the 1930s when a country immersed in economic depression sought comfort in theoretical strength. This might be a positive movement, such as the you-can-do-it message of Dale Carnegie's *How to Win Friends and Influence People* (1936) and the nation's rallying behind Roosevelt's National Recovery Adminsitration blue eagle, or a negative movement, such as eugenicists' oppression of the genetically "inferior" (see *Tomorrow's Children*) and the moralists' struggle to distance society from images of sexual degeneration. As Thomas Laqueur states of the 19th-century phobias of prostitution and masturbation, "the perverted sexual body haunts society and reminds it of its fragility, as it had done in other ways for millennia." [11]

Censorship rhetoric elaborates the idea that these films' "immorality" could be spread like a disease and that merely looking could contaminate the healthy mind, and then, the healthy body. Pennsylvania Judge Michael Musmanno stated of the marijuana soaper *She Shoulda Said 'No'!*:

> How will the punishment of the exhibitor heal the lacerating wounds made in the delicate sensations of children and sensitive adults who witness a picture of lewdness, depravity and immorality? [12]

This belief that sexual depravity was the Achilles heel for a nation fighting to regain its vitality and economic health is epitomized by the 1937 exposé of an abortion racket, *Race Suicide*, in which a coroner, intent on busting up an illegal abortion ring, cues the audience to the symbolic importance of preventing abortion. As the coroner intones, it is a slothful, decadent branch of white, otherwise respectable womanhood—the good breeding stock—who are, the subtext suggests, limiting their race's progress by aborting their children, while the spread of the Black, the Hispanic and other minority races proliferates unchecked. As the coroner sees it:

> The pitiful part of it is, they prey mostly on women who should have children: silly shopgirls who should get married, wealthy women who are too lazy or too busy with their social affairs to bother with bringing up a family, risking their health and their lives to escape their responsibilities. I tell you, it is little short of race suicide... It's our duty to the race to protect these women, if possible, from the results of their own folly.

The blight of the Depression, compounded by the escalating war in Europe, only increased this sense of the high stakes involved in keeping the country morally vigilant. The 1941 sex hygiene picture *No Greater Sin* has a crusading health commissioner and newspaper man uniting to expose the virulent sexual diseases originating at a local roadhouse. The newspaperman, the alliterative J.J. Jarvis, is at first reluctant to publish the scandalous story until he begins to consider the nearby Army camp which may catch the syphilitic spillover if unchecked. Jarvis recognizes his "responsibility of protecting the men from infection who are preparing to defend their country."

Sometimes the threat of contamination wasn't quite so literal but was cloaked in a xenophobic

Distilling many of the fears facing 1940s America, *No Greater Sin* showed the small-town fallout of roadhouse brothels being located too close to Army bases.

81

policy of keeping our national borders unsullied and free of subversive infection. The 1944, brutally racist propaganda piece *Samurai* (about a Japanese child adopted by an American couple who grows into an Axis spy, eventually betraying his country and murdering his parents) treats the outsider—the foreign born—as a potential infectant. The child's political insurrection is transmitted as insidiously as syphilis or gonorrhea.

In many of the feverish exploitation film's imaginations, infection, insubordination and drug use threaten to devastate home and family. Young girls drinking beer in a film's inception are, by the denouement, cocaine fiends. Girls who start out as uninformed virgins are transmogrified into wanton sluts. Morality must therefore be swift, strong and harsh in exploitation's weltanschauung, if the country is to be made strong through the eradication of disease. The threat to the democratic way of life posited in between-the-war American society was not only explicitly, but also *implicitly* sexual in discussing drugs, which represented a perversion of normalcy steeped in carnality. Marijuana's possession or use was made a federal crime in 1937, in answer to paranoia about the drug's ability to introduce users to heroin, cocaine and madness. A rash of scare stories in the 1930s, appropriated by exploitation films, fanned middle-class fears about marijuana as leading to sex crimes, homicide and moral degeneracy and the popular image of a pusher luring school kids to their ruin with a few puffs, even though a 1938 study by New York mayor Fiorello La Guardia found marijuana's effects minor, and its use restricted to bohemian and inner-city enclaves. But the campaign against marijuana was seen as part of a larger morality crusade aimed at legislating a religious-based morality to private lives.

Social historian Michael Schaller writes:

> The campaign against (marijuana) was portrayed as a grand battle for the salvation of America. The reformers, going beyond the tone of the earlier anti-alcohol campaign, saw marijuana use as a total threat to American civilization. This view persists today, where a public official has said of marijuana: "Time has run out. The jungle is closing in on this clearing we call civilization." [13]

The hyperbolic film-within-a-film in the exploitation classic *Reefer Madness* shows New York police officers wading through a vacant lot overgrown with marijuana plants. This drug bust, the narration tells us, helped stop the supply of marijuana sold in "schools and army posts," the moral incubators and training grounds of tomorrow's future. The stakes of the war on drugs are so high, these films intone, because of what they represent of our national well-being. It's easy to see the fear that could occasion the propagandistic suggestion of playgrounds and barracks filled with maniacally cackling, lascivious reefer-smokers.

The statement in President Roosevelt's 1933 inaugural address, "The only thing we have to fear is fear itself—nameless, unreasoning, unjustified terror which paralyzes needed efforts to convert retreat into advance," [14] was perhaps the inspiration of the opening scroll of Dwain Esper's *Maniac*. In the most ominous tones it could muster, the film's prologue suggests the corruptive possibility of fear for the nation.

At the local soda shop, another innocent teen (Warren McCollum) is drawn into a world of corruption by a cunning dope peddler (Carleton Young) in *Reefer Madness*.

> It is because of the disastrous results of fearful thought—not only on the individual but on the nation that it becomes the duty of every man and woman to establish quarantine against fear. Fear is a psychic disease which is highly contagious and extraordinarily infectious.[15]

Irrelevant as it was to the tale of a madman's experiments with reanimation, the text was like a pledge of allegiance which excused the film's excessive treatment of murder, rape, drug use and lingeried working girls. Similarly, Kroger Babb's *Mom and Dad* (released during WWII) prefaced its narrative with a sing-along of the national anthem (complete with waving flags and Washington crossing the Delaware), as if the subsequent tale of premarital pregnancy was undertaken as a contribution to national security.

Characterized by a growing intolerance for matters of sexuality and vice, the 1930s also experienced intense dialogue concerning the moral effect of films on youth and immigrant populations. Groups such as the Committee on Educational Research of the Payne Fund, the Motion Picture Bureau of the International Federation of Catholic Alumnae and the National Council of Women exerted strong pressure upon the industry and rallied popular support through their memberships. This popular protest was backed by high-profile political influence from such figures as Senator Brookhart, and industry publications such as Martin Quigley's (a Production Code co-author) *Motion Picture Herald* and *Harrison's Reports*, which commonly blackballed films of the lowbrow exploitation genre. In 1934, *Enlighten Thy Daughter*, *Narcotic, Road to Ruin* and *Tomorrow's Children* were classified by Quigley as:

> Immoral and indecent and entirely unfit for Catholic patronage; and since the list circulates also among non-Catholics, it may be said that they are unsuitable for any decent person. [16]

Part of the growing concern with mass entertainment, and the need to safeguard its audiences, was the solidification of the Production Code, which unwittingly ushered in the most prolific era of the exploitation film. Not subject to the regulations of the PCA, exploitation used the Code's guidelines with a kind of inverted logic, basing its narratives on the PCA's formally specified taboos:

> The treatment of low, disgusting, unpleasant, though not necessarily evil, subjects should be guided always by the dictates of good taste and a proper regard for the sensibilities of the audience. [17]

While the Production Code sought to guarantee a middle-class mass audience by policing the morality of the movies, social movements like eugenics hoped to homogenize culture into an acceptably mainstream body. Codified between 1919 and 1930, the "science" of eugenics is either an overt theme of many exploitation films or is more subtly cloaked in its conventions, such as exploitation's equation of immorality with the city. According to the influential eugenicist Madison Grant, speaking in 1913: "Cities are consumers of men and the countryside producers of them. So we still have a chance for the future if we are able to keep the blood of the countrymen pure." [18] Advocates of eugenics like Grant often linked moral degeneracy and criminality to the city and argued that the feeblemindedness, pauperism and criminality bred there were hereditary, and that the "degenerate" lower classes reproduce at a greater rate than the genetically superior population. [19]

Andrew Bergman, writing about Hollywood films of the Depression, has discussed how prominent the morally corruptive dimensions of the city became in the early '30s when "during the nadir of the Depression... corruption must have seemed like an old and trusted friend." [20] In Bergman's Hollywood, cities like New York are the province of the "shyster," the crook and the slick politician, while in exploitation films, a more pervasive, amorphous evil defines the city.

Exploitation films like *Sex Madness* and *The Pace That Kills*, [21] whose heroines are contaminated by urban disease, prostitution and drug addiction after leaving home, actualize this fear of the city as morally corruptive. Far from merely an atmosphere of vice which contaminates naive girls, films such as *Slaves in Bondage* and *Mad Youth* paint the country/city dichotomy in more black and white terms, demonstrating how young girls are procured from the country like livestock for sexual use in the city. In

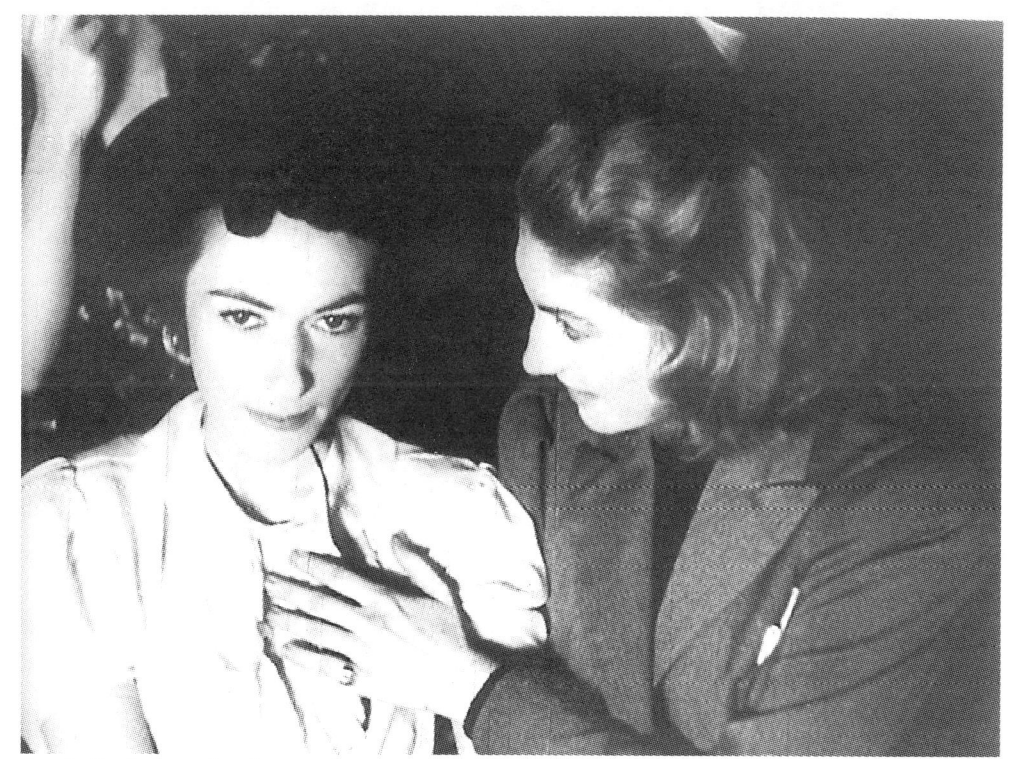

A relatively tame burlesque show opens up a Pandora's box of sin in its audience members, including a polite office girl and her secretly Sapphic co-worker in *Sex Madness* **(frame enlargement).**

exploitation films from *Slaves in Bondage* to *Race Suicide*, young girls travel to the city to become manicurists or show girls, where they then become involved in white slavery and abortion. The subtle inference is that girls who leave their quiet hometowns for the glamour of big city life are bound to wind up ruined by their wanderlust and naive thirst for excitement—like the anonymous manicurist whose death from an illegal abortion opens *Race Suicide*.

Such films demonstrate the profound fear occasioning America's shift from an agrarian, family-centered community in the '20s and '30s to a capitalist, industrial, diversified economy and the fear, along with this shift, of losing control over young America's sexuality. It was generally women's sexuality which concerned not only the exploitation films, but also the American population who were obsessed with how changes in the society would affect women.

Exploitation, true to form, *exploits* the relationship of sexuality to society, and suggests that the control of sexuality, especially female, is crucial to the proper functioning of society. Daughters, sisters, mothers in exploitation films are corrupted and changed by the modern emphasis on freedom from parental and social constraints, equal access to work and sexual equality especially as experienced in the libertine city. To not control women represents a more fundamental, devastating lack of control of the family and, by extension, the economy and the nation. Daughters, whose course from father to husband was once unmediated, are shown in the Payne Fund studies and a range of moralizing literature of the day as distracted by a range of options—sexual and otherwise—no longer contented to operate within the family economy where virginity is the

85

greatest honor a daughter can grant her father and her future husband. Whereas the novel represented a threat to the Victorian woman's honor with its window into a tempting, potentially corrupting fantasy life outside the protective womb of marriage and the family, film was the feared entertainment form of the modern, machine age.

Like all genres, from the Western to the post-war detective film, exploitation is less a reflection of "real life" as a mythmaking to contend with it. What America fears—what America desires—all transpire in exploitation. Just as John Ford's Westerns use the old West as an allegorical expression of the democratic, law-and-order American mind-set defeating the lawlessness and corruption of the natural world, so too exploitation's moral universe presents women as unoccupied, barren territory to be corrupted or preserved by the men and women with whom they come into contact. A mark of exploitation's difference from the neat, optimistic resolutions of Hollywood is that an uncontaminated, uncompromised woman is *not* the guaranteed outcome.

Of acute concern during the 1930s was the impact that the golddigger archetype of celluloid lore (*Manhandled, Orchids and Ermine, Possessed, Baby Face, Red-Headed Woman*) might have on girls who flocked to Hollywood, New York or Chicago in the hopes of somehow participating in this luxurious myth, and the moral fallout when—out of luck and money—they confronted the gritty reality behind Hollywood's glamorous facade. Exploitation tended to handle this eventuality in the most brutally frank terms, expressing in its typically hysterical fashion, a very real fear of the day. In *Slaves In Bondage* an urban beauty parlor serves as a white slavery front, its owner luring women with a promise of manicurist jobs, then trapping them in prostitution. In *Mad Youth* a lonelyhearts matchmaking advertisement in a movie magazine draws a teenage girl to the city to meet and marry a pen-pal husband, who is in fact the recruiter for a brothel. In *The Pace That Kills*, an exchange between a reunited brother and sister, both having become "hopheads" in the city, illustrates the heavy price a move away from home exacts, especially for women.

> Jane: You must get away, back to the country and sunshine. It isn't too late for you.
> Eddie: Yes, yes we'll go home now.
> Jane: No, it's too late for me. Girls can't come back.

Events in exploitation have a quicksand predestination and unfold in a nightmarish fashion, in a universe where escape and salvation are cut off, its characters left flailing in the mire of their own bad judgment. With women, a moral lapse is the most egregious and unresolvable crime which is often only escaped in suicide or a painful death from sepsis or disease. The sacrosanct nature of female flesh is illustrated in an exchange between a narcotics official and physician in *Reefer Madness*, in which the gravity of female disgrace is spelled out. The narcotics agent states, "Just a young boy. Under the influence of the drug, he killed his entire family with an ax." He then proceeds to a more troubling incident, "the most vicious type of case." He remarks, "Here...a young girl, 17-years-old [was] taken [into custody]. A reefer smoker. Taken in a raid in the company of five young men. Here is a particularly flagrant case." The actual and fictionalized debate over the vices of both city and small town seemed to demand a greater control over young girls, and their perishable innocence, if only for their "own good."

The police raid a dope den, capturing two "reefer addicts" (Lillian Miles and Thelma White) and a killer (Dave O'Brien) in *Reefer Madness*.

Film scholar Lea Jacobs, in her look at the Payne Fund studies of the 1930s, points to a moral subtext in the censorial establishment's treatment of filmgoing, and their belief that certain audiences are unable to intellectually contend with an immoral cinema.

According to Hollywood's Production Code:

> Most arts appeal to the mature. This art appeals at once to every class, to mature, immature, developed, undeveloped, law-abiding, criminal... The exhibitors' theaters are built for the masses, for the cultivated and the rude, the mature and the immature, the self-respecting and the criminal. Films, unlike books and music, can with difficulty be confined to certain selected groups. [22]

Evident in such a statement is a growing class bias played out in the movie house, that assumes one segment of society may interpret and appreciate art or entertainment while the other merely misreads and uses film for immoral or deviant purposes. The social Darwinism making the rounds in 1930s America proposed that some groups, especially immigrants, were unfit to participate in the same social institutions the "fit" took for granted. Immigrants and the working class were considered less able to handle

A remote roadhouse is the starting point of a high school girl's downfall in *Marihuana: Weed with Roots in Hell* **(1936).**

the imagery Hollywood parceled out to large audiences of viewers regardless of character or upbringing.

The idea that moral watchdogs must be vigilant against a class that chooses "circus" (an especially apt term for exploitation) above "bread" is a common claim.[23] Several exploitation films ironically literalize phobia into actuality by depicting the sort of decadent subject matter to which the middle class objected, as well as its grim consequences. *Sex Madness* has various audience members engaging in promiscuous sex, lesbianism, child molestation and murder, all based on watching a single burlesque show. The tragedy-bound hero of *The Pace That Kills* squanders the money he saved while working on the family farm at a nightclub with a lavish stage show. Displays of the female body in dance and the cabaret show are also depicted as the preamble to a life of sin for both dancer and audience. Performance itself could corrupt the vision and scruples of the audience, these films suggest, in a schizophrenic logic that validates the claims of the film reformers.

Young women's—and men's—patronage of adult roadhouses and gin joints in films like *Marihuana* and *Road to Ruin* often provides the means for their meeting older, more sophisticated men who introduce them to drugs and sex. The roadhouse was a locale frequently cited by exploitation filmmakers as the site of youth's corruption. Usually located in an aging tavern on the outskirts of town, the roadhouse was the menacing doppelganger of the neighborhood malt shop, providing a place for jazz-crazed youths to escape parental supervision and fall prey to pushers, pimps and other corrupters of innocence. Though their dangers were exaggerated by the reactionary press and the sensational exploitation film, the roadhouses illegally sold beer to minors, often served as fronts for gambling and prostitution and were, because of their rural location, conducive to driving while intoxicated. In a 1929 exposé of roadhouses in the newsweekly *The Survey*, Mary Ross noted that, "For the most part the patrons are the young—anywhere from 15 or 16 up to the ancient levels of 35, with the preponderance in the 'teens or very early 20s, despite the signs on the walls, 'No Minors Allowed.'" In his 1937 vice expose *Here's To Crime*, Courtney Ryley Cooper described a typical roadhouse:

> Music blared from within. Through the half-open door we could see a struggling mass of young couples on the dance floor, legs entwined, hands on buttocks, bodies pressed tightly together. Many "tongued" each other as they danced, lips clasped in a light suction. Outside the door were three young people beside an automobile. One, a 15-year-old girl, was vomiting; two boys, both sodden drunk, were holding her head.[24]

While censors feared such scenarios of liberated youth would inspire girls to ruin, actual viewers of these films often attested to a different effect. A 14-year-old "truant and runaway" interviewed as part of the Payne Fund's study of the link between film and delinquency had this to say:

> A play I saw, namely, *Is Your Daughter Safe?*, for adults, has taught me how to beware of boys, especially if I should ever take a pick-up ride, which I have taken only once. Well, this play taught me—and now I know the jokes that fellows play on some girls. They take girls out sometimes and make them walk—that's if they're good girls, they'll walk.[25]

The phenomenon this anonymous teenager is referring to is undoubtedly the one presented in *Marihuana*, where Burma's refusal to "park" with her boyfriend means she has to walk home. Other subjects in the Payne Fund echo this girl's sentiment, citing exploitation films as instructional guides down the proper path, though perhaps a little late as this 16-year-old "sexual delinquent" attests:

> Movies were not to blame by any means for my misbehavior. It was when I'd see passionate plays, I'd go home and then resolve to behave. The girls always become diseased and then if they had a child it was blind or deformed. These plays always seemed to teach

A school girl's willingness to "park" with her beau is the second step down for Burma (Harley Wood) in Dwain Esper's *Marihuana: Weed with Roots in Hell*.

> me a lesson... When I see pictures of women going wrong I think that I'll behave because I wouldn't want it to be blind or deformed. I certainly do think that such pictures are true to life. [26]

Of the 252 delinquent girls interviewed for the Payne Fund, "47 percent acknowledge that motion pictures taught them not to be sexually delinquent because they might have a child or get diseased." [27] What exploitation taught the rest, the statisticians don't say. And while girls may have taken the morals of exploitation to heart, and have seen their own ruin in exploitation's tales of tainted women, boys often cited the films as inspirational and titillating, as a 16-year-old "Italian" in a high-rate delinquency area noted:

> I didn't care for love pictures, and I don't like them. I'd rather see a funny picture or "hot" pictures for adults only. I like to sit next to a girl when they'd show them. I'd get sexually aroused. Once in a while I'd take a

Petting parties, such as this one in *The Road to Ruin*, where Ann Dixon (Helen Foster) succumbs to a suitor's amorous advances inevitably have tragic consequences in the universe of exploitation.

> girl to a show to get her warmed up but after the show I couldn't get very far. When I saw [in a film, a girl] went in the water, and her bathing suit came off. The girl was warmed up and so was I, and I started to play around. I got pretty far.[28]

As this teenager's testimony suggests, exploitation filmmakers may have been protecting themselves from even greater public scorn and potential legal action by insisting upon sex-segregated audiences, thus avoiding the problems of a mixed-sex audience "warmed up" by their pictures. While the majority of exploitation films show young girls being led astray by an urban sophisticate (e.g., Tony Santello in *Marihuana*), it is motherhood which is ultimately indicted for its failure to educate and guard its daughters from vice.

The use of the "reformist voice" in many exploitation films is found in characters—almost always mothers—who serve as mouthpieces for the moral sacrament of the day and who are normally reprimanded by film's end for failing to instruct their children in the realities of life. The reformist voice is sent up as an outdated, negligent and counterproductive element in the fight for true reform and education. Enlightenment is better provided, these films suggest, by a man—the policemen, newspaper reporters and fathers whose interest in eradicating vice is rational and sincere rather than hysterical and self-serving. *Guilty Parents*, a sex education film boycotted by the Catholic Church of Detroit, takes this common motif in exploitation films to extremes. A young woman's mother is formally indicted by a court of law for her failure to educate her child, which has resulted in, successively: underage drinking, premarital sex, pregnancy, her boyfriend's death, her flight to the city, near suicide, pimping of other young women and finally, murder. In *Road to Ruin* mothers again incur the blame for their daughters' fall from grace. A social worker tells a mother, whose daughter Ann has been diagnosed as a "sexual delinquent," "Your responsibility is to do what's best for your daughter. She's going to need a lot of help. And you mustn't fail her *this* time." We are to assume the mother then fails a second time when Ann's sexual degeneracy culminates in death from a botched abortion. On her deathbed, Ann asks her,

> Ann: Mommy, are you asking God to forgive me?
> Mother: I've failed you so utterly...can *you* forgive *me*?

In *Modern Motherhood*, a young man's perceptions of marriage and family are distorted by a mother who is not too conservative, but excessively liberal, condoning birth control and a non-traditional "modern" lifestyle:

> Mother: You know, Ted you can't support a wife.
> Ted: I don't have to: Molly makes a good salary. We'll just be living together instead of two different places... In-laws and babies are tabooed!
> Mother: Yes—a baby WOULD play havoc with your plans, WOULDN'T IT.
> Ted: And everything else! What's the good of a wife if she's tied down and can't go places with you?
> Mother: (Thoroughly in accord) That's when the OTHER woman gets the break. I remember when YOU were born. Your father—but then—he was very nice about it.
> Ted: (appreciatively) Gee, mother, you're a peach!

Protect Your Daughter/Reckless Decision puts the terms of maternal negligence more bluntly, in the opening scroll which intones, "Modern mothers are inclined to be over-suspicious of their daughters. This is dangerous. The young girl, feeling she is suspected, oftentimes lets go and says to herself—'What's the use—I might as well have the game as the name.'" Though these women's voices can be seen as an expression of exploiteers' sexism, they can also be seen as a tongue-in-cheek and often politically relevant depiction of the hypocrisies of the day.

It is possible that the sex hygiene film (those dealing with VD and birth) was speaking to a viable public need and a class that even the health care industry tended to ignore. Hildagarde Esper, an exploitation screenwriter and wife of director Dwain Esper, has described the popularity with women of films like *Modern Motherhood*, which concerned abortion and sex education: "...it seems that men weren't so interested. But the women liked it so we used to have special matinees and the theaters would do good on those."[29] A photograph of a line of women snaking along the sidewalk for a daytime screening of *Modern Motherhood* illustrates the investment women, in this image mostly middle-aged, had in the messages these films promised. Films like *The Birth of A Baby*,

In this remarkably successful publicity stunt, women were encouraged to bring their children to the theater playing Dwain Esper's *Modern Motherhood*. **A newsreel camera captures the moment. (Courtesy of Millicent Esper Wratten)**

Mom and Dad and *Narcotic*, which feature birth footage, enlightened a generation of women who in earlier years would have assisted in home births, but no longer had access to such information with the rising institutionalization of childbirth in the 1930s. With their narrative admonitions about the dangers of sexual ignorance often dramatically intercut with appropriated childbirth footage, this sub-genre of the exploitation film provided a graphic depiction of this increasingly hidden function of the body.

As childbirth historian Nancy Schrom Dye asserts, "By the middle of the 20th century, women knew very little about the process of birth and had no alternative but to accept physicians' authority... American women came to depend on medicine as the only source of knowledge about a central female experience."[30]

Maternity was not the only facet of life claimed by science with "progress." Writing about the history of American public health, John Duffy states that during the first 30 years of the 20th century, "A few county health units were beginning to function in rural areas, but most rural Americans scarcely knew the meaning of public health, and a great many seldom if ever saw a physician."[31] In terms of education, "the gradual elimination of federal grants for venereal disease after the war led to closing most of the clinics, and by 1930 the veil of silence had once again descended... Reluctant to move

A paternal doctor (Joseph Crehan) provides the voice of logic (and authority) to Wanda McKay in Howard Bretherton's *Because of Eve*.

into a sensitive area, public health officials contented themselves with performing laboratory diagnostic services."[32] It is the contention of Joyce M. Ray and F.G. Gosling, writing in the *Journal of Social History*, that advances in the dissemination of birth control and birth control information during the 1930s and 1940s may have been largely restricted to the middle class, who could afford the service of private practitioners and family physicians.

> Out of fear that their colleagues in private practice might disapprove of their work, clinic physicians may well have felt constrained to adhere to the strictest moral standards in providing birth control information, certainly enforcing stricter standards than at least some private practitioners despite the support of public opinion and the non-interventionist policy of federal law.[33]

Being a dominant force in American politics, the middle class had obvious advantages over the minority and low-income population, and used its influence to establish and defend a (conservative) system of moral values.

Such class bias was illustrated in a 1936 letter from the editor of the Alamosa, Colorado, *Daily Courier* to government officials urging marijuana legislation:

I wish I could show you what a small marijuana cigarette can do to one of our degenerate Spanish-speaking residents. That's why the problem is so great: the greatest percentage of our population is composed of Spanish-speaking persons most of whom are low mentally, because of social and racial conditions.[34]

The middle class feared marijuana and its influences in spite of their ignorance of the drug and its effects. In this instance, the exploitation film did not contradict this assumption but played into society's worst fears (as exploiteers would whenever such toe-the-line hysteria was to its own financial advantage). In Dwain Esper's *Marihuana*, for example, a group of apparently wholesome high school students are enticed by a pair of sophisticated older men to try marijuana at a party, and become skinny-dipping hedonists and are eventually involved in a murder cover-up.

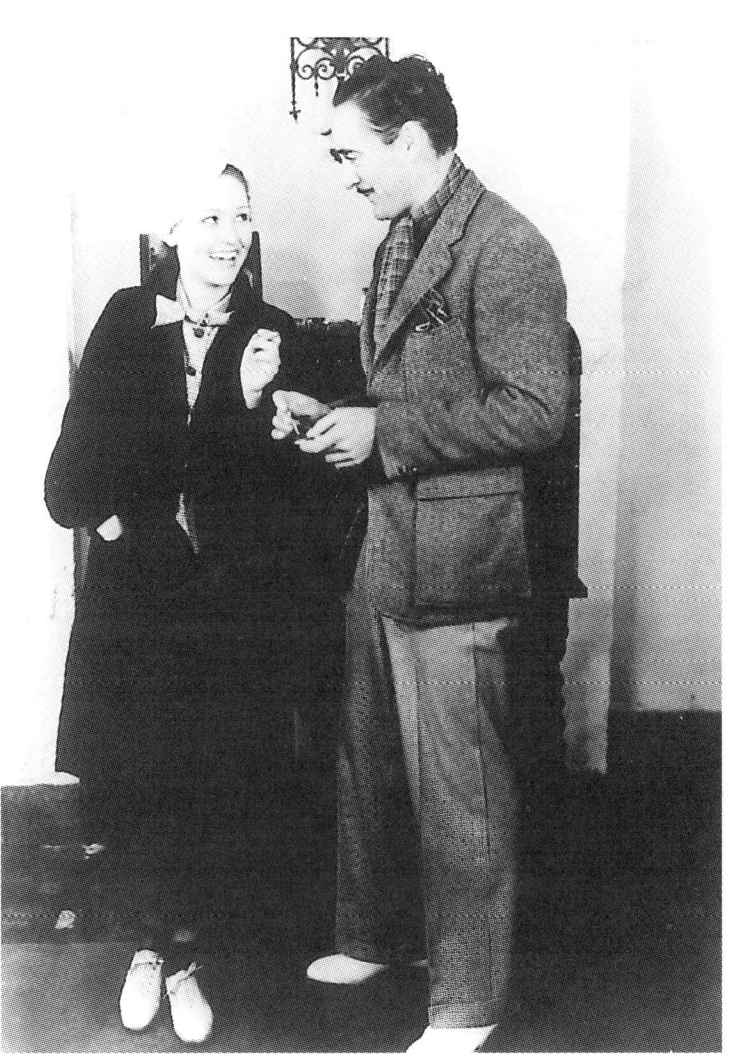

Fallen from grace: Burma (Harley Wood) enjoys a puff alongside her significantly older seducer (Patrick Carlyle) in *Marihuana: Weed with Roots in Hell*.

Though the makers of exploitation films often took the high moral ground (especially in the self-righteous title scrolls that opened—and in some ways excused—each film), the filmmakers seem to have had no true moral compass. Instead, their actions seem to have been dictated by the taboo desires of the audience and their own abilities to adapt controversial topics to the screen.

95

Chapter Five

THE SHOW ON THE ROAD

In the not-so-distant past when exploitation was king, an enigmatic figure appeared beneath the glare of the Main Street marquee. An emissary of sexual enlightenment, an apostle of Ehrlich, his solemn presence at the small-town moviehouse was meant to insure that the film's earnest message would not be lost amid the banners and bombast.

He invoked the names of medical specialists, government health agencies and even the creator Himself as a bulletproof vest deflecting ridicule and prudery. This powerful orator, remarkably effective in his campaign to spread the gonorrhea gospel, soon inspired filmmakers to tailor their motion pictures around his hypnotic presence. Rather than allowing the narrative to build to its climax and then taper away in closing credits, producers made films which were intentionally halted at their emotional pinnacle. The projectors were shut off, the lights were raised, as this valiant lecturer seized his opportunity to address his captive audience before the film's shocking resolution.

During this suspension of the drama on-screen, while the audience was communally held in a moment of heightened anticipation, the medical missionary mounted the podium, or if necessary paced along the aisles, and delivered his impassioned plea against sexual ignorance. Had there been any doubts as to the legitimacy of the film—or the theater's motives in presenting it—they were quickly dispelled in the lecturer's heartfelt harangue.

He reminded the viewer of the seriousness of the film's message. He daringly elaborated upon the mysteries of human reproduction that had so stymied the common man and woman. He even deciphered the blood-shrouded mysteries of the woman's menstrual cycle, differentiating between the fertile and infertile periods, scoffing at those who degraded this natural cycle by relying upon it as a means of birth control—in the dangerous lottery known as "Vatican roulette." For those who were interested in learning more about a woman's menstrual cycle, he prepared a chart so the phases of fertility could be mapped to the day, and generously offered this grid to his listeners... for a small sum of money.

This sum entitled the viewer to a booklet stocked with unimaginable wisdom which frankly addressed such taboo topics as mastur-

This sex-hygiene manual was sold to the men who attended screenings of Street Corner.

Drawn like moths to a flame, a group of women prepare to be enlightened by eminent sex lecturer Curtis Hayes. (Photofest)

bation, impotence, syphilis, various methods of childbirth, as well as the appearance and function of genitalia. The lecturer modestly prepared two books, one for women and another for men, but graciously sold both to any interested party.

This snake oil peddler of the exploitation circuit was known by many names, for there were many types of the exploitation film "salesman."

To his peers he was known as a roadshowman. And to exploitation's opponents he was a fallen angel, unveiling medical marvels of reproduction outside the respectable arenas of the home and the doctor's office.

In the '30s and '40s the roadshowman was, indeed, always a man, although frequently a man *and* woman shared certain tasks.

And gracious as he may have appeared, this emissary of forbidden knowledge was more serpent than saint.

When he stepped from the stage to the theater manager's office, his kind benevolence contorted into a more natural expression of financial ruthlessness. In addition to being a spokesman for sexual hygiene, he was also the agent for the film's distributor, a jack of all trades with a chameleon's ability to assume whatever guise best suited his needs.

In towns unreceptive to films of this unsavory genre, he acted as a diplomatic representative of the film's producers (even those companies that attempted to rise above criticism with names such as Social Guidance Enterprises, Inc., which released *The Story of Bob and Sally*). He argued on behalf of the film's noble intent and explained the redemptive effects of letting innocent eyes loiter on the ways of the wicked. If all other efforts failed, he resorted to bribery and chicanery to fulfill his mission.

The roadshowman was responsible for the success of an exploitation film, insuring the delivery of the print from theater to theater, overseeing the delivery of revenue from viewer's pockets to box office attendant to manager's office to distributor's desk, and insuring the proper size of the audience by employing promotional techniques drawn from P.T. Barnum's 19th-century showmanship, elixir salesmen of the Old West and the wily serpent of biblical legend, piquing the curiosity of his fig-leaved audience.

This WPA photograph shows one of the more creative mobile methods of exploitation promotion. (Library of Congress)

Crass commercialism and mass manipulation made flesh, the roadshowman is a remarkable icon of the 20th century, bridging the dying era of the sideshow spieler and ushering in the dawn of modern hype with his brilliant salesmanship of colorfully packaged lies.

To truly understand the multitudinous responsibilities of the roadshowman, it's vital to examine the entire process by which exploitation films were circulated. Complicated as this system was, it proved highly profitable; so much so that many of its facets and techniques were subsequently "borrowed" by more mainstream distributors and exhibitors. This system of production, distribution and exhibition distinguishes the exploitation genre. The outrageous content and ingenious approach of the films aside, the exploitation movement would still be a fascinating phenomenon just for the mechanics of its operation.

The process would begin with the completion or the acquisition of a new sordid potboiler of sin-and-sorrow by a distributor. Booking representatives then contacted theaters in big cities to secure a foundation of initial engagements, giving these more profitable venues the preferred weekend playdates. A route through the territory was then charted on a road map, with theaters in smaller towns (decorating the ribbon of highway that separated the metropolise) vying for weeknight playdates.

Regardless of its size, when a theater booked an exploitation film, it received far more than the rental of a 35mm print. Each screening was publicized with brazen showmanship in colorful one-sheets (the standard 27x41 movie poster; as few as four, as many as a thousand), a couple of large posters (41x81 three-sheets or 40x60 placards) for the lobby, one hundred window cards (14x22 cardboard posters with the theater name and playdate stamped on the space across the top which were placed in shop windows of barbers and grocers who appreciated a few passes in exchange) and 3,000 to 5,000 heralds (cheaply printed pamphlets foisted into the hands of pedestrians by victims of unemployment treated to a free shave, a day's work and a movie to follow). A set of stills and a preview trailer were also dispatched to the theater.

The size and quantity of newspaper ads (usually 66 agate lines, or about 4 3/4 column inches) were agreed upon by distributor and exhibitor at the time of booking. The cost was often deducted from the former's share of the box office. In bigger cities or longer runs, much larger blocks of advertising space would be purchased.

The more sophisticated operations split promotional duties in half, with an advance agent traveling along the route, plastering posters and placing newspaper ads just a few days ahead of the film's arrival. Smaller fry operations relied on the promotional acumen of the theater's crack publicist (who was, in many cases, the owner/manager). If the roadshowman found the film hadn't been sufficiently publicized, he would paste up a last-minute flurry of paper to take up the theater's slack. After all, the distributor's take was based on a percentage (usually the standard 35%) of the total box office gross rather than a flat prepaid rental fee; and with ticket prices wavering around 25 cents, it was in the roadshowman's best interest to pitch in some of his own time to stir up interest in the picture.

If a theater manager buckled, and had second thoughts about running such a scabrous picture, the roadshowman could seek out a new venue (if the distributor had not already done so), have the publicity materials quickly modified and continue the tour without interruption.

While this town-by-town method of promotion and distribution may seem disorganized and ineffectual, roadshowing—when properly performed—was quite profitable.

This garish and colorful window card, with no fewer than three references to the killer weed, exemplifies sensational salesmanship at its best.

Roadshow spouse June Ormond, who traveled with her husband pitching exploitation films, recalls that *Untamed Mistress*:

> Was the first roadshow picture we handled, and we made $90,000 in three months in Texas. So we were off and running... I knew all the drive-in people. You had to know them. The best territories for our pictures were Cincinnati and North Carolina. Georgia was also good. The South was the country for this kind of stuff.[1]

In addition to the local censors and other drum-beating forces of reform, the roadshowman had to contend with another potential foe: the theater manager. Knowing they were dealing with small companies who wielded little clout in the business

A doctor and his two medical assistants prepare for a women-only screening of *Sins of Love*, a Mexican film imported and retitled by Dwain Esper. The two men at the extreme right are probably roadshow agents or the satisfied theater owner and manager.

world, unscrupulous owners often attempted to bilk the distributor out of their due share of revenue by falsifying ticket records, squeezing in unauthorized screenings or never bothering to mail in their rental checks. To prevent all these things, the roadshowman lingered about the ticket booth, manager's office or a nearby bar and grill, quietly overseeing operations, counting heads, appearing during the final show to help calculate the day's totals and carry away on his person the distributor's share of the take... in cash, always in cash. The revenue (less expenses and the roadshowman's standard five-dollar *per diem*) was then wired back to the home office along with a report on the screenings, the condition of the print, etc.

The roadshowman's nightly fin covered meals and lodging—in a tourist cabin, boarding house or on the highway shoulder. Proper payment for services rendered would follow upon the successful completion of a roadshow circuit. A tank of gas, quart of oil or patching of tire, print inspection fees, shipping and telegram charges were deducted from the distributor's share.

When a roadshowman pulled into town in the late morning, he usually appraised the local situation, checking the newspaper for ads or signs of gathering political storm clouds. Arriving at the theater, he cordially greeted the manager and staff, then set to work examining the house, the lobby and marquee. Returning to his black sedan, or the small two-wheel trailer in tow, he unearthed the tools of his garish trade. Painted canvas banners—40x60s for the lobby, a long narrow apron for the marquee—extolled the sensationalism of the film in vivid verbiage and equally grandiose type.

A sheaf of 8x10 glossies were slipped into cardboard still displays and propped up near the entrance. He supervised the usher as he or she adjusted the red plastic letters on the yet to be illuminated marquee to his satisfaction. Then, untying the bundle from his automobile's rooftop, he brought in the *pièce-de-résistance*: the lobby display. For the smaller roadshow circuits it might be little more than a pair of tabletop glass cases of hypodermic needles, spoons pinched from a cafeteria, simulated reefers and assorted tools of the drug smuggling trade. Larger tours, circulating, say, a jungle picture, might have six-foot tall, vertical glass-front cabinets with "authentic" spears, shields, bones and the requisite shrunken heads. Lobby displays were not usually designed for specific films but meant to accompany films of a particular exploitation sub-genre, such as drug pictures, sex-ed treatises, jungle "documentaries" and vice-laden crime thrillers.

Buried in the roadshowman's trunk beneath all these accouterments lay, almost forgotten in the grimy octagonal Goldberg can, the film itself. With such a tight booking schedule, the distributor could not chance an unforeseen delay in the schedules of film transit companies and logically added print transport to the roadshowman's roster of duties.

The entire show, with the exception of advance publicity materials, was contained in a single vehicle. A picture's success could easily be jeopardized by engine failure, a drunken binge, a misread map or unexpected incarceration—though such fiascoes were uncommon. The roadshowman's resourcefulness was his stock-in-trade and every good exploiteer was armed with as many ploys and counterploys as there were problems to be faced.

One of the most effective tools for keeping the moral watchdogs at bay (outside of the roadshowman's own devices) was the introductory scroll—the seemingly endless text that opens every true exploitation picture. Invoking the names of doctors, police departments, drug enforcement agencies, Presidents and Jesus Christ himself, the scroll declares in florid, self-righteous tones its noble intentions, as in this excerpt from *Guilty Parents*:

> Sex ignorance, the black plague of adolescence, continues to augment the mass of innocent youth in the abyss of despair.

Chanted at the beginning of the film like a mystical incantation of self-protection and prosperity, the scroll defused the reformist spoilsports who attempted to thwart the roadshowman's interstate highway crusade against vice and VD. How could a critic claiming to defend the community's morals effectively argue against a film that openly dedicates itself to the very same cause, especially when bolstered by the mighty weight of Federal, State and Police Narcotic Officials (*Marihuana*)? That the film either contradicted or, more often, simply ignored its formally stated purpose was an issue of aesthetics that few public officials felt qualified to address. Only Willis Kent's silent version of *The Pace That Kills* offered specific constructive advice. A closing scroll announced:

> Write to your Senator and lend your support to the Porter Bill for the segregation and hospitalization of

Original title treatment from the theatrical trailer of Dwain Esper's *Maniac*, a not-so-delicate examination of mental illness.

> narcotic addicts—the greatest constructive measure
> ever offered for the abatement of the narcotic evil.

A simple splice transformed a sleazy, exploitive film into a noble treatise on humanity's suffering. Dwain and Hildagarde Esper's *Maniac* succinctly illustrates this esoteric exploiteer talent. A modern-day, wildly expressionistic retelling of Poe's "The Black Cat," *Maniac* was a departure from the usual formulas of exploitation, and therefore unfit for survival in the specialized exploitation market. The psychological horror film was brought up to speed with the insertion of a typically verbose Esperian introductory scroll ("...It is because of the disastrous results of fear thought not only on the individual but on the nation, that it becomes the duty of every sane man and woman to establish quarantine against fear..." William S. Sadler, M.D., F.A.C.S., Director of the Chicago Institute of Research and Diagnosis) and definitions of mental illness terminology which spasmodically intruded upon the action. Surprisingly, such fitfully presented information never seemed to clash with the film's tone, such was the near-schizophrenic style of the Espers' work. *Maniac* thus became *so* respectable that its distributor, Louis Sonney (Roadshow Attractions Co.), figured he could afford to spice it up a little by renaming it *Sex Maniac*, thoroughly rejuvenating its earning potential.

Some ingenious exploiteers devised the perfect legitimizing tool: a generic introductory scroll that lifts the picture from gutter to glory without specifically mentioning the film's actual topic. Thus the scroll could be taped onto the head of any feature in which wayward youths suffer moral ravishment (an effective synopsis of every exploitation film ever made). This all-powerful and all-purpose invocation can be found on a print of *Highway Hell*, which reads:

> There never was—never will be another picture like this presented in our city. We are truly proud to present the dramatic thunderbolt that ridicules false modesty and exposes the shame of misguided youth.
>
> The story that is happening in your town today—could be your son—our daughter. We hope that by the grace of God youth may be saved from this horrible SIN and SHAME and guided down the road of clean living after screening this picture.
>
> "Be not deceived; God is not mocked: for whatsoever a man soweth, that shall he also reap."
> —Galatians 6:7
> The Management

Exploiteers strived to secure formal endorsement of their films by respected authorities and, once attained, the seal of institutional approval was trumpeted loudly, often more loudly than the organization preferred.

When Mrs. James Looram, Chairperson of the National Legion of Decency (the Catholic organization that fought for the establishment of the PCA and stricter censorship laws), wrote to Harry Blair, the producers of the VD film *Damaged Goods*, commending him "for the delicate and restrained manner with which they handled a rather difficult subject,"[2] Blair integrated her comments into the ad campaign, especially her "hope that all adults and young adults will see this film." Less than two weeks later, Looram, belatedly realizing the potential embarrassment of having her good name associated with oozing chancres and filthy party girls, retracted her praise, saying:

> We deeply regret that you did not consult with us before quoting from our communication... the film, although executed in a delicate and restrained manner, is not *entertainment*, and should not be exploited as such. Secondly, the film, in our opinion, was definitely *not* for general audiences.[3]

In all fairness, *Damaged Goods* (also released as *Marriage Forbidden*) is a tasteful, well-made, emotionally involving drama. *The New York Times* wrote:

> The public has been fooled too often, mainly by being lured into the theater with prurient promises or extravagant lobby slogans unjustified by the actual content of the picture. It is very important then, in the case of a picture like *Marriage Forbidden*, to understand that there is nothing "sensational" about it... *Marriage Forbidden*... would undoubtedly do tremendous good in the educational campaign against syphilis, if only the public could be persuaded to go and look at serious pictures.[4]

In spite of this ad's promise of "wild orgies," director Patrick Carlyle insisted his *Polygamy* was sticking to the moral high ground, and strictly for "the thinking world."

It wasn't so much the film that the Legion of Decency refused to be associated with as the hell-raising manner in which it was promoted. The exploitation genre was one of such ill repute that producers were forced to conceal their association with the enterprise until after the film had been shot or the endorsement granted. Director Patrick Carlyle downplayed the sex angle of his film *Polygamy*, instead suggesting that his filmic gutter-crawl was an earnest, blunt educational instrument meant to separate no chump from his paycheck. During the PCA's consideration of *Polygamy*, Carlyle pontificated, "We are not striking at the angle of morbid sex to reach the masses and attract the 'Main Street' crowd." He lied; "We are aiming directly at educators... the sociologists, the psychologists... the thinking world."[5]

A similar bit of dissociation occurred after the release of Bryan Foy's *Elysia*. The president of the nudist colony where the film was shot divorced himself from the project because, "The message of health and sunshine and release from morbidity... was construed by a great portion of its audience in an entirely different fashion than was intended."[6]

In addition to legitimizing the evening's entertainment, it was often necessary for the roadshowman to perform a task with the opposite effect.

If a film was *too* educational, failing to meet the sordid expectations of the audience, it was sometimes necessary to placate nervous theater managers and rowdy crowds unsatisfied with their allotment of T&A before they began punching holes in the seat cushions or ripping speakers from posts. As an unadvertised coda to the performance (assuming all potential censors had long since vacated the premises), a roadshowman might conjure a reel or two of some more exotic spice: a nudist short, a cinematic striptease or the gross-out coup de grace, the birth reel.

Known as a square-up reel, these more explicit shorts were guaranteed to send the audience home happy, with a little taste of depravity to cushion their slumber. "The square-up reels were used only to keep the audience quiet if they hadn't seen anything in the main feature," recalls David Friedman in the outstanding video documentary *Sex and Buttered Popcorn* (Kit Parker Video, 1991), "To square 'em up, you square a beef, you make peace with 'em, you make 'em happy. That's what a square-up reel was... These were all made in the late '20s, very early '30s, and were taken around by the roadshowman. Half the time if there were no problems in the main feature... you could show the bare breast, maybe a bare behind... you didn't even have to use it."[7] Some historians refer to the prologue scroll as a square-up since it placates the opponents the same way the spicy reel satisfies the viewer, but for the sake of clarity, this book will apply the term only to the odd reels of distilled prurience used by roadshowmen as an audience pacifier.

If the sensational advertising, pious title scroll, road-to-ruin story (with all its mixed messages) didn't thoroughly discombobulate the audience's moral compass, the spectacle of a harem veil dance following a VD film, or a cesarean delivery tacked onto a drug menace picture was sure to thoroughly confuse the thrill-crazed viewer—who probably took home far more than he or she ever bargained for.

Over the course of his cross-territorial trek, the roadshowman was perpetually gauging an unpredictable public's reception of the exploitation film, adjusting the tone of advertising from town to town, sometimes even altering the content of the program to accommodate varying regional standards of taste and codes of censorship: more skin in the steamy South, less in the puritanical North. The content of a single exploitation title often varies from print to print, with visible splices where more lurid shots had been sandwiched into a scene or where segments of celluloid had been crudely excised. "Spicy" shots were routinely filmed during production (with the original cast, on the same sets) and set aside for "special" occasions. In some instances, predating the contemporary cinema's ratings-and-broadcast consciousness, producers filmed two versions of a single scene: one palatable to the eagle-eyed censor ever on the lookout for fleshy provocation and the other version more liberal in the degree of undress. This phenomenon is illustrated in *Sex and Buttered Popcorn*, which intercuts two versions of such a scene from *Escort Girl*, its cast alternately attired in skimpy lingerie in one version and more modest robes in the tamer version.

The producer usually tagged these substitute shots onto the last reel of the negative, so that each new print would be equipped for alteration. Also included in this supplementary material were modified opening credit sequences—identical but for the title of the film—that could be subtly swapped for the film's original titles. This enabled the more unscrupulous exploiteer to more quickly repeat his tour with the same film. It wasn't until the film was unspooled and the audience was tormented with *deja vu* en masse that the roadshowman's ploy could be discovered. *Polygamy*, for example, was also exhibited under the title *Child Marriage*. *Damaged Goods* was also released as *Forbidden Desire* and *Marriage Forbidden*. Even a film as well known as *Mom and Dad* graced the screen as *The Secrets of Love and Birth*. "Every time we didn't have a good title," Dan Sonney explained, "we'd put another one on it."[8]

Exploiteer David F. Friedman remembered Atlanta producer/ distributor/ roadshowman Ted Toddy as the master of the "title switch":

> He would play off a picture in every theater that would book it, take the picture out of release for six months, splice on a new main title, and rehash the route. Every Toddy movie had three sets of posters and ads.[9]

Title-switching was not always the distributor's ploy, but also a favored device of the less honorable roadshowmen who duped their competitors' prints, slapped on a celluloid alias and traveled the countryside selling someone else's property.

Films were also outfitted with a wide variety of slogans that trumpeted their importance (and sexual frankness) in capital letters. The following are several "catch lines" offered by the pressbook of *Enlighten Thy Daughter* (which might have been used for just about any sex-related exploitation film):

> Mothers need no longer tell their daughters. Send them to see "Enlighten Thy Daughter." It reveals the truth in a gripping, moving drama.
>
> A vivid, soul-searching drama of reckless youth faced with the inescapable consequence of mad romance.
>
> A tragic lesson in love.
>
> Does your daughter know the facts of life?
>
> Your child is sweet, good, and innocent. But is she safe?
>
> A revealing dramatization of a vital social problem that every mother, father, son and daughter should see.
>
> Reckless revelry breeding disgrace, disease, and even death.
>
> It is the duty of every mother and every father to see this picture.

But perhaps more noteworthy than his skills as a promoter was the roadshowman's performance as the lecturer. Sporadically in the 1930s but quite consistently in the 1940s and even into the 1950s, the roadshowman doubled as guest speaker before the respectful eyes of the audience. It began as pure pretense, dating back to Muybridge's magnanimous discussions of his contributions to science while audiences thrilled to the sight of men, women and children circumambulating on screen without benefit of clothing. The VD films of the 1910s had their sanctimonious lecturers, lest anyone mistake the educational pictures for mere entertainment. So also the roadshowman was called upon to lend moral weight to his wares.

It wasn't long before the roadshowman developed the lecture into a fresh source of revenue, one that did not necessarily have to be split with the house (or, as far as anyone knew, with the home office either): the sex hygiene booklet. These cheaply printed tracts, cribbed from medical textbooks and government pamphlets, didn't deliver much more than the films did, though their line drawings of bisected groins and a few photographs of syphilitic faces and genitalia could be enjoyed at leisure in the privacy of one's home.

It was also soon ascertained that sales (and legitimacy) were heightened if the talker donned white lab coat and tacked on a counterfeit "Dr." at the head of his name. White smocks were doled out to half a dozen local women who posed as nurses and assisted the fine doctor in his educational crusade. The exploitation practice of lecturing reached its peak with the 1944 film *Mom and Dad*, produced by Kroger Babb's Hygienic Productions. Babb standardized his advertising materials and simplified the publicizing of the film by having all lectures performed under the wonderfully respectable pseudonym Elliot Forbes.

An ad for every occasion: the original pressbook for Kroger Babb's *Mom and Dad*.

"Here's how it worked," Dave Friedman later recalled:

> Just before beginning the lecture, Elliot Forbes would count 50 books out to each "nurse"—25 women's copies, 25 men's. At the conclusion of the pitch, Forbes would say, "The attendants will now pass among you. If you care to take home a set of these books, simply raise your hand and they will be brought to you, I will have additional copies in the lobby after the show, and will be delighted to meet you and answer any questions you might have." Each bookseller then brought back to the lecturer cash for the books sold plus the unsold copies. On big dates each attendant would replenish his or her supply as needed. In indoor situations, the book sale took about 10 minutes; drive-ins required about 20." [10]

These ready-made ads provide a concise illustration of exploitation's unique methods of exhibition, which left no promotional stone unturned.

The educational lecture also afforded women the opportunity to involve themselves in roadshowing, when it was discovered that female audiences purchased more educational booklets when addressed by a female lecturer. During its first year of release, six of *Mom and Dad*'s doctors and nurses were husband-and-wife teams: Rocky and Betty Andrus, Bill and Ella Weinberg and Charles and Ruth Zimmerman.

June Ormond, who with husband Ron roadshowed an exploitation picture entitled *Please Don't Touch Me* in the late 1950s, recalled, "We would make up to $1,000 per night on book sales alone." [11] But Ormond adds, "You've got to *work* in exploitation—you can't be that dainty. It's a masculine business." [12]

All the true roadshow films had their esteemed, impersonated lecturers. *Because of Eve* had Alexander Leeds, *Street Corner* had Curtis Hayes and *The Story of Bob and Sally* featured Roger T. Miles. "The most euphonious and easily remembered names," Babb once told Friedman, "are short Anglo-Saxon names ending in 's.'" [13] The silent films had yet to learn this trick. *Love Life* toured with Dr. Benjamin A. Allan, while *Married Love* featured a lecture by Dr. M. Sayle Taylor.

If the roadshowman was exploitation's generic mouthpiece for the film's moral intentions, pimping the salacious wares to a sensation-starved crowd, the men behind the roadshow—exploitation's Kingpins and Dons—were anything but interchangeable. The principal role these small-town entrepreneurs and steak-eating he-men played was of the All-American, well-fed shyster, a vaunted tradition of hustle and hype seen in enterprising entertainers from Howard Hughes to Robert Ripley, from P.T. Barnum to Elvis Presley.

Mom and Dad's creator—its financier, producer, distributor, lord and master—Howard Kroger Babb, was just such a man. Babb—the definitive hearty, jovial demi-capitalist and one of exploitation's true titans—proclaimed himself "America's Fearless Young Showman" and, on the strength of his flair for Barnumesque ballyhoo, enjoyed a few years of remarkable prosperity during the late 1940s.

Like so many of the more daring exploiteers, Babb was born in small-town obscurity but cultivated a penchant for the sensational, dazzled no doubt by the thunder and glare of every circus, carnival and con act to roll its way through Lees Creek, Ohio. After busy careers in sports writing and as a referee for local basketball and football games, Babb tried his hand at special promotions during the early years of the Great Depression, at one point hyping the exploits of "Digger" O'Dell, the living corpse. As often as Babb could find a virgin town and a vacant lot suitable for banners and streamers and a portable ticket booth, "Digger" would be ceremoniously interred and dramatically resurrected after six days of staring up a narrow airshaft into the eyes of the curious.

In 1934 Babb became director of advertising and publicity for a movie theater chain based in Springfield, Ohio. Success fueled ambition, and in the early 1940s, Babb left the security of a weekly paycheck to join the wily, peripatetic fraternity of the motion picture roadshowmen, jamming the seats of small-town American theaters with youth starved for knowledge and thrills, rewarding their enthusiasm with raw spectacles of child bursting forth from woman.

As the story goes, Babb's inspiration for *Mom and Dad* came in 1943, when he sat in on a town meeting called to halt the reputed mass-impregnation of Burkburnett, Texas schoolgirls by the G.I.'s of a local military base. "It was a hell of a meeting," Babb later recalled, "You had all those old biddies squabbling and roasting everybody, they wanted to declare the whole Air Corps off limits... Then the idea hit me that would make a hell of a movie."[14]

The wisest decision of Babb's career was to produce *his* birth feature with a modicum of polish. With the help of J.S. "Jack" Jossey, Babb raised enough cash to form Hygienic Productions. With their $62,000, they hired former Hollywood director William Beaudine, a cast of struggling actors and a handful of musical variety acts to give the picture a touch of class—1940s dinner-club style—so that it rose above the common exploitation film by "passing" as a respectable feature.

From Babb's mistress, Indianapolis film critic Mildred A. Horn, a competent screenplay was coaxed. Ms. Horn would also compose the sex-education booklets sold during each "performance" of the film. A few reels of birth and VD footage from a medical supply company completed the package and, on January 3, 1945 in Oklahoma City *Mom and Dad* was born. Before the end of the year, Babb was jovially holding court a steak banquet in Columbus, Ohio, handing out cash bonuses, cigars and congrat' tions to his prosperous family of lecturers, nurses, "highwaymen" (account: "bywaymen" (publicists) and "legal squabblers" (lawyers).

Babb developed the overreaching, yet nonetheless effective, small-town marketing technique of dispatching a four-color handbill to every household with a mailbox. Like the traveling carnival's freak show—10 acts for a dime—posters billed *Mom and Dad* as "10 shows in One," including "When Life Begins," "Historic Moments in Surgery" and "A Cesarean Section." Special promotional literature sent to the exhibitor by Hygienic Productions instructed the theater owner on how to handle the anticipated record-breaking crowds of expectant men and women. A special tour was set up for race-segregated theaters, with an African-American Elliot Forbes and nurses, and a modified ad campaign.

By 1949, *Time* magazine was reporting *Mom and Dad*, "a knowing mixture of syrup, spice and corn," had grossed $8 million from 20 million ticket-buyers, with an additional $7 million income from booklet sales.[15] Of *Mom and Dad*, exploiteer/raconteur David F. Friedman opined, "Although the figures never have really been published... I would estimate that the picture took in, by today's dollars, close to 90 million dollars. I'm talking about by today's dollars. Actually, it was somewhere in the neighborhood of 32, 33 million dollars between film rentals and book sales."[16] *Mom and Dad*'s hysterically hyperbolic pressbook boasted earnings of $80 million ("second only to *Gone With the Wind* in total gross").

A healthy dose of exaggeration was a necessary ingredient in the exploiteer's formula for success, but the numbers are not as inflated as they may at first seem. Partial financial records exist of *Mom and Dad*'s box office returns during the years 1946-1956, and offer some indication of the film's true monetary impact. In California during this period, the film earned $518,034 in gross receipts. In smaller states such as Arkansas, Connecticut, Michigan and North Carolina, the film earned $84,773, $40,079, $259,881 and $192,159 respectively. Thus for these five diverse states, *Mom and Dad* pulled in $1,094,926.

To date, it has probably earned between $15 and $20 million, since it played steadily throughout the following decade and into the drive-in era of the 1960s. As evidence of the film's staying power, it was submitted to the MPAA ratings board in 1971 in order to play theaters that permitted only features with ratings; it was awarded an "R."

"In Hamilton, Ohio, they came like a stampede of wild animals," Babb recalled with his typical flair for hyperbole, two-and-a-half years before his death in 1980. "They took the box office right off its foundation, they moved it clear through the glass doors into the lobby, and the girl inside with it.

"The first time we played (in New Orleans), the priests from the various parishes came down early that morning and put themselves in a chain by locking arms. They put a complete chain around the front of the theater and no one could get through, it was like a football line... Well, various women said they weren't Catholics and went up to the line of priests and demanded to get through. When they refused, some woman hauled off and slapped one of the priests and it started a real fist fight. It was a sort of knock-down, drag-out situation and the priests finally yielded."[17]

Much of the film's success can be attributed to its rather strange and ambiguous title. At first glance, its innocuous title almost dared censors to find fault with such a clean-cut, traditional relationship. But considered as a sex picture, the title promises to lead the child into the parents' locked bedroom and reveal the hidden secrets of this primal scene. By referring to one's "Mom and Dad," it suggests sexual enlightenment tainted by family. Viewers must have experienced some ambivalence... excited to be educated on matters of sex but slightly repulsed by the choice of tutors.

The film was not merely Babb's most successful, it probably racked up higher grosses than any other exploitation film ever made. Yet in spite of his prosperity, Babb maintained the demeanor of an average Joe, albeit a Joe who wore a $3,000 ring, owned two airplanes and traded in cars for new ones once the smell of the new upholstery faded. "Just a country boy with a shoeshine," he liked to tell his cohorts with a grin.

In his prime, Babb ran a crackerjack organization, a quintessential postwar independent businessman, sharply dressed, overweight, back-slapping, steak-loving, Cadillac-driving American man. But Babb had a tragic flaw that limited his potential as king exploiteer. Instead of cultivating his gift for bringing the taboo to the screen and making it sellable, the respect-hungry Prince Hal of exploitation turned his back on the Falstaffian genre with misguided attempts to find fame and fortune with films decidedly less lowbrow.

So successful were Babb's techniques that he became a stellar attraction in his own right... at least as far as theater owners were concerned.

After *Mom and Dad*'s primary release, he changed the name of Hygienic Productions to Hallmark Productions. Though he occasionally made genuine exploitation films (all of the same high caliber as *Mom and Dad*), he squandered his hard-earned assets on poorly conceived family pictures. The strangest of these was *The Lawton Story*, a small-town, heart-warming religious drama perhaps offered as atonement for his multi-million-dollar-earning *Mom and Dad*.

The Lawton Story involves the exploits of a six-year-old girl who spreads love and cheer among the jaded and crotchety residents of Lawton, Oklahoma. Instead of inserting a birth sequence or a VD reel, Babb brought his film to a found-footage climax with Cinecolor shots of a passion play staged annually by Lawton's residents (Babb purchased four hours' worth of and whittled it down to fit into the story).

Babb prepared lavish 8 1/2 x 12 color program books with text by Horn (who could write about the life of Christ with the same ease that she penned VD pamphlets) to be

Cloying cuteness with just a hint of the perverse: Ginger Prince was often advertised in *The Lawton Story* with the tag "soap washes off dirt, but only God can wash away your sins!" (Photofest)

sold during a lengthy break between the cornpone drama and the Biblical reenactment. Miniature Bibles were also hawked in the aisles.

It was Babb's belief that every churchgoing person in America would attend the film at least once. *The Lawton Story* was praised in such ecclesiastical terms that to miss it would be sinful, but Babb didn't realize that non-churchgoers couldn't be less interested in a film about a small-town passion play, and many churchgoers (especially in rural areas) considered motion pictures of *any kind*, even those with religious themes, blasphemous.

While playing to an imagined demand for religious films, Babb hoped to create a star to fill the shoes of Shirley Temple, who had since passed into ungainly adolescence and unemployment. The instrument of his aspirations: Ginger Prince. A native of Atlanta, Georgia, Prince (who could only have been a relative of Babb's) was hyped beyond reason ("42 inches and 42 pounds of Southern Charm") and allowed to perform an unforgivable four musical numbers. It is baffling that the man who devised the most cunning sex-ed film of all time expected throngs to rush the box office of a film sold thusly (and with a straight face): "In Lawton, there lived a little minister who carried the Bible in his hand... and his love for LITTLE GINGER in his heart."

Even when screened under the title *Prince of Peace*—with new ads that resembled Sunday school literature and with the southwestern accents of Christ and his disciples redubbed by professional voices—*The Lawton Story* couldn't pass box office muster.

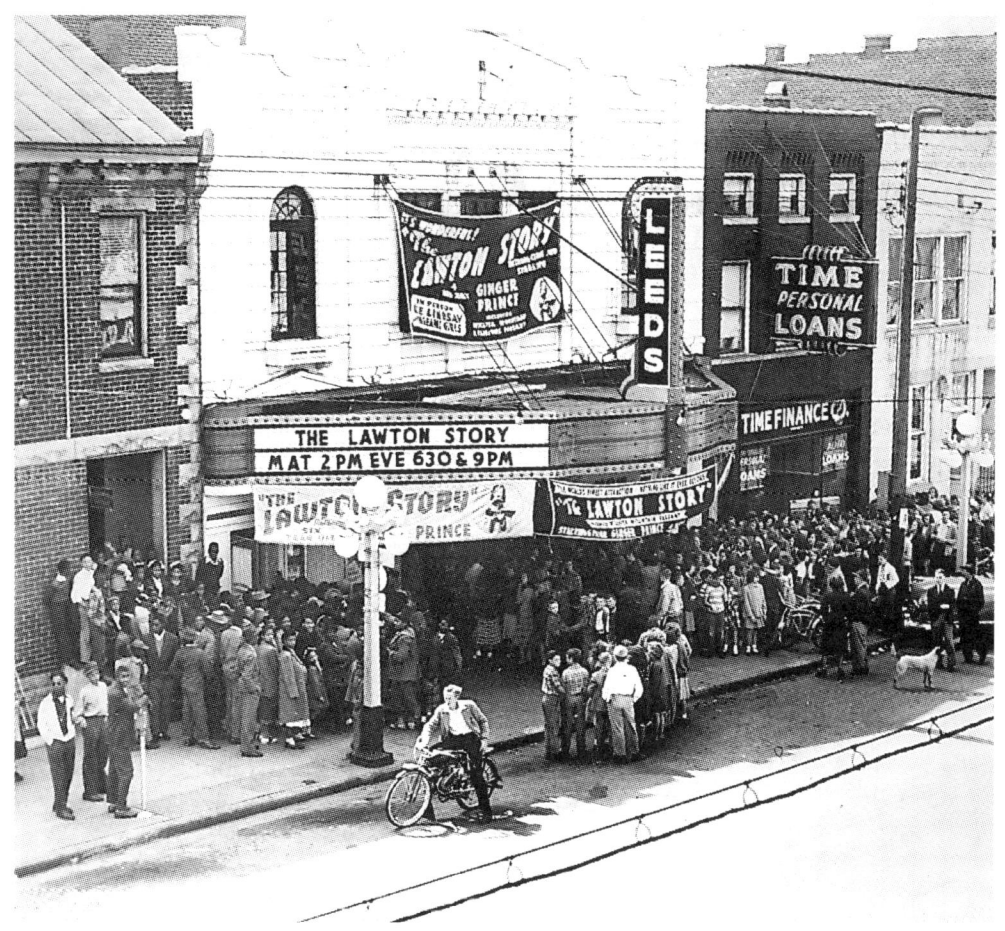

A healthy crowd—possibly in Lawton, Oklahoma—scrambles for a slice of big-screen inspiration. *The Lawton Story* (Photofest)

Ultimately, Babb cut some of his losses by applying some of the crafty tricks that had made *Mom and Dad* a success, apparently unconcerned by the clash between selling style and subject matter.

"PRAISED BY MILLIONS... Criticized by the Customary Few," some ads proclaimed, playing the anti-censor card. The ads became less pious and some were downright sexually suggestive, as one pictured little Ginger in a bubble bath saying, "Soap washes off dirt, but only God can wash away your sins!"

Babb even jazzed up the program by replacing the kindly Bible-and-souvenir-booklet salesman with "Lee Lindsay, the Wichita Mountain Speaker" and "The Pageant Girls," selling religion with a taste of sex.

Ginger Prince showed up in Babb's next two films, both produced in 1951. One was something of a return to the producer's roots—*One Too Many* ("The Important Story of Alcoholism")—while the other turned out to be another debacle of *Lawton*-ian proportions: *The Secrets of Beauty*, a film which instructed women on how to groom themselves and climaxed with the opportunity to purchase $10 beauty kits from the live representatives at the theater. The film was almost two hours in length, dragged down by a dry 35-minute demonstration of beauty secrets by Hollywood makeup artist Ern Westmore. Babb removed the beauty lecture, edited the film down to 70 minutes,

After the facelift: the revamped pressbook cover of *The Lawton Story*, newly titled and poised for prosperity.

tacked on an assortment of new titles (*Why Men Leave Home, Redheads and Blondes, The Marriage Bed, Man and Wife*) and sold it not as a women's picture, but a movie for men ("ONE out of 4 Marriages Crack-up! Divorce figures today are on the startling increase everywhere. Here's WHY...!"). Then, in perhaps his most bizarre promotional ploy, Babb released it on a double bill with *The Prince of Peace*, where it again foundered. By the summer of 1953, Babb was sued by two of his *Beauty* investors for fraud.[18]

One Too Many, one of Babb's last true exploitation films, was less successful than *Mom and Dad* because it lacked the playful edge that made the 1944 film so tantalizing and rewarding to the carnally curious. Among the film's primary flaws is the very vice being explored. It is considerably less enthralling to witness the aftermath of drink than narcotics since, according to the laws of exploitation, drugs—any drugs—lead to sexual abandon and general avarice, whereas alcohol—at least the way Babb represents it—leads to sleep, hangovers and guilt. Babb and Horn also erred by allowing the stern lectures to far outweigh the reckless behavior that warrants them. Even casual drinkers are treated to verses of scripture and A.A. platitudes delivered by none other than the local bartender who, by proximity to the spirits, seems to better understand their moral ramifications. When the medical lecture finally occurs, it's illustrated with bar graphs and pointless charts, with nothing as mesmerizing as the birth of a baby or the decay of a nude body. To cap it all off (the chaser to the watered down shot), he also thrust little Ginger Prince to center stage, allowing her again to sing several musical numbers, and thus tainting the entire narrative with a buoyancy and whorish sentimentality hardly befitting a hard-hitting expose of alcoholism.

Babb's dreams of being a big-time legitimate producer were so great that they blinded him to the potential of the genre in which he could have thrived. One occurrence in 1953 sadly illustrates this flaw. On November 29, he sped through a red light in California and was charged with driving while under the influence. Babb refused to take a sobriety test and attempted to bluff his way out of the arrest. Instead of owning up to his own accomplishments, he claimed to be the eastern producer for *Your Show of Shows* and the Bob Hope television specials. The officers were not impressed by the gaudy ring he wore, the $500 cash in his pocket or the Cadillac he was driving (which was driven from the scene by a significantly unnamed woman).[19]

The press quickly caught wind of his lie and rubbed his nose publicly in the truth, revealing to the public the types of films responsible for the independent mogul's prosperity. Babb lived the life of a high roller but couldn't live down the reputation of his profession.

Besides *Mom and Dad*, Babb's most successful pictures were traditional exploitation films: *Wild Weed* (aka *She Shoulda Said 'No'!*), *One Too Many* (aka *The Important Story of Alcoholism*) and *Halfway to Hell*. He entertained the idea of producing an uplifting film about new advances in cancer treatment but before the cameras could roll he realized the folly of his pretensions and dropped the project.

Babb died on January 28, 1980 in his retirement home in Palm Springs.

Exploitation filmmaker Dwain Esper, more than any other individual (especially when his work is considered along with the contributions of his screenwriter wife Hildagarde) epitomizes the aggressive spirit, crass sensationalism and reckless artistry that define the exploitation showman at his scandalous best.

Himself a veteran of carnival life (he began his show business career as "Fearless Chick," steering a motorcycle up the vertical wooden walls of a traveling motordrome), Esper lived his life and conducted his business by the laws of the midway, exuding a brand of flash and charm that won the reluctant admiration of many (even those who were aware of how dangerous he could be in a court of law). But if a dollar was to be had, Esper let nothing stand between himself and it. If he couldn't better someone in an honest transaction, his second act was usually to drag the other party into a court of law and engage his hapless victim in a series of protracted trials that sometimes resulted in the depletion of both parties' funds—which, in an odd way, seemed to be satisfying to Esper. In the course of his life, Esper sued or countersued not only his rivals but his partners, the government, his grandson and even his own mother. On a number of occasions, Esper's ruthlessness bordered on the suicidal. In Chicago in the 1960s he flaunted the powers of labor unions and organized crime and, for this transgression, was the repeated victim of arson, frequent death threats and on at least one occasion removed an explosive device from beneath the hood of his Cadillac. In pursuit of personal victory, Esper risked everything and spared nothing. Whether involved in a $100,000 land deal, distribution rights to a motion picture or even a casual dinner-table conversation, Dwain Esper held back neither tooth nor nail in his crusade to win. Life was the boardwalk, he was behind the counter, and the world was little more than a holiday throng of suckers and boobs parading naively past his booth—just asking to be taken. To most, Hildagarde appeared the model wife of their generation: quiet, supportive and demure. "She was definitely a very lovely lady," remembers form

To commemorate the 1934 holiday season, the Esper family sent loved ones a custom-recorded 78 rpm disc with a family portrait sandwiched within the acetate (l-r: Hildagarde, Dwain, Dwain, Jr. and Millicent Esper). (Courtesy Millicent Esper Wratten)

exploiteer Dan Sonney, who first met the Espers when he was a young man in the 1930s. She was "a very smart lady—a writer." Others, however, have indicated that less gracious qualities lay behind Hildagarde's urbane, attractive smile. According to one relative, Hildagarde "was a devil. She's the good guy and he's the bad guy and he did all the dirty work... She knew how to pull [Dwain's] strings." This opinion was seconded by another, who deemed her "a snake in the grass." But if Hildagarde was the vamp, Dwain was a willing victim, for they shared a hunger for prosperity and (ironically, considering the industry in which they worked) respectability. They complemented each other's strengths perfectly and balanced each other's weaknesses. Alone, neither might have achieved notoriety. Combined, they were legend.

Hildagarde's zeal is plentifully evident not only in the sensational, unflinching screenplays she penned, but also in the headstrong correspondence, lawsuits and appeals that constituted a considerable portion of her writing career. Dwain's aggressive spirit is displayed in the films themselves, which ignored the traces of pretense occasionally found in the screenplays and committed the narrative to film with all the finesse of a meatpacker. Dwain and Hildagarde's "butcher shop," as it were, came to them as a result of their real-estate investments, which were a source of extra income in the 1920s, when Dwain was a building contractor. According to surviving relatives, when a debtor defaulted on a loan, Esper seized the man's collateral: a motion-picture processing facility. A compulsive tinkerer and occasional inventor, Esper could not stop himself from experimenting in the lucrative motion-picture industry. He developed a portable sound recording system (Radiotone, which was used in the location shooting of independent films, primarily Westerns), founded his own production facility, Phono-Kinema Studios, and by 1932 had produced his first feature film: *The Seventh Commandment*, billed as "Hollywood's First All-Talking Sex Picture." In the course of the next five years, he directed and/or produced four features and one short film, and also worked as a distributor of other people's films, usually retitled and promoted more sensationally than the original filmmakers had intended. Esper actively produced films between 1932 (*The Seventh Commandment*) and 1937 (*How to Undress*). After this period, he focused his attention primarily on operating a succession of movie theaters, many of which supplemented big-screen fare with a procession of live strip shows. By the 1970s, the live performances had vanished, and the screens were converted to straight hard-core pornography, sold without the hyperbole and

With one exploitation film (*Damaged Lives*) under his belt, Edgar G. Ulmer (right) ventured briefly into big-studio terrain, pictured here with Boris Karloff on the set of *The Black Cat* (1934).

zeal of his earlier efforts. Finally, the images on-screen were more sensational than marquee-and-lobby hype ever could be, and the carnivalesque salesmanship was no longer necessary. If anything, such promotion scared away the "respectable" middle-class clientele eager for a furtive glimpse into the boudoirs of other men's wives. Even though Esper made no narrative films after 1937, he occasionally produced features that were compiled of found footage and supplemented with new titles, narration, and a few scenes of freshly shot material. At the time of his death, he was in the process of producing *Day of the Despot*, which recycled footage from his film, *Hitler's Strange Love Life*, and was to document the rise (and grisly war crimes) of Hitler and Mussolini.

The exploitation genre was not exclusively the domain of self-taught entrepreneurs, nor was it the final toiling place for Hollywood veterans whose careers were following downward trajectories.

The son of vaudeville headliner Eddie Foy and member of the legendary "Seven Little Foys," Bryan Foy pursued a career in film as an adult, becoming a gag writer for silent comedies and, in 1928, directing the world's first fully synchronized sound feature, *Lights of New York*. Eager to graduate from writer/director to producer, Foy stepped out of the major studio system and established Bryan Foy Studios at 9147 Venice Boulevard, where he engineered such films as *Tomorrow's Children* (addressing the issue of forced sterilization) and the nudist film *Elysia*. Impressed by his gutsy determination, Warner Bros. hired him to produce their lower-budget features and he began earning the moniker bestowed upon him by his 1977 obituary, "Rajah Of 'B' Pics."[20] Though he never returned to exploitation (in fact, his accomplishments in the genre are nowhere to be found in his official Columbia Pictures bio sheet of 1956), he remained somewhat true to the spirit of the genre as producer of such sensational films as *House of Wax* (1953, 3-D), Anthony Mann's *T-Men* (1948), *I Was a Communist for the FBI* (1951) and the prison pictures *Inside the Walls of Folsom Prison* (1951) and *House of Women* (1962).

Well-known director Edgar G. Ulmer was an artist in his own right, having trained in the theater under Max Reinhardt, and served as set designer at Universal, Fox and the

German UFA Studios, where he worked with F.W. Murnau, Fritz Lang and William Dieterle, among others. One of his earliest films as director came in 1933 in the midst of the legendary feud between Harry and Jack Cohn, the bi-coastal brothers who struggled for control over Columbia Pictures. Jack decided to fortify his financial position while ruffling Harry's feathers by producing a syphilis film (ostensibly as a public service on behalf of the Canadian Social Health Council (CSHC)). Ulmer later recalled:

> Jack Cohn, whom I knew very well, brought up the subject one night... We met the Canadian health minister who needed a picture for Canada. He told me about a play by Brieux called *Damaged Goods*, translated by Bernard Shaw... I knew that play and I said I could make a picture out of it... I wrote a script, the Canadian health minister was delighted. He didn't know a thing about pictures. I came back to the Coast and shot it. Harry, because he was fighting with his brother Jack, wouldn't let me on the Columbia lot. I had to go to General Service Studios, and I made the picture there in eight days... And it made a fortune. At that time the picture made $1,800,000, played ten weeks at the Central Theatre on Broadway.[21]

The victory Jack scored was a brief one. Harry took undisputed control of the studio and refused to distribute *Damaged Lives* (as the film had become known) through its usual channels and concealed all signs of its involvement in the production of the film—instead crediting the Weldon Pictures Corp. Nevertheless, *Damaged Lives* received a good deal of theatrical play in Canada, where the CSHC promoted it as the first Canadian film produced in Hollywood and the first Hollywood picture to have its world premiere in Canada (Toronto in May 1933).

For the most part, *Damaged Lives* is, in terms of content and style, a routine, low-key B picture. But at the close of the narrative, when the female protagonist attempts suicide by gas, the film becomes remarkably graceful and haunting, and one witnesses the depth of talent of the man who would later direct such stylized cult films as *The Black Cat* and *Detour* (under similarly constraining budgets and schedules).

The exploitation film's foremost raconteur was David F. Friedman, who chronicled his involvement in the business and his brushes with the "Forty Thieves" (the most colorful and notorious figures in the roadshow rackets... "a collection of crafty, individualistic, fiercely competitive sharks"[22]) in the book *A Youth in Babylon*. Friedman was one of the crucial links in the evolution of the exploitation film to new genres, beginning as a roadshowman but becoming more involved in distributing European art films (on the selling point of their liberal depictions of sex), making burlesque shorts, nudie pictures and gore films with such notorious underground filmmakers as Herschell Gordon Lewis. Prior to that he was a traveling lecturer under Kroger Babb and rubbed shoulders with virtually all the significant players in the exploitation demimonde.

Friedman's summation of exploiteer Howard "Pappy" Golden was of an irresponsible, inconsiderate grifter who routinely practiced the "scorched earth policy." That is, he *so* drastically misrepresented his product, left audiences *so* dissatisfied with this variety of film and was *so* contemptuous of theater owners and public officials that it was virtually impossible for any other exploiteer to "turn a tip" in his wake.

S.S. Millard was equally aggressive but abided by the unwritten code of conduct of the exploiteer, though he stepped on enough toes in the course of his career (which spanned back to the early exploitation of the late 1920s, when he was roadshowing *Sex, Is Your Daughter Safe?* and *Scarlet Youth*) to generate a fair amount of ill will. A 1928 *Variety* article took pleasure in resurrecting Millard's prison record (he had been paroled from San Quentin the year before) and in revealing the businessman's real name: Elid Stanch. This bit of "dirt" implied that he was now conducting business under an alias, which is a curious indication of *Variety*'s bitchiness toward exploitation, since the newspaper certainly did not reveal the actual names of the legions of "legitimate" film personalities who adopted new monikers with the same venomous glee.[23] Millard's incarceration for an unspecified felony charge was also mentioned in a 1927 *Variety* article, which states that the imprisonment interrupted his promotion of "a pageant in Detroit."[24]

The official spokesman of the "Forty Thieves," David H. Friedman, aka Alexander Leeds.

George Weiss was probably the most active exploitation producer of the late '40s and early '50s. His production concern, Screen Classics, released *Test Tube Babies*, *The Devil's Sleep*, *Glen or Glenda?* and the 1954 short film *Sinner-ama Cuties*. As soon as the restrictions of censorship began to loosen, he, like Friedman and Dan Sonney, abandoned the traditional exploitation film for sexploitation. No longer required to be clever in their integration of sex into the narrative, the "Nudie Cuties" they produced are lacking in imagination and far more tedious (and considerably less erotic) than their "educational" predecessors.

One of the tragedies of Ed Wood, Jr.'s career is that he so quickly abandoned the social commentary melodrama for a crude, formulaic form of crowd-pleasing entertainment. When he made *Glen or Glenda?* (aka *I Changed My Sex*), he invested in the film a great deal of his own feelings and opinions, resulting in a motion picture that is a true, unqualified original, his awkward visual stylings aptly suited to the bold, hallowed pronouncements being voiced. A tortured plea for social acceptance, *Glen or Glenda?* addressed Wood's own penchant for cross-dressing in a wildly disorganized but deeply impassioned film. Not long after, Wood seemed to give up on the idea of expressing himself through cinema and resigned himself to pandering to the masses, in a series of schlock horror films (*Bride of the Monster*, *Plan 9 from Outer Space*, *Night of the Ghouls*), mildly topical potboilers (*Jailbait*, *The Sinister Urge*), then in several nudie pictures (*Orgy of the Dead*, *Love Feast*) with a few other genre films thrown in between. While in the latter films he did manage to integrate some of his passion for transvestitism, and in all the films his wry, self-aware sense of humor evidences itself, Wood's films never achieved the profoundly engaging synthesis of style and content found in *Glen or Glenda?*

Had he entered movies 20 years earlier, Edward D. Wood, Jr., (pictured here in his beloved angora) might have revolutionized the exploitation film instead of being drained of his idealism and vision in the awkward post-exploitation, pre-porn era.

Several noteworthy exploitation figures share common origins in the making of low-budget independent Westerns. Wood, producer Willis Kent, producer/director Dwain Esper, director/actor Patrick Carlyle and director of photography William C. Thompson are but a few of the prominent exploiteers who first worked in cowboy pictures. Though the frankness and cynicism of the exploitation film may seem to be antithetic to the escapist, idealistic '30s Western, the two genres bear many other similarities. The two are closely bound by the minuscule budgets with which they were produced and the ease with which their scenarios were written (both closely adhering to well-established, tried-and-true narrative formulas). Both genres targeted specific factions of the general audience. For Westerns, it was the juvenile crowd and, for exploitation, the post-adolescent bachelor(ette). One of the greatest differences, aside from subject matter, is the "release life expectancy" of films in each genre. Westerns—be they serials or features—were produced in an assembly line format, cranked out with Fordian precision (Henry, not John) in order to meet the demands of the small town theater which needed a steady supply to fill the bill of weekly Saturday matinees. Films were shot, shown and shelved in rapid succession and the modest profits (carefully calculated in advance by the producer) quickly pocketed. Exploitation films were filmed with equal speed but much more carefully marketed so that a single film could remain in active distribution for more than a decade, if periodically rejuvenated by a title switch. The initial investment was approximately the same (slightly more since they generally involved more studio shooting) but the profit potential was far greater, which is why so many filmmakers made the transition from Old West to modern vice. Because in exploitation the emphasis was on promotion rather than production, fewer films were made for the market. Thus dozens of exploitation films were made compared to hundreds of Westerns.

Perhaps the most personal and eccentric of the latter-day exploitation films, Wood's *Glen or Glenda?* featured many of the genre's traditional ingredients: surgery, stock footage, headlines, authoritative doctors and histrionic melodrama.

Many exploitation films were shot by and cast with Saturday-morning-Western veterans, which explains the slapdash look and feel of many of the features. *Maniac* is perhaps the best example, its director, cinematographer, actors, sound engineer and editor all taking a departure from the cowboy picture in order to create a serious film about mental illness that moves at the frenzied pace of an adventure serial.

Once the lobby emptied itself into the theater, the banners would be folded, the display cases stacked near the exit and the roadshowman would join the theater manager for a little cash-counting. After the screen was dark, the print would be canned and dropped into the trunk of the exploiteer's car and he—money in pocket—would drive the highways to the next town, and the next playdate, usually the following night.

ROADSHOW SCHEDULES

The frenzied and circuitous route of the roadshowman is well illustrated in this map of Texas, which charts the course of the Dwain Esper film *Marihuana: Weed With Roots in Hell* over the course of one year.

MARIHUANA

A (roadshowman enters Texas)

Theater	Location	Playdate
Palace	El Paso, TX	June 17-19, 1936
Royal	San Angelo, TX	June 21-22, 1936
Lyric	Big Springs, TX	June 23-24, 1936
Strand	Del Rio, TX	June 26-27, 1936
Prince	San Antonio, TX	June 29-July 5, 1936
Royal	Laredo, TX	July 7-8, 1936
Palace	Robstown, TX	July 9, 1936
Palace	Corpus Christi, TX	July 10-11, 1936
Tremont	Galveston, TX	July 12-14, 1936
Queen	Austin, TX	July 18-19, 1936
Palace	Mexia, TX	July 22-23, 1936
Bell	Temple, TX	July 24-25, 1936
Ideal	Corsicana, TX	July 26-27, 1936
Majestic	Tyler, TX	July 28-29, 1936
Lamar	Paris, TX	July 30-31, 1936
Capitol	Dallas, TX	Aug. 1-7, 1936
State	Wichita Falls, TX	Aug. 9-11, 1936
Pictorium	Vernon, TX	Aug. 12-13, 1936
Mission	Amarillo, TX	Aug. 14-15, 1936
Ritz	Sweetwater, TX	Aug. 19, 1936
Lyric	Eastland, TX	Aug. 20-21, 1936
National	Breckenridge, TX	Aug. 22, 1936
Columbus	Ranger, TX	Aug. 23, 1936
Rialto	Harlingen, TX	Aug 25-26, 1936
Palace	San Benito, TX	Aug. 27, 1936
Queen	Brownsville, TX	Aug 28-29, 1936
Queen	McAllen, TX	Aug. 6, 1936
Ritz	Weslaco, TX	Sept. 1-2, 1936
Rio	Mercedes, TX	Sept. 3-4, 1936
Pope	McKinney, TX	Sept. 12-14, 1936
Star	Dennison, TX	Sept. 18, 1936

B (roadshowman leaves Texas)
C (roadshowman re-enters Texas)

Theater	Location	Playdate
Iris	Houston, TX	Feb. 15-17, 1937
Texas	Crockett, TX	March 1-2, 1937
Lyric	Terrell, TX	March 3-4, 1937
Palace	Fort Worth, TX	March 6-9, 1937
Palace	Stephenville, TX	March 7, 1937
Gem	Mineral Wells, TX	March 10-11, 1937
Gem	Brownwood, TX	March 12-13, 1937
Majestic	Abilene, TX	March 13, 1937
Ritz	Ballinger, TX	March 16, 1937
Dixie	Coleman, TX	March 17-18, 1937
Lyric	Dublin, TX	March 19, 1937

Majestic	Comanche, TX	March 20, 1937
Harlem	Dallas, TX	March 20, 1937
Ritz	Lemalde, TX	March 22-23, 1937
National	Capital City, TX	March 26-27, 1937
Plaza	San Antonio, TX	March 24-27, 1937
Roberta	Taft, TX	March 29, 1937
Orpheum	Waco, TX	March 30-April 1, 1937
Texas	Smithville, TX	April 2, 1937
Century	Dallas, TX	April 3, 1937
Jay	Tyler, TX	April 4-5, 1937
Ritz	San Antonio, TX	April 4-6, 1937
Queen	Victoria, TX	April 7-8, 1937
Strand	Yorktown, TX	April 9, 1937
Ritz	Columbus, TX	April 10, 1937
Roxy	Boling, TX	April 12, 1937
Queen	Wharton, TX	April 13, 1937
Floyd's	El Campo, TX	April 14, 1937
Edtex	Edna, TX	April 15, 1937
Rex	Port Laraca, TX	April 16, 1937
Colonial	Bay City, TX	April 19-20, 1937
Jewel	Texas City, TX	April 21, 1937
State	Pittsburg, TX	April 21, 1937
Alvin	Alvin, TX	April 22, 1937
Cleveland	Cleveland, TX	April 23, 1937
State	Atlanta, TX	April 25, 1937
Ritz	Dangerfield, TX	April 26, 1937
Ritz	Denton, TX	April 27-29, 1937
Gayety	Ft. Worth, TX	April 30-May 1, 1937
State	Slaton, TX	May 2-3, 1937
Texas	Monahans, TX	May 5-6, 1937
Grand	McCamey, TX	May 7, 1937
Palace	Pecos, TX	May 9-10, 1937
Texas	Royalty, TX	May 11, 1937
Palace	Crane, TX	May 12, 1937
Grand	Ft. Stockton, TX	May 13, 1937
Granada	Alpine, TX	May 14, 1937
Texas	Marfa, TX	May 15, 1937

D (roadshowman leaves Texas)

In general the theater was loaned one trailer, a set of B&W 8x10s. The theater was required to pay for newspaper advertising (66 column inches usually [actually agate lines]) and distribute heralds (3-5,000) and window cards (100 on average, usually dated) supplied gratis by the distributor. The theater was given four one-sheets and two three-sheets. Sometimes the distributor would allow newspaper costs to be deducted from the gross.

None of the contracts were ever approved by Esper; only Roy Reid or Ed Mapel.

Special thanks to David Pierce, from whose collection of exploitation materials this information was assembled.

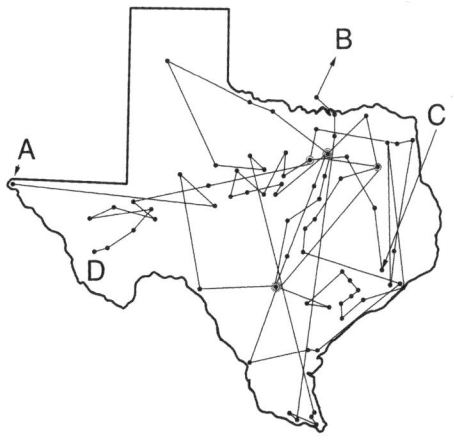

Chapter Six

SIDESHOWS AND SKINSHOWS

When presented in its full glory—with live lecture, booklet sales, square-up reel, lobby displays and garishly decorated theaterfronts—the exploitation film was more than a movie. It was a theatrical performance on a grand scale, with a pomp and circumstance all its own.

As might be expected, the theatricality of exploitation had little in common with the highbrow pageantry of opera or the legitimate stage. Even the coarse variety shows known as vaudeville seemed downright respectable compared to the theatrical medium that was exploitation's kindred spirit: the carnival freak show.

With its reputation for chicanery and deception, its phantasmagorical banners promising the exposure of lurid extremes in human life, its unapologetic exploitation of the physically different (obese, diminutive, misshapen, scaly, pierced, stretched and tattooed), the freak show was the focus of much criticism during the 1930s. The carnival sideshow and urban dime museum were succumbing to the forces of repression just as the exploitation film was enjoying its ascendancy. The exploitation film can be viewed, then, as a continuation of the freak show tradition, picking up the standard of its fallen comrade and carrying it across new battle lines of American culture.

Though the origins of the freak show are traceable back to medieval mountebanks and Renaissance fairs, the American freak show was officially inaugurated by one of the country's most famous showmen, P.T. Barnum. Barnum opened his American Museum in 1940s on New York's Broadway promenade, exhibiting all manner of natural and unnatural flora and fauna with the rousing barker's call: "See 10 Wonders for One Thin Dime!"

But like exploitation, the deceptive advertising practices of the urban dime museum and its growing perception as unwholesome and socially unacceptable inspired its ever-resilient showmen to take their fat ladies and Siamese twins on the road. The freak show profited on the traveling circus and amusement park circuit of the late 19th century, and even in "respectable" world's fairs and education expositions. But by 1940s what had once been a highly profitable amusement enjoyed by a variety of social classes, was on the ropes. Doctors and eugenicists repulsed by the notion of the physical in the hands of the uncouth and uneducated publicly condemned this suddenly abhorrent entertainment. Adding to this sense of the freak show's exploitive aspects were more practical blows to its rein, like the onslaughts of the Great Depression and a growth in competitive amusements like radio, the movies, vaudeville and burlesque.

And where the freak show's lowbrow tradition left off, exploitation was ready to take its place.

Bright and jubilant on the outside, dark and sinister on the inside, both the freak show and the exploitation film offered a unique blend of entertainment, education and horror, punctuated with unexpected moments of humor and artistic finesse.

The use of medical figures as lecturers and the dramatic impact of childbirth were two exploitation ingredients shared by the freak show. (Library of Congress).

The feeling of flushed anxiety that swept over the ticket-buyer as he or she placed a quarter on the box office counter and began to contemplate the carnal revelations within could not have been much different from the nervous anticipation of the carnival-goer just before stepping through the canvas doorway into a darkened tent of worldly wonders.

There was little to differentiate the front of a properly dressed exploitation theater from the well-appointed freak show bally. Both were bedecked with banners, pennants, posters and all forms of hyperbole, promising more thrills and curiosities than could possibly be provided by the attractions within. The banners that decorated a Plant City, Florida carnival bally in 1939 ("Exposing Birth Control" and "The Man Without A Skull—Alive") find cinematic kin in ads for *Sins of Love* (begging, "How Can Happiness Best Be Guarded?" and offering "The Truth About Love and Sex... True and Authentic in Every Detail").

In some of its advertisements, *Mom and Dad* was billed as "10 Shows in One." While this referred to the educational sequences within the overall film, it also brought to mind the structure of the dime museum and carnival tent show (known as the Ten-in-One), which offered 10 varied attractions for the price of a single ticket.

The technique of roadshowing—which gives exploitation its unique character, somewhere between cinema and carnival—is also based largely on the nomadic circulation of the carnival freak show. Where physical oddities were once exhibited in urban halls (such as P.T. Barnum's American Museum, which became the model for "dime museums" throughout the country), they responded to opposition from social groups and the medical community by traversing the country on an unpredictable path meant to shake the freak show's naysayers. A 1908 *Nation* editorial was just one voice among many condemning an entertainment seen as outmoded, viewed as "pathological" profiteering of deformity for dollars. The magazine called for the freak show's end as part of the "humanizing of our amusements."[1] Roadshowmen discovered this "hit-and-run" approach was as effective with films as it was with freaks.

$1,000
In Prizes for 'Hustling' Managers!

Each year, Hygienic Productions will award at Christmas-time, a total of $1,000 in cash prizes to the 10 'hustling' Managers, who in the opinion of an impartial Board of Judges, did the 10-best campaigns, respectively, on their engagement of "MOM and DAD".

Only bona fide managers, who operate their theatre day-in and day-out, are eligible.

If an Exhibitor owns and manages his own theatre, then he is also eligible.

Prizes will be awarded as follows:

1st Prize—$500.00 in cash.	6th Prize—$25.00 in cash.
2nd Prize—$200.00 in cash.	7th Prize—$25.00 in cash.
3rd Prize—$100.00 in cash.	8th Prize—$25.00 in cash.
4th Prize—$50.00 in cash.	9th Prize—$15.00 in cash.
5th Prize—$50.00 in cash.	10th Prize—$10.00 in cash.

To participate, eligible managers must make-up a scrap-book of their complete campaign and submit it for entry NOT LATER than 30 days after the close of their engagement of "MOM and DAD."

All entries received AFTER December 1st, each year, will be entered and judged the following year.

The impartial Board of Judges will decide the winners.

The thoroughness of your campaign... the tie-ups promoted without cost, or at little cost, to your theatre... the population of your town... the seating capacity of your theatre... the surrounding territory you have to draw from... the actual box office results of your engagement—all these things, and others, will be taken into consideration by the Judges before rendering their impartial and individual verdicts.

EVERY MANAGER, OLD OR YOUNG
IN A LARGE CITY OR SMALL TOWN
HAS THE SAME FAIR, EQUAL CHANCE!

"Mr. PIHSNAMWOHS (Showmanship)," Kroger Babb, used cash incentives to spark motivational fires in theater managers.

Nineteen years after appearing in *Freaks*, Siamese twins Daisy and Violet Hilton starred in *Chained for Life* and later toured as part of an exploitation roadshow package. (Photofest)

The most obvious link between freak show and exploitation film is found in the perpetrators of these lost, disreputable arts. Kroger Babb was not the only exploiteer who had cut his promotional teeth in the world of the carnival. Dwain Esper was a former motorcycle daredevil, while his wife Hildagarde used to dance for a truckbed medicine show in Frisco. Producer/distributor Roy Reid was a vaudeville theater manager and his wife a professional unicycle rider. Lecturer Scott Hall was once a sideshow barker, his wife Evy a circus acrobat. Roadshowman Card Mondor was a professional magician, his spouse Donna a professional dancer.

Other casual connections are found within the films themselves. *Mad Youth* features footage of an actual freak show, as does Esper's *Narcotic*. *Chained for Life* (1951) is an exploitation romance built around the personalities of world famous Siamese twins Daisy and Violet Hilton, while another veteran of the film, dwarf Angelo Rossitto, appears briefly in *Child Bride*.

All the popular arts—from fiction to film, music and theater—share an ability to whisk an audience into distant lands, eras and cultures, and allow them to vicariously indulge in new experiences. Rarely, however, do they exercise their transportive powers... to confront those outcasts who, willfully or genetically, violate the societal norm. Both the freak show and the exploitation film made this exposure of social deviation

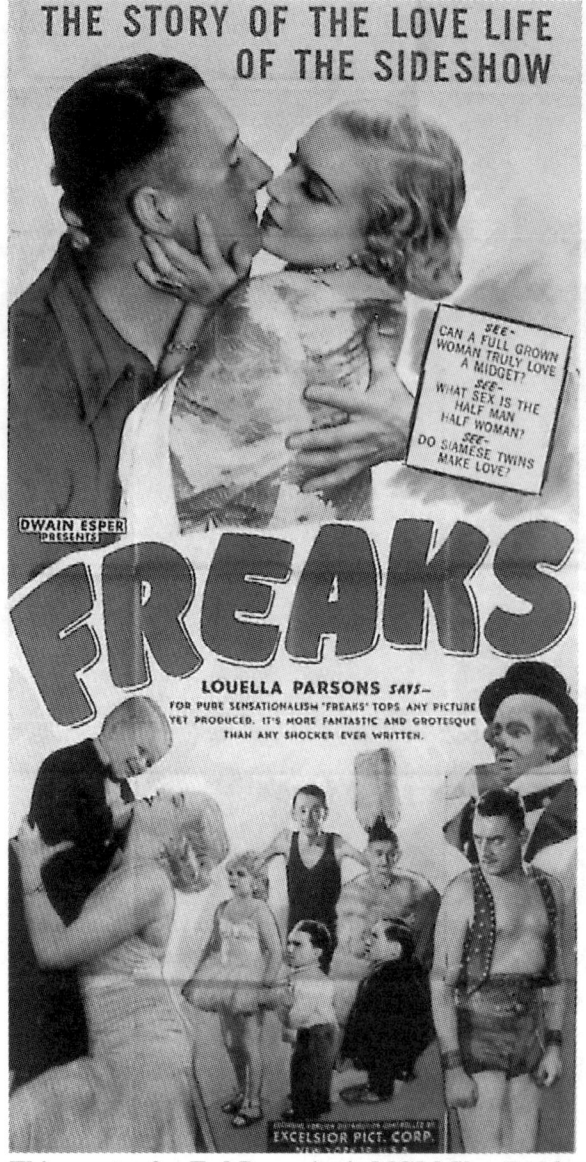

This poster for Tod Browning's MGM film *Freaks* shows how Dwain Esper later exploited its scandalous subject matter on the exploitation circuit.

their primary mission, and for their transgressions they were widely reviled and condemned by "respectable" society.

A prime example of the general contempt for the lowly freak show occurred in 1931 when, fresh from the success of *Dracula*, director Tod Browning was recruited by M-G-M and given complete freedom to make another horror film. But the respect and trust of the studio was quickly withdrawn when the cast of his new film—culled from carnivals and freak shows across the continent—attempted to dine among the platinum and bronzed actors in the M-G-M commissary. After numerous complaints were made, the freaks were forced to eat outdoors on a makeshift picnic table beyond the cafeteria premises. When test screenings of *Freaks* yielded wildly mixed responses, the film was thoroughly recut and given only a marginal release. Browning was never offered carte blanche again, so profound was his defiance of standards of "good taste." As one reviewer stated of *Freaks*, "Anyone who considers this entertainment should be placed in the pathological ward in some hospital." [2]

In the mid 1940s, Dwain Esper mysteriously acquired the rights to Browning's *Freaks* and the line between exploitation film and freak show was virtually eradicated. The sidewalks beneath the marquee were carpeted with sawdust. Esper even roadshowed the film with live "curiosity acts" in attendance, and was perhaps the anonymous promoter who, in 1962, brought Daisy and Violet Hilton to a drive-in in Charlotte, North Carolina to accompany a screening of *Freaks*, then coldly abandoned them after the show. Fortunately the duo found employment at a local supermarket and lived there the remainder of their lives.

Esper's former son-in-law, Mark Woods, occasionally acted as a Hollywood anchor man while Dwain and Hildagarde were on the road and assisted in putting together Dwain's exploitation freak show:

Laced with sexual innuendo, Tod Browning's *Freaks* dared to acknowledge the humanity of the physically deviant... and was condemned as a result. (Pictured: Browning [center] and the cast of *Freaks*.)

"Once, they must've been showing *Freaks*... Dwain decides he wants to have a little more advertising in the market," Woods remembers, "Calls me up and he says 'I want you to put a man on the train in L.A.'... So I go down and here's a big black man who used to do a show down at the amusement park at the beach (where) he had a monkey, he was dressed with a leopard skin, had stuff in his nose. You'd go in and he'd run after you, scared you."[3]

J.D. Kendis' *Slaves in Bondage* (1937) offered one of exploitation's most startling (if less literal) allusions to the freak show. Duplicating the sequential attractions of the canvas ten-in-one, the film's madame, Belle Harris, leads white slave "initiate" Mary Lou down a hallway lined with open doors which reveal a succession of women in

Akin to a sideshow banner, this poster for *Highway Hell* sets no limit to its sensationalism.

various states of undress. Belle points out a woman seated at a vanity table powdering her lingerie-clad body and explains, "This one is reserved for bankers, a haven for retired businessmen." Indicating another girl reclining in bra and panties, as the camera moves insinuatingly from her legs to face, Belle chirps, "And this one is for lawyers." This compartmentalized museum of iniquity culminates with two women lying on a huge bed taking turns spanking each other in the "Oriental" room. The sequence has the feel of a walk down the carnival midway, with the similar surprise waiting around every corner and behind every door. It also mirrors a more obscure carny attraction, the *tableaux vivants* show, in which patrons walk along a series of booths wherein live models recreate famous works of art—almost all of which are classical nudes.

Edgar Ulmer's *Damaged Lives* offers a nearly identical sequence, although the host is a white-smocked scientist and the row of doorways he beckons a young man to peer through reveal assorted cases of venereal disease. This guided tour of physical decay is very similar to the freak show's dramatic structure. Usually the carnival exhibitions were narrated by a lecturer who, like the Elliot Forbeses of exploitation, legitimized the taboo displays by posing as doctors or professors, and proclaiming the grotesque spectacles purely educational.

And just as the roadshowman concluded each lecture with the sale of sex hygiene booklets, the performers in freak shows routinely sold souvenir photographs of themselves (known as *cartes de visite*), and in some cases autobiographical booklets. Any opportunity to squeeze another penny from a gullible mark was taken, whether in the freak show or its bastard stepchild, exploitation. In the name of public enlightenment, exploiteers hocked everything from true-crime booklets to plastic wheels with which women could predict their menstrual cycles.

In his definitive history of the freak show, habitué of the outré Robert Bogdan describes an actual medical doctor, Martin Arthur Couney, whose lectures at Coney Island's Luna Park were almost identical in content and form to the exploitation variety. Couney operated a display of "Incubator Babies," premature babies of poor women who could not afford hospital care and so entrusted their preemies to Couney. "The exhibit was decked out like a hospital, with all those in attendance wearing hospital uniforms,"[4] Bogdan remarks, an image not far removed from the lab-coat-adorned Doctors Forbes and Leeds and their staffs of booklet-pitching nurses.

Defiantly fighting the forces of repression, doctors like Leon Ames in *No Greater Sin* (1941) were often the heroes of exploitation films. (Photofest)

Damaged Lives, a 1933 treatment of venereal disease, was unusual in that it toured with the doctor who appeared in the film, Dr. Leonard (Murray Kinnell), who provided a 29-minute speech "crammed with facts, plus frequent use of diagrams and illustrations."[5] More common seemed to be the traveling lecturer[6] who merely reiterated the moral crux of the film, as expressed by other "doctors" and representatives in the narrative. Such was the case with a 1938 "Sex Madness" show, which featured a double bill of *False Shame* and *Tomorrow's Children* and was accompanied by a lecture from a generic "expert" billed simply as "Radio's Friendly Advisor."[7]

Before the freak show fell into disfavor with the scientific community for cruelly "exploiting" freaks the medical community wanted sole access to, medical professionals were often willing to endorse the exhibitions, and their opinions and observations were often added to the pitch. According to Bogdan, "to the showmen's great delight, physicians and other scientists were particularly interested in human anomalies, and their commentary provided good advertising copy."[8] In the same way, exploiteers courted the support of any group that might help deflect criticism from their more controversial works. Positive quotes from nudist groups accompanied the release of *Elysia* (though they quickly withdrew their endorsement upon seeing the film), while promotional

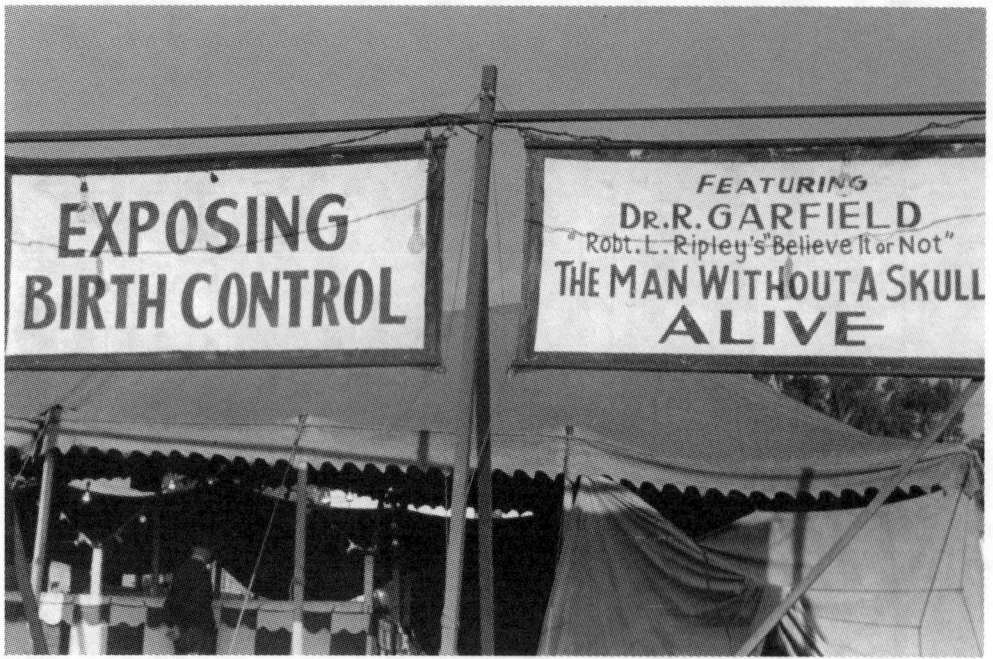

In the traveling freak show, the basic sexual functions of the body were presented alongside more bizarre medical conditions. (Library of Congress)

materials for *Polygamy* featured letters of support from numerous Mormons attesting to the benefits of multiple wives.

When such endorsements from respectable members of society could not be obtained, exploitation relied on the pretense of enlightenment offered by its "talker." The talker at freak shows and also in exploitation films tempered unpleasant or offensive subject matter with soothing moral guidance and, in some cases, humor meant to lighten the dreary line-up of syphilitic showgirls and gonorrheal bridegrooms.

While some exploitation films lacked the extra-filmic lecturer, almost all contained within the film one or several camera-directed addresses by a doctor, lawman or other authority figure who fulfilled the same educational and narrative purpose as the freak show lecturer. In a similar vein, the introductory title scroll which accompanies the majority of exploitation films also suggests the legitimizing influence of the freak show lecturer, translated into filmic terms.

One of the more bizarre spins on this voice-of-authority is the Bible-quoting, amateur psychologist and Central City bartender Sully (Rhys Williams) in the dipsomaniac potboiler *One Too Many* (produced by Kroger Babb), who not only lectures his customers on the evils of alcoholism but provides charts and statistics on this national plague.

Child Bride also features several instances of direct-camera address courtesy of the crusading school teacher. campaigning as vigorously as Sully, to eradicate the evils of child marriage from a mountain community.

Honky Tonk Girl takes this technique of "expert testimony" to extremes, opening with a typical title scroll, then fading in on a police officer who speaks into a dispatch microphone but is clearly addressing the film's audience:

> Calling everyone, calling everyone...stop, look and listen, and this means [indicating audience with a finger

> pointed at camera] you and you and you...The producers of this picture have drawn directly from the official police records the amazing almost unbelievable story presented in *Highway Hell*.[9]

And if the warnings of this lawman didn't wake audiences up to the severity of the hitchhiking trollops problem, there was a third lecture to the audience contained in the film itself, in which the paternal figure known as "Pop" begins instructing his son on the pitfalls of life, then pivots to deliver the remainder of his speech directly to the camera:

> You see Bob, experience is the foundation on which we build. For instance, this "highway love"—the oldest profession in the world in a new setting—the modern highway kind, the kind that takes you unawares and in unexpected places, is the most vicious in this pleasure crazy world. [turning toward camera]
> But it's something we cannot close our eyes to if it would build character. To overcome it, we must act quickly. Let us keep our highways, the byways of life clean. And we can do it, if each and every one of you will do your part.

Even exploitation films of the silent era were not without the authoritative lecturer. *The Road to Ruin* opens with Captain Leo W. Marden of the Los Angeles Juvenile Bureau mouthing stern warnings to the youth of 1928.

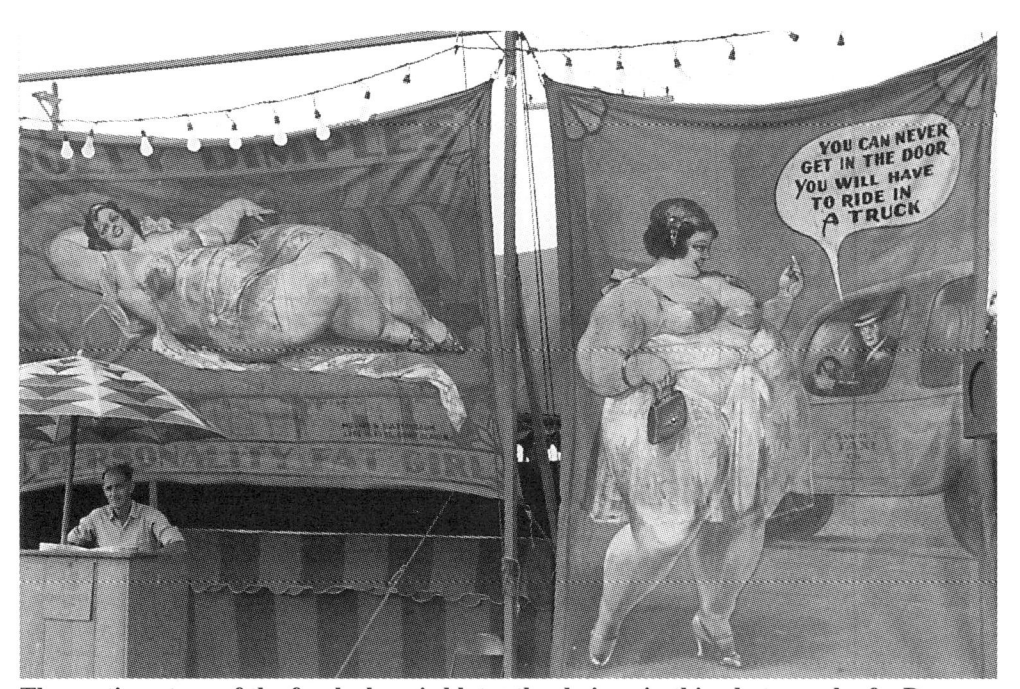

The erotic nature of the freak show is blatantly obvious in this photograph of a Depression-era midway banner. (Library of Congress)

133

The true-crime expose was often played out on vaudeville stages in addition to exploitation movie houses. (Library of Congress)

Reefer Madness duplicates this direct-camera and audience address in its opening and final scenes, as the anti-marijuana crusader Dr. Carroll tells an audience of concerned citizens, "The next tragedy may be that of your daughter or your son, or yours or yours or *yours*," his final words emphasized by pointing out to the film audience followed by the superimposed final edict, "Tell Your Children." This acknowledgment of audience in the testimonial address places exploitation in a strange limbo between the freak show and Hollywood, borrowing conventions from both, but presented in an entirely new form.

The similarities between exploitation film and freak show are spiritual as well as structural. Many carnival shows featured attractions beyond the physically aberrant in sexualized performances which foreshadowed the carnal lure which was soon to be an integral part of its cinematic cousin. Every sideshow worth its sawdust had some sort of erotic spectacle among its garish attractions, a place where the physical ideal was celebrated and sexuality was thrust unashamedly to the foreground. Similarly, exploitation films occasionally turned their attention away from bodies spotted by chancres and offered viewers a glimpse of a healthier specimen of feminine beauty. Filmmakers did this by either inserting shots of characters disrobing, or else by integrating footage of burlesque performances into the fabric of the narrative (as in the trip to a music hall in *Sex Madness*).

The always audacious Esper made burlesque and striptease the very substance of his film *How to Undress*, yet still dared to excuse the exhibition as educational (though the introductory scroll was definitely written with a comical slant):

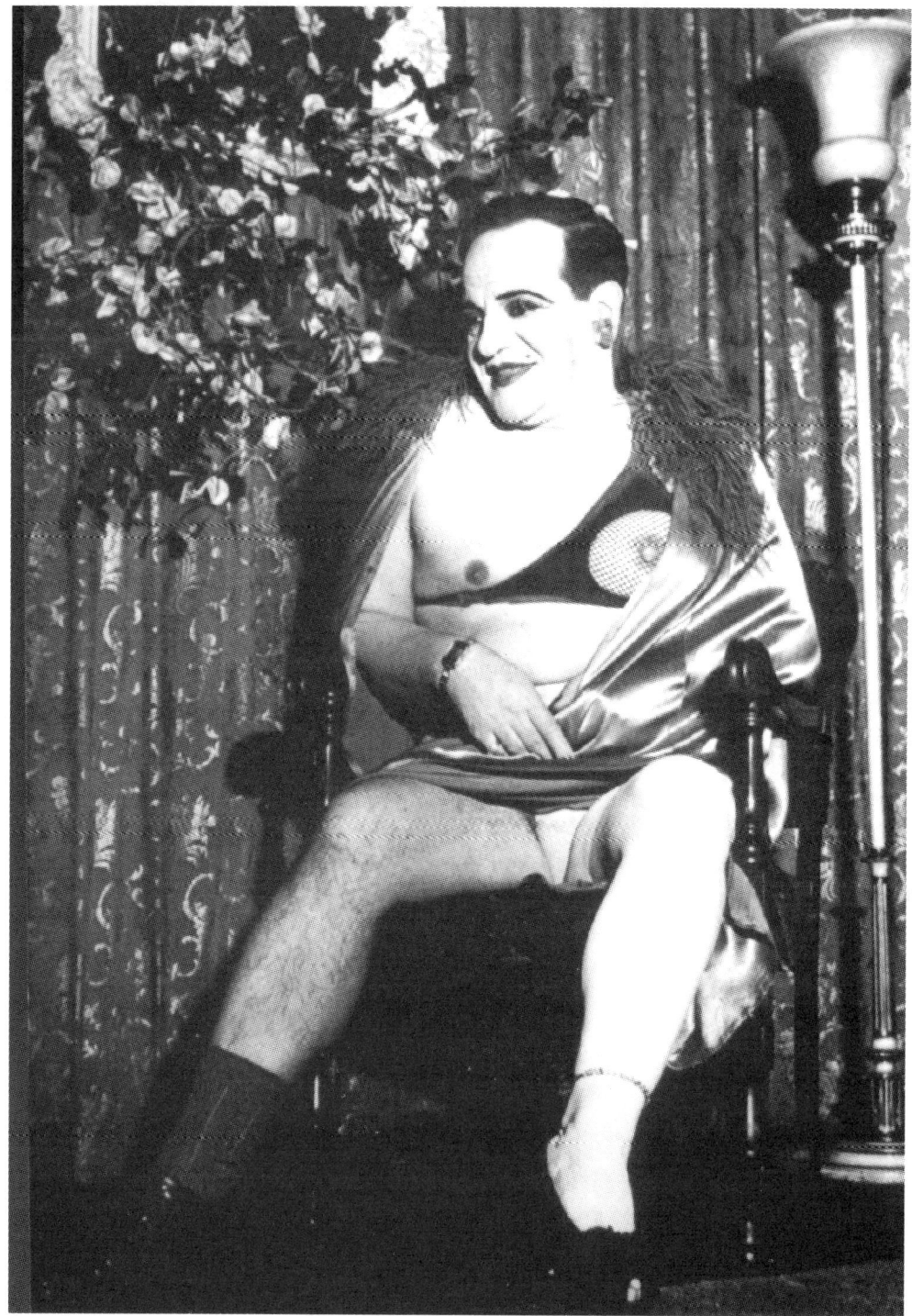

As this dime museum hermaphrodite proves, eroticism and revulsion were strangely wed in the American freak show.

The old marriage institution has limped along for centuries, burdened by boredom—men have submitted, suffered and supported long enough. Therefore: We have decided to do our bit toward the relief of marital boredom. LESSON ONE:—TO THE LADIES—"HOW TO UNDRESS IN FRONT OF YOUR HUSBAND"

Burlesque was allowed to thrive in big city venues such as New York's Republic, Central and Gaiety Theatres, while smaller cities and towns often suffered a void in men's entertainment. Perhaps in recognition of this highly profitable omission, many exploiteers found excuses to incorporate female performance, thereby satisfying (and profiting from) yet another version of the skinshow.

Such complex relationships between showmanship, sex and science can be found in more arenas than the exploitation film.

One prime example is the notorious Little Egypt's "cooch dance," the most popular carnival showcase of female pulchritude, introduced to a salivating, ethno-curious American public at the Chicago World Fair's Colombian Exposition of 1893. Recognizing it as a profitable new draw, many burlesque entrepreneurs began to integrate Little Egypt "cooch dances" into their own shows in what was clearly a precursor to striptease so that, "by the turn of the century, the cooch dancer had become a standard feature in burlesque companies." [10] These showmen exempted themselves from criticism by referring to the exotic show's educational value as a demonstration of "native" culture. This link of science with an implicit sexual display mirrors the design of the exploitation film and the anthropological and sexual display of freaks such as the Hottentot Venus.

Even though her body is whole and her beauty evident, the cooch dancer was as much a freak as the hermaphrodite or bearded lady. All these performers were linked by their displays of the body which were viewed in both popular and legislative terms, as "dirty." As ex-freak show sword-swallower and fire-eater Daniel P. Mannix points out:

> In 1969, when World Fair Shows opened in North Bay Village, Florida, the freaks were forbidden to appear, the prohibition being based on a 1921 state law that classed them with pornography. [11]

And while even the freak show allowed for some degree of ambiguity and androgyny in depicting sex, the exploitation film tended to make "sex" synonymous with woman. Exploitation exchanged the implicit sexuality of the freak's body (male, female, or androgynous, draped or undraped) for that of the female body (giving birth, covered with chancres or engaged in sexual performance).

The pretense of scientific inquiry which surrounded the freak's display also cropped up in the medical treatment of the cooch dancer, who was a forerunner of exploitation's sexually and medically displayed woman. In smaller traveling carnivals, where cooch dancers generally performed bolder, more licentious shows beyond the cursory glimpse of breasts and genitalia:

> The performance might end with a gynecological anatomy lesson as the performer caters to what Arthur

Forbidden to dine alongside the glamorous employees of M-G-M, the cast of *Freaks* was forced to eat outdoors during the film's production.

Lewis calls "insatiable male curiosity about the exact nature and geographic disposition of 'women's parts.'" At one show he witnessed, several regular marks brought flashlights with them. These they used in businesslike fashion in order to examine, clinically and under laboratory conditions, what they "couldn't see at home." [12]

It is indicative of the prejudices of our culture that displays of deformity are no longer acceptable, though displays of "genetic success" like beauty pageants, are. A culture that made room for difference has been obliterated by a present-day beauty culture which tends to fetishize the unnaturally "perfect" female body (anorexic, lips injected with collagen, breasts swollen with silicone) in advertising, pornography and entertainment, making women into the symbolic Other—the modern-day corollary to the circus freak.

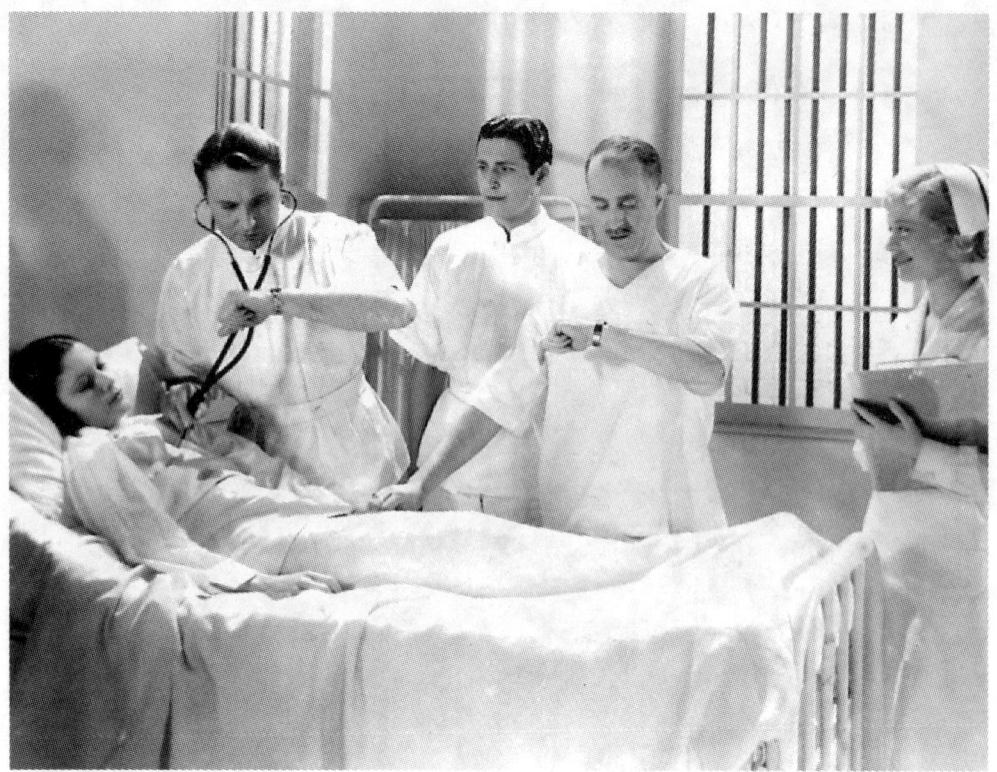

Whether or not the scalpel would penetrate the reproductive organs of an innocent girl (Diane Sinclair) was the perverse dramatic fulcrum of Bryan Foy's *Tomorrow's Children*.

Freak shows and the exploitation cinema are alike in that the bodies they put on display are often blighted by disease, disability and pregnancy, posing an uncomfortable threat to the medical establishment which was claiming the physical, the flesh as its professional domain. Just as the exploitation cinema would one day be attacked for its unwholesome, unhealthy tendencies, there was a growing sentiment fostered by an elitist medical community that certain displays of the abnormal body were distasteful, morbid and the rightful domain of science rather than commerce. Using his pointer to indicate the lesions or extra appendages on a freak to his medical colleagues, the doctor was not too different from the freak show barker and the exploitation lecturer, though the doctor's "pitch" was delivered in the more respectable venue of the medical amphitheater.

Censors' reactions to similar medical displays in exploitation films echo this disgust with entertainment infecting education in a nation increasingly erecting a barrier between the two. The freak show not only gave the disabled an autonomy and presence eugenicists preferred they not have, the economic nature of the business made deformity profitable, encouraging freaks to have children, or carnival owners to procure freaks for their shows, thus threatening the balance of "inferior" and "superior." The perception of the "freak" had shifted, according to Robert Bogdan, because of a number of turn-of-the-century phenomena: the aforementioned rise of eugenics; medical advances which demystified some of the claims of the freak show; and the professionalization of medicine.

Based on the promotion of healthy genetic stock and the extermination of tainted, degenerate bloodlines, eugenics was insistent that even the most private, intimate en-

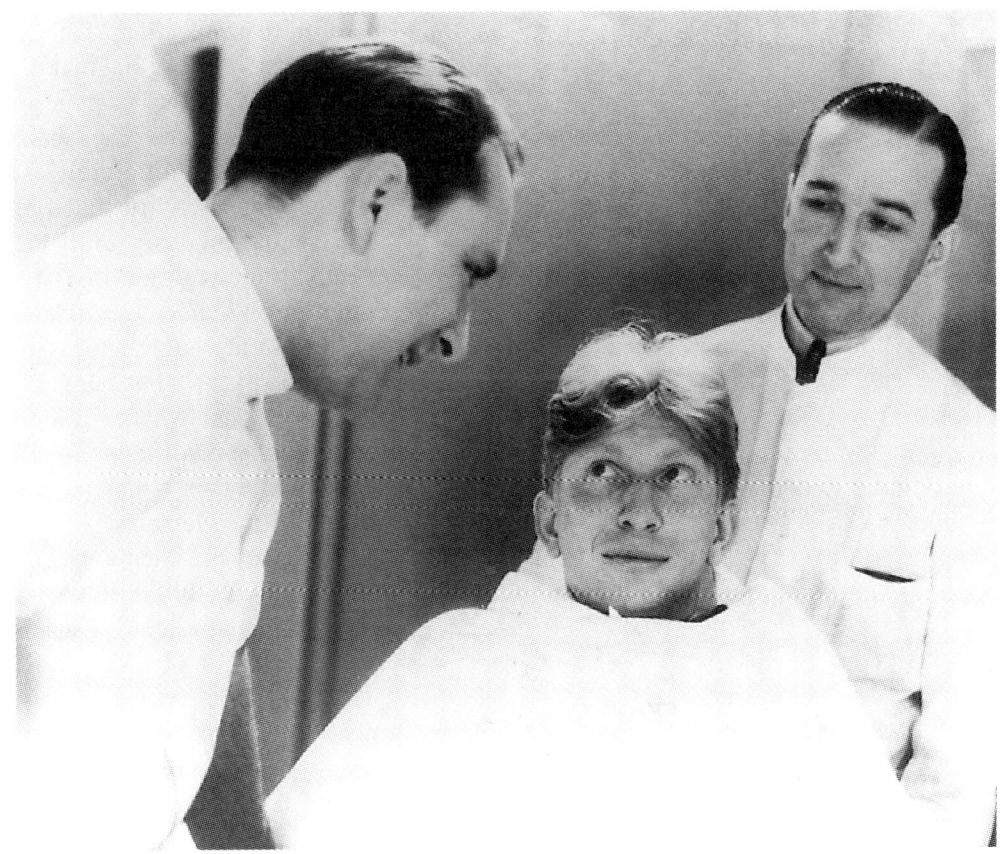

Better known as the voice of Winnie the Pooh, Sterling Holloway (center) provided comic relief in the forced-sterilization saga *Tomorrow's Children*.

tity—the body—could be regulated. By the beginning of the 1930s, thousands of Americans were affected by the new legislation of this pseudo-science, and forced to undergo sterilization so that the nation could guard against a contaminated gene pool. This increasing censorship of private life, of reproduction and sex was evident in the often hysterical reception of exploitation films. But the warning bell had been sounded decades before, in forums like that *Nation* editorial, which also called for the restriction of the American freak show.

While doctors and scientists claimed to be saving the freak from exploitation and humiliation, their ranks often exhibited an even greater cruelty in the terms with which they spoke of their new charity. When discussed in medical terms, freaks are commonly referred to as "monsters," as in a 1934 paper delivered at the American Society of Clinical Pathologists entitled "An Anatomical Study of a Thoracopagus Monster Delivered Dead at Full Term,"[13] and treated in a manner that often makes these professionals seem more Frankensteinian than compassionate caregivers.

An example of how cruelly the scientific community could treat freaks is the illuminating case of the Hottentot Venus, a South African woman brought to England in 1810 as an anthropological curiosity. The Hottentot Venus was famed for her large thighs and buttocks, which were seen as dramatic physical evidence of the distinction between the "primitive" and the "civilized" world. The Venus was adopted as a medical curiosity by not only a curious public, but Parisian scientists, including Georges

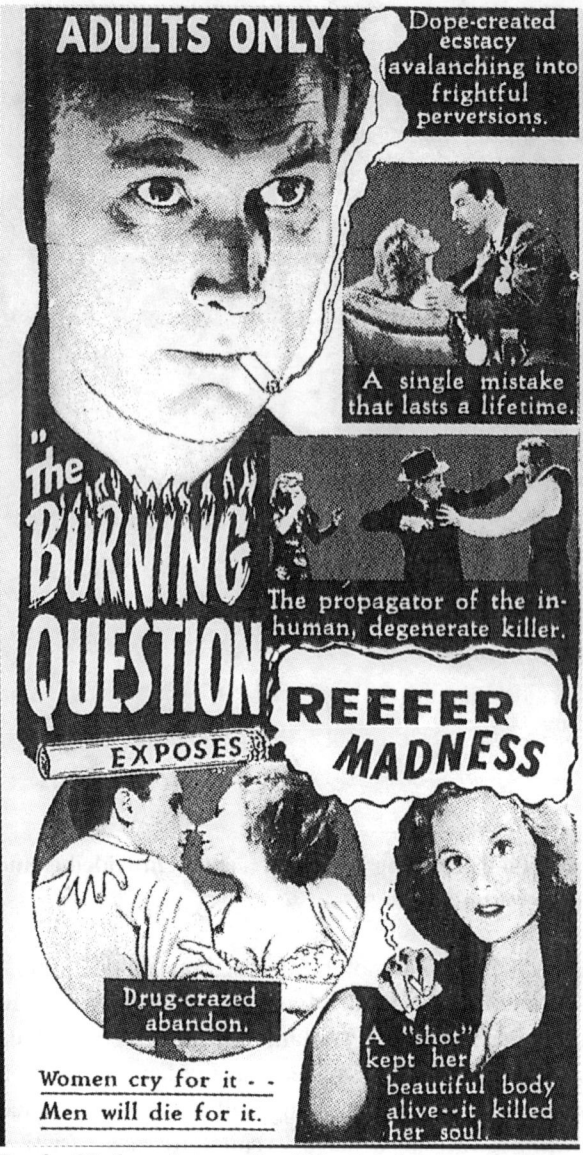

Reefer Madness **internalized the live lecturer by integrating brief monologues by the fictitious Dr. Carroll into its narrative.**

Cuvier, chancellor of the University of Paris, whose singular desire was a peek at her gynecological endowments. The French professor's scientific curiosity was unfortunately frustrated by the Venus' modesty until her death from smallpox in 1815, after which Cuvier was able to perform a thorough autopsy of his muse. Like a butcher carving an animal for the dinner table, Cuvier readied the Venus' corpse for posterity, making wax molds of the woman's genitals and anus, casts of her body, and preserving her brain, skeleton, skin—and in the acme of scientific lewdness—her genitals. The case of the Hottentot Venus not only demonstrated the grotesque treatment of the freak by the medical community, it represented a standard means of looking at difference as a medical, dissectable problem, a riddle to be solved by application of scalpel and formaldehyde. And though both the freak show and exploitation film used a similar educational, scientific language to speak about the body, at the very least they allowed it to remain a populist, accessible forum.

The refusal of the freak show to cloak abnormality is the same outpouring of the repressed found in exploitation. The use of taboo, "educational" childbirth footage and glimpses of bodies crippled by venereal disease are some of the most explicit examples of exploitation's links to the freak show in terms of spectacle and displays of the taboo. An ability to see what science preferred remain hidden was accompanied by a show biz hustle emphasizing the spectacular nature of such imagery. What critics of freak shows objected to ("that human oddities were not benign curiosities, they were pathological—diseased" [14]) was also suggested in the censors' condemnation of exploitation, where disease, birth, nudity are visual manifestations of what society has deemed improper. Implied in critics' common objection to the freak show as a "perversion" was the element of sexuality which exploitation film made explicit.

In one of the more peculiar but genuinely subversive scenes of *Freaks*, sideshow clown Wallace Ford flirts with a pair of "pinheads."

Existing prints and advertising materials from exploitation films indicate a continual fascination with the body, even if the topic of the film is not directly sexual. The body, in all of its incarnations, healthy or deformed, was contaminated by sex because of medical and eugenic rhetoric which encouraged Americans to see flesh of any kind as an affront to the national health, and a contamination of the populace.

In exploitation, it is women's bodies that remind viewers of the dangers of an unclean life. *Sex Madness*, which describes the downward spiral of a showgirl's life after contracting syphilis, suggests the permanent damage done to her husband and her child by the woman's sexual transgression. And while in exploitation's typical patchwork conclusion a cure is "found" within the film's last few minutes, the notion that sexual dishonor and history can be worn on the body like a scarlet letter or a withered limb is a powerful reminder of the folk traditions of the freak show, which posited that maternal shock and experience was often registered in the body of the freak. John Merrick's (the "Elephant Man") severe deformities were believed the result of his mother's having witnessed an elephant stampede while pregnant. In an interesting spin on this Victorian belief, one reviewer of *Freaks* even suggested psychological consequences for pregnant women who saw the film.

Objections to particular exploitation films could therefore be raised, not only due to overt presentation of the body, but because of an exploitation film's fixation with sex often centered on a "morbid" medical treatment, as the critical reception of Browning's

Well into the 1960s, films such as *The Story of Birth* were still being circulated to drive-ins and grindhouses across America (in this case hitched to the purely innocuous 1941 film *No Greater Sin*).

Freaks suggested. The Child Conservation Conference, quoted in a 1938 *Variety* article, stated that the sex education film *Birth of a Baby*, "caters to a *morbid* curiosity, is an insult to innate modesty of refined women, and physicians and nurses do not need the information conveyed."

Banned in New York in 1937, *Tomorrow's Children* epitomized the moralists' attitude toward exploitation. At the time of its production, 27 states had sterilization laws on the books, with the procedure performed on a variety of persons, ranging from the syphilitic, epileptic, child rapists, repeated sex criminals and the "feebleminded, [who] would produce children with an inherited tendency to crime, insanity, feeblemindedness, idiocy or imbecility." In *Tomorrow's Children*, one of the most innocuous examples of the genre, scandal seems to lie in the sexual connotations of sterilization. The court's objections centered first on the context in which the film was exhibited:

> Many things may be necessary in surgery which are not proper subjects for the movies. The teaching and demonstration of many facts may be necessary to the

This clipping from the *Mom and Dad* pressbook shows how theater managers could either sell the film as a public hygiene crusade or as a cavalcade of glitzy showbiz.

> classroom of the law school, the medical school and clinic, the research laboratory, the doctor's office, and even the theological school, which are not proper subject matter for the screen.

Secondly, the film's thematic concern with sex and sexual surgery suggested the possibility of even non-representational sex offending moral standards. The New York State Supreme Court stated of *Tomorrow's Children*:

> Throughout the picture the minds of the audience are centered upon the subject of sterilization of human beings, curiosity is aroused as to the operation on the sex organs and the effect of sterilization, and the audience awaits the picturization of the operation on the young criminal and that is about to be performed on the sex organs of the young girl.

Just as the medical profession sought to quarantine the freak's exhibition, so too, public watchdogs battled to keep depictions of the body out of exploitation. As with the freak show, it was *context* which was paramount. A film like *The Birth of a Baby* was only labeled indecent, "when presented in places of amusement." [15] Likewise, the 1948 film *Mom and Dad*, was, according to the Newark, New Jersey, director of public safety, "suitable only for noncommercial showings under educational auspices." [16]

Chapter Seven

NO MORE MAKE BELIEVE

With its stark naturalism, its embrace of contemporary social issues and its frequent reliance upon scientific footage, it was inevitable that the exploitation film would at some time assume the form of the full-fledged documentary.

Though they never rivaled the narrative feature in terms of quantitative output or box office performance, reality-based films were as much a part of the exploitation scheme as newsreels, travelogues and human interest shorts were a part of the well-balanced studio release roster. And just as the narrative exploitation film injected narcotics, disease and depravity into the veins of the conventional melodramatic form, so was the lifeblood of the respectable mainstream documentary polluted by all the hard-edged lasciviousness that characterized this renegade film movement.

Rather than recording the speeches of international statesmen and reporting the marvels of modern science, the exploitation newsreel reenacted the crimes of the century, offered stolen glimpses of apprehended felons and depicted the wages of sin with morgue-slab footage of bullet-riddled badmen. Reputable travel documentaries such as Robert Flaherty's *Nanook of the North* and Merian C. Cooper and Ernest B. Schoedsack's *Grass* chronicled the primitive existence and everyday struggles of exotic cultures, whereas their uncouth siblings found ethnographic interest in societies that espoused bestiality (*Forbidden Adventure, Bo-Ru the Ape Boy*), cannibalism (*Gow, The Killer*) and other assorted barbarities (*Karamoja*), alternating between footage taken by legitimate expeditions and scenes photographed among the canyon scrub of Los Angeles. Human interest pieces extolled the benefits of nudism, and an

Often considered the first true "documentary," Robert Flaherty's *Nanook of the North* was a largely staged drama of survival in the Arctic, with many similarities to the less scrupled exploitation documentary.

instructional film taught the ladies of the audience the proper techniques of disrobing before their spouses.

The exploitation documentary was an integral tool of the roadshowman. While their fictional siblings armored themselves with breastplates of education, the real-life film excused itself from reproach by asserting that it was not sensationalism, but merely a celluloid representation of reality. When *The March of Crime* was submitted to the New York Censor Board in 1946 (it had apparently been circulating prior to that time without a certificate of approval), the Board refunded Classic Pictures Inc.'s $18.00 payment on the grounds that—"under the provisions of paragraph (2) Section 1083 of the Education Law"— newsreels did not require a state seal.[1] Vision Pictures, Inc. was not

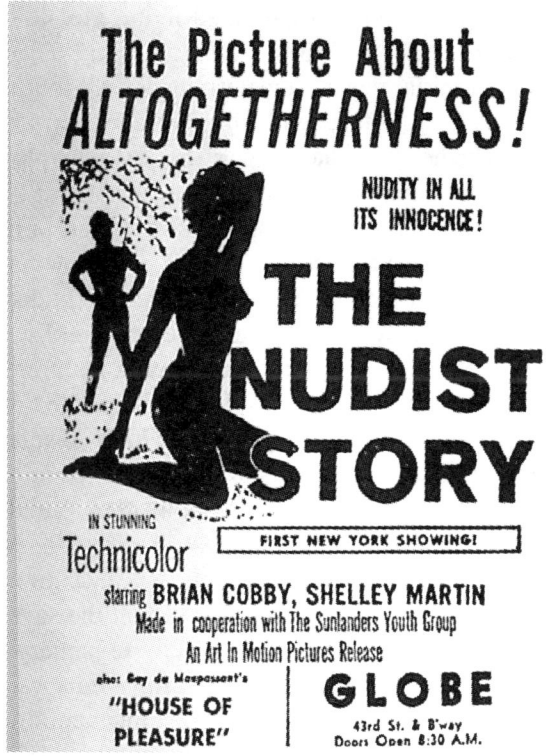

Not all nudist films sold themselves as scientific documentaries about alternative life-styles, as this poster illustrates.

so fortunate. Its 1933 film *This Nude World* was banned by New York censors, even as Vision legal counsel Louis Nizer "declared it resembles a newsreel of nudist activities."[2] A trade ad for the film declared its authenticity, "This is not a Hollywood-made picture BUT—ACTUAL scenes of the foremost Nudist Colonies in Germany—France—America. Photographed at the source. Thousands of men, women, children—NUDISTS. How they live, their morals, their beliefs, etc. STATES RIGHTS NOW AVAILABLE."[3]

Death could be freely represented and the flesh undisguised as long as they were cloaked in newsworthiness and anthropological interest—much the way the general exploitation film dressed up its sex, drugs and disease in vestments of education and moral enlightenment. Or, as Kroger Babb bluntly put it, "The folks with the scissors don't care about nudity in pictures as long as it's the natives who are naked."[4]

In addition to being almost censor-proof, the documentary exploitation film was, from a production standpoint, a cinch. An entire feature could be assembled without cranking a camera, compiled in toto from the stock footage that was already so valuable a tool to the cost-conscious exploiteer. Like Depression-era Dr. Frankensteins, exploitation documentarians scavenged film vaults for usable remains, searching for the celluloid abnormalities that would form a somewhat cohesive whole capable of rousing the interest of the village mob. Once enough material on a particular topic was compiled, a fresh unsynchronized soundtrack of stock music and sketchy narration was laid over the visuals. New titles (and a bogus copyright notice) were slapped on the head new ad slicks and posters were printed and a new exploitation film was born.

Prime examples of the found-footage exploitation documentary are *The Exposé of the Nudist Racket* (1938), *Nudists at Play, They Wear No Clothes* and *Why Nudism* (years of initial release undetermined). All four films consist of the same reel of bland nudist colony footage, with different titles and soundtracks and some variations in editing. Whether the material was shot by an exploiteer or a well-meaning proponent of nudism remains a mystery, but once prints hit the roadshow circuit, seemingly every distributor swiped a copy and constructed his or her own version. Having a nudie short was a professional necessity. Every roadshowman, especially those trafficking in low-grade product, had to have a "square up" nudist reel on hand to graciously appease dissatisfied audiences and quell the chance of a siege on the box office for refunds in the wake of a particularly disappointing feature.

The exploitation newsreels were exhibited much in the same way as the fictional exploitation feature. If anything, the lobby displays became even more elaborate when promoting the exotic thrills of darkest Africa or addressing the pressing social concern with crime. The jungle picture *Gow* often toured with a series of four six-foot display cases containing human skulls, stuffed reptiles, weapons, tools and accouterments of the "world's most vicious people." Roadshowers of *Untamed Mistress* unpacked a gorilla suit for every screening and sent the savage ape out amongst the spectators (a promotional ploy later immortalized in Flannery O'Connor's *Wise Blood*).

The lobbies where *Forbidden Adventure* was screened were often crowded with taxidermied leopards, a lion, snakes, mannequins of imperiled explorers, a fake alligator, terrariums and the typical preponderance of 27x41 one-sheets and 40x60 posters. Among the sell-lines splashed throughout the lobby of the Miami Theatre in New York were, "See unheard of orgies of wild women and beasts! See love-starved women

The most rabidly promoted jungle film was *Forbidden Adventure*, whose lobbies were filled with stuffed animals, mannequins, lewd banners, nude photos, display cases and plenty of decorative palm fronds.

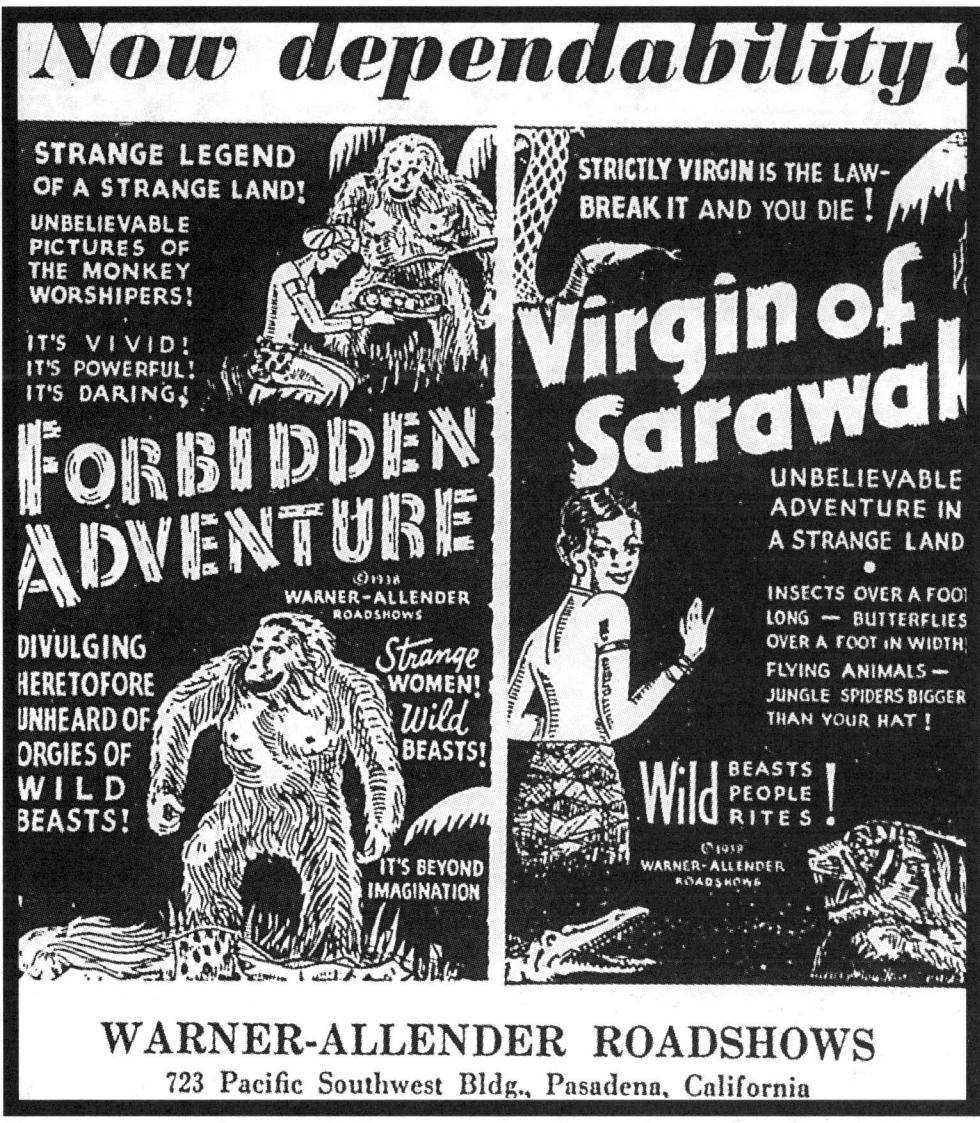

This trade ad, offering states rights to potential distributors, shows the more sordid side of the ethnographic film, and the intimations of bestiality that often circled around it.

break their bonds! Intimate practices of a love-starved race! Where men dared not go women sought new thrills! True! Authentic! Educational!" A bust of a Neanderthal man, meant to suggest the "missing link" (or perhaps the product of women mating with apes) was prominently exhibited. The ticket booths were occasionally dressed in a facade of bamboo and thatched palm and the velvet ropes replaced with rough wicker fences. Some screenings were attended by Buster and Betty, two lion cubs leashed to a pith-helmeted traveling showman. According to New York Censor Board agent Frank Dermody:

> Inside the lobby there appeared a large figure of an ape, which, by reason of some electrical device, caused the jaws of this figure to open and close intermittently

This poster for a live "Spook Show" borrows many of the advertising ingredients of the exploitation documentary.

and at the same time illuminate the breasts of this ape-like figure... There were also a number of stills of an ape carrying a woman, as well as several stills in which the exploitation of women's breasts were shown.[5]

For the exhibition of the drug-related films *Narcotic, Marihuana* and *Dope Dens of the Orient*, Dwain and Hildagarde Esper's daughter Millicent recalls:

> Dad bought her a board... and he wanted mom to put all the different heroin, cocaine, opium, all this, behind glass... a lobby display. So my mother used sugar, flour, salt, what have you. She packaged them identically the way they were packaged. She put the coke in the bottle. She had this thing all fixed up, and she had headache powders made out of flour... beautiful... so good that the FBI came out and took it away from her. And they never returned it. She told them it's all sugar, water and salt. And he said, 'It's too realistic. People will know what they're looking at.' That was true but people had to go into the lobby, it wasn't out where children could see it. They never did give it back. It's a dirty shame, too.[6]

So effective was the crime show lobby display that theaters playing mainstream product got wise to the tumble and adopted the promotional technique. To accompany screenings of *Special Agent* (Warner Bros., 1935) at the Majestic Theatre in Dallas and to assume an exploitation-style appearance, "Inclined shelves were placed around the walls, displaying weapons, police equipment and other paraphernalia... Each pistol, dagger and tool was tagged with [a] complete history of the criminal who used it and the crime committed. Everything from a sub-machine gun to an ice pick, used for murder, was displayed, including a pair of knotted silk stockings used by a burglar to strangle a prominent society matron... Apparatus and methods used in the smuggling of dope created much interest..."

The public's interest in these theater-lobby chambers of horror obviously went beyond a sociological interest in primitive cultures and crime prevention. America had, and continues to maintain, an insatiable appetite for true crime stories in the most raw form allowable, largely because the "reality" of such entertainments endows them with a legitimacy and a visceral potency that pure fiction can never replicate.

There was also, in the throes of the Depression, a growing fascination with the nature of crime. The 20th century's fixation on eugenics offered some explanation for the 1930s true crime phenomenon, as academics and crime-fighters speculated on the genetic causes of criminality. It was essential flaws, not in upbringing, but in the parents' brains and bodies which pegged them for defective or exemplary progeny even before conception, such theories suggested, giving a religious-based, original sin quality to the genesis of evil.

But there's also reason to suspect in a country plagued by deprivation, that the bank robber or kidnapper represented denied impulses given full, glorious rein. Just as a contemporary fascination with serial killers seems bound up, both with disgust for the excesses of crime and the psychological interest in the home as incubator of criminality, there is some expression of misanthropy, a disgust for human life which the serial killer acts upon, and which appeals to a commonly shared temperament.

Once J. Edgar Hoover fortified the FBI and put an ingenious media spin on the agency, the Depression-era criminal began to function as a scapegoat—a means for an entire nation to forget its own troubles for the more satisfying, communal sport of finger-pointing, attributing the decay of civilization, the erosion of values to a Dillinger or a Bonnie and Clyde. What other explanation for the bloodthirsty, intense glee with which Bonnie and Clyde's bullet-riddled car or footage of Dillinger's corpse were exhibited, but the sacrifice of one figure for the nation—like a primitive offering made to the gods to stave off more suffering? One way or another, there was a vicarious participation via newspaper, true crime digest or exploitation film, in the adventures of America's celebrity criminals.

The independently produced true-crime documentary capitalized on the growing 20th-century fixation on celebrity fiends and was a staple of the exploitation film movement.

When it played at Denver's Palace Theatre in 1928, the exploitation newsreel *Edward Hickman, the Fox* was accompanied by "the most spectacular brand of out-front ballyhoo seen here in years."[7] Hickman kidnapped, murdered and mutilated 12-year-old Marian Parker, then accepted $7,500 in ransom from her father in late December, 1927. By late January, *Edward Hickman, the Fox* was already being spread across America's screens. Prior to his death by hanging in San Quentin on February 4, 1928, Hickman was something of a celebrity, as the press exaggerated his youthful good looks, arrogance, vanity and viciousness (much as they had with Nathan Leopold and Richard Loeb in 1924, and later would with Charles Starkweather in 1958 and Ted Bundy in the mid-'80s). The thousands of curious spectators who jammed train stations from Seattle (where he was apprehended) to California (where he was tried) for a glimpse of "The Fox," served as a clear indicator to the exploiteer of the money-making capacity of crime reportage.

Even before sentencing, Hickman's likeness was rigged up to the true crime exploiteer's favorite chassis—the essential electric chair trucked from theater to theater. That Hickman was actually executed by hanging was largely irrelevant in the sensationalism-over-truth exploitation scheme. The Palace Theatre "had a dummy strapped in an electric chair, with metal headpiece adjusted for the 'burn,' sitting in front of the b.o." Apparently the tableaux was too enthralling. Too many pedestrians crowded around the electric chair instead of buying tickets for the film, and the show closed after two days.[8]

So notorious was Hickman that the mayor of Minneapolis banned *Edward Hickman, the Fox* from his city's screens. Advertisements for the film promised "the complete story of the most famous crime in modern times and to present the principal incidents in its perpetrator's career," even though it was released while Hickman was still on trial.[9]

Among the most oft-employed sidewalk promotional devices on the exploitation circuit was the Bonnie and Clyde "death car," sometimes toured solo, sometimes alongside exploitation compilations of newsreels in a cavalcade of criminality. Any 1934 Ford sedan could be riddled with bullets and passed off as the authentic death coach, and several such vehicles are still exhibited today, each claiming authenticity. In one of many parallels between exploitation cinema and the carnival midway (explored in greater detail in the previous chapter), the true-crime show, such as "Russell's Penitentiary Portrayal," was also a staple of the nomadic amusement camps of the 1930s. One carnival crime outfit, touring with United Shows of America in 1935, one-upped its death-car competitors by presenting along with the "authentic" vehicle Emma Parker and Mrs. Henry Barrow (the slain fugitives' mothers) and John Wilson Dillinger (father of the notorious bandit).

When small-town America received a visit from Ted Toddy's *Killers All*, it came surrounded by a "$25,000 Lobby Display: Wax Figures of Gangsters, Electric Chair Reproduction, Death Car 160 Bullets, See It Free at Theater... Plus The Crime Doctor You Will Remember As Long As You Live." The second feature on the bill was a "Daring Marihuana Exposé" entitled *The Devil's Killer* which, knowing Toddy's frequent use of the title switch, could have been any number of drug scare pictures.

The popular fascination with sociopaths was not limited to national borders. The car of choice the following decade would be Adolf Hitler's personal 1937 Mercedes-Benz. "In 1949," says Friedman, "at least 25 American carnivals also had Hitler's 'personal car.'"[10]

True to the formula of exploitation, the true-crime subgenre was not without its educational pretense. Its validity as a constructive social force was bolstered by the government's occasional appropriation of the medium in the fight against crime.

In the early '30s, it seemed to many that film might be a powerful new tool in law enforcement. One of its functions was as a cinematic dragnet to flush out contemporary badmen. The film dragnet was cast across regions where a criminal might be at large, as in television's later application of "America's Most Wanted." Police officials in Detroit worked with the Metropolitan Motion Picture Co. to prepare a newsreel on the murderer of 11-year-old Lillian Gallaher. The short featured closeups of Ward Goodrich (the suspected murderer) and his wife, as well as the alleged culprit's fingerprints—in case there were any exceptionally talented and ambitious amateur crime-fighters in the audience.[11] Likewise, home movies of Charles Lindbergh, Jr. were integrated into newsreels that blanketed New York City shortly after the child's disappearance.

The Fox-Hearst Corporation demonstrated the versatile application of its Movietone process by creating moving, talking mug shots of several suspected criminals and presented them "before a gathering of lawyers, police chiefs, judges and criminologists" in

Philadelphia. *The Survey* optimistically estimated the impact of "a Movietone Rogues' Gallery":

> Aside from its value to the witness and the police, the movietone could serve as a broadcasting agency for arousing the interest of the general public... What man planning to commit a crime would not think seriously of his chances of detection and escape when he may appear, walking and talking, before the eyes of thousands scattered throughout the country? To what extent these factors of public interest and crime prevention may develop cannot be forecast.[12]

The hard-boiled criminals featured in most true-crime exploitation pictures had long since been apprehended, so the function of such films was limited to "arousing the interest of the general public."

The exploiteer most adept at making crime pay was Louis Sonney. Instead of a film producer dabbling in true crime, Sonney was a former lawman who found a second career on the roadshow circuit once he discovered its potential. While working as a policeman in Centralia, Washington, Sonney in 1921 single-handedly captured well-known bandit Roy Gardner. In addition to a $5,000 reward, he appeared in a short newsreel and was offered a moment in the limelight by a theatrical agent who paid him to appear on the Pantages stage circuit as "Officer Sonney, The Man Who Captured Roy Gardner." By the time Gardner was released from prison, Sonney had quit the vaudeville racket and organized a touring show of his own—*The Crime Does Not Pay* show—free of agents' commissions and high overhead.

Taking out short-term leases on unoccupied storefronts, Sonney would, with the help of his two sons, uncrate a truckload of curiosities, foremost among which were 150 wax figures in a bizarre combination of the nation's most reviled and most celebrated figures, of America's greatest criminals and presidents (some of the former being shown in *The March of Crime* and the opening credits of *Maniac*). According to David Friedman, Sonney:

> Had a portable prison cell that he would put up in the lobby of the theater and hire the local town drunk or something and put him in a prison costume and have him sit there all day. And he had an electric chair in the lobby, and people would sit in that and he'd give them a little shock with a Ford spark coil, and he sold a book on 'Crime Does Not Pay,' and also sold a photograph of himself posed with Roy Gardner after he captured him.[13]

Dan Sonney remembers his father trolling the sidewalk to drum up business. "He used to stand out in front of the theater and handcuff people when they'd touch the electric bars. He'd shake hands with them and all at once put the cuffs on" (a deft bit of police chicanery that can be seen in *You Can't Beat the Rap!* and *The March of Crime*).

This cheaply printed booklet was sold at screenings of Dwain Esper's *The March of Crime* and probably offered as a souvenir at Louis Sonney's traveling true-crime show. (Courtesy Millicent Esper Wratten)

It was at a gaudily decorated theater front such as this, promoting Dwain Esper's matrimonial potboiler *The Seventh Commandment*, **that Louis Sonney was inspired to delve into the world of exploitation cinema.**

"My dad had two 4x8-foot plywoods with a frame and velour inside," Dan says, "It was wired together and would open and different kinds of guns were in there; old and new ones, swords, things like that." [14]

The most bizarre item in this menagerie of criminals and presidents was the actual corpse of Oklahoma bandit Elmer McCurdy, which was given to Sonney by a freak show proprietor as collateral on a loan (which he later defaulted on). Friedman remembers:

> Even when I was a kid I used to read *Billboard*... and you would always find these mummified bodies of corpses for sale. And they were real mummies. What would happen, back in those days, 1910, turn of the century, they'd capture some guy, the posse would shoot him, the local undertaker would embalm the body and then stand it up in the local undertaking parlor and people would come in and pay a dime to see the embalmed body of whoever was shot. After the novelty of that wore off, he'd sell it off to some carnival guy and take it out on the road. [15]

One day, circa 1916, a man entered the shop where McCurdy was perpetually lying in state, identified himself as the gunman's brother and demanded that he be given his sibling's cadaver for a proper burial. Little did the mortician know that the indignant brother was actually a crafty carnival man who later exhibited McCurdy's body for nickels and dimes behind colorful canvas facades.

In addition to appearing in Sonney's traveling exhibit, Dwain Esper toured McCurdy through the lobbies of dozens of American movie houses and even used him as decoration at parties for his children and their schoolfriends. "We had (Elmer) in the garage for about six years," says Esper's daughter Millicent, "Dad put a blue light over him for a Halloween party... Dad made a big production about this... opened the casket... the kids screamed. You could've heard them for blocks." [16]

After the death of Louis Sonney and the golden age of exploitation, Dan Sonney (who had by then graduated to pornography and was operating a chain of Pussycat Theatres) sold the mummy to the Hollywood Wax Museum, which in turn closed its doors in 1971 and passed McCurdy along to Long Beach's Nu-Pike Amusement Park, where he found a home in the "Laff-in-the-Dark Funhouse." In 1976 a camera crew, filming an episode of *The Six-Million-Dollar Man*, was shocked to discover the authenticity of the dried corpse and reported it to the local authorities. An examination by celebrity coroner Thomas Noguchi confirmed McCurdy's identity, whereupon his body was turned over to the Oklahoma Territorial Museum of Guthrie, which ceremoniously interred the badman at Boot Hill.

Sonney's transition to film from live appearance and wax effigies came circa 1933 when he stumbled upon a theater in Los Angeles showing Esper's *The Seventh Commandment*, often hyped as "Hollywood's first all-talking SEX PICTURE." Impressed by the throngs of ticketbuyers crowding the box office, Sonney bought half an interest in the film and co-founded Roadshow Attractions Inc., a short-lived partnership with Esper that resulted in some of the most engaging and peculiar exploitation films ever made, including *Maniac, Marihuana, The Curse of the Ubangi, Modern Motherhood* and *The Expose of the Nudist Racket*.

The March of Crime, produced by Sonney and Esper in 1937, is the paragon of true crime exploitation films. Cobbled together from the 1921 newsreel that began Sonney's entertainment career, the circa 1931 sound film *You Can't Beat the Rap!* which reunited criminal and cop upon the former's release from Alcatraz (allowing Gardner to thank Sonney for guiding him to the straight and narrow), the 1922 anti-capital punishment film *Found Guilty, Edward Hickman, the Fox*, other unidentified crime-related newsreels, footage of Elmer McCurdy's mummified corpse, assorted picture postcards and wax dummies from Sonney's collection and a fair amount of freshly photographed reenactment footage, *The March of Crime* is a crazy quilt of American death. Chaotically organized and haphazardly edited (title cards from silent footage were never completely removed), *The March* is sewn together by commentary written by Wedgwood Nowell and delivered with all the verve and incessant speed of a thundering newspaper press spinning out a five-star final. Nowell's furiously paced spiel is so unrelenting in its effort to fill every inch of the soundtrack with fervent verbiage that one can hardly absorb the avalanche of words, especially when the images they accompany are so distracting: photos of a family of four's suicide (motivated by the rape of the two daughters), bodies of two accused murderers who have been stripped and lynched (their genitalia modestly inked out) and novelty postcards of beheaded Chinese men (with the tasteful caption "easy to 'lose' your head in China" still legible across the bottom).

Shots of bullet-riddled corpses (such as this image from the newsreel *Cry of the World*, 1933), were a standard ingredient of the true-crime documentary.

Near the end of *The March*, Nowell's voice intensifies and rises to the brink of glossolalia as a criminal is executed and the narrator intones "Crime doesn't pay, crime doesn't pay..."

Perhaps as a means of offering viewers relief from Nowell's relentless monologue, the 50-minute *March* was later broken down into a series of one-reel shorts used to supplement features in need of some bite.

Just as the general exploitation film serves up a convoluted, often contradictory mixture of vice and moralizing, so is *The March* an eerie combination of voyeurism, bloodlust, patriotism and piety. Viewers are given privileged glimpses of the victims of crime (e.g., Marian Parker's shrouded, legless body on a morgue slab) as well as the victims of justice (John Dillinger's fly-specked corpse). Criminals are characterized as "vicious degenerate fiend(s) of the lowest type," but the film boasts, "due process of law must be faithfully followed," adding cheerfully, "that's the American idea of fair play!" In its opening prologue, *The March* delivers its strangest warning, an indication of the Depression fixation on eugenics and the incipient American interest in how criminality arises, by nature or nurture: "Many criminals are the offspring of mismated parents... choose your life partner carefully."

The newsreel was as old as the cinema itself, and some of the very first filmic subjects were reenactments or actual recordings of topical events (e.g., the 1897 inauguration of President McKinley and execution of his assassin in 1901). With the rise of the narrative film, a division formed between the feature film and the news short, the main attraction and the supplementary reel. Though newsreels were generally subordinated to the feature, they remained a fixture of every well-rounded evening's entertainment until television rendered them impractical in the 1950s.

In the early 1930s, the newsreel industry became a vicious battleground as studio camera teams (now armed with sound recording capabilities) aggressively competed not only with each other but also against the print and radio media for the fastest, most sensational coverage. Newspapers had the sensationalism advantage but were handicapped by the time it took to print and distribute new editions and radio wielded the power of instantaneous transmission though it lacked the increasingly visceral impact of the visual.

The 1932 Lindbergh baby kidnapping case was the proving ground of the newsreel, and an opportunity to demonstrate its superiority to all other forms. The only son of celebrated aviator Charles Lindbergh and Anne Morrow, the child was abducted from its New Jersey home and held for ransom, though it was speculated the baby died at some point on the night of the abduction. A massive amount of press attention followed the case as it unfolded, capturing the burgeoning thirst for celebrity in America as the nation's beloved hero met up with America's incipient anti-hero, the celebrity criminal. As testament to the swiftness and increasingly up-to-the-minute American press machine, the child was noticed missing just before midnight of March 1, and by the following afternoon, 49 New York theaters were unspooling reports from the Hopewell, New Jersey scene of the crime.

The efficiency of the crews was at first looked upon by the film industry and the legal system with pride and admiration, but as the cameras' presence in the courtroom became more obtrusive and the style of coverage more sensational, opinion on the newsreel began to sour. As later famous court cases like the Menendez brothers and O.J. Simpson trials illustrated, the American thirst for play-by-play access to news has often rubbed up against a prudish and hypocritical desire to hide the illicit, a back-and-forth fluctuation between desire for and fear of information.

Oftentimes newsreels mimicked the tabloid press exemplified by the smut-trafficking New York newspaper *The Evening Graphic* and boosted circulation by reporting the unsavory. By the mid '30s—coincident with the rise of the PCA—public outcry began to rise against the sensational newsreels which reached new heights in representing the macabre.

One film documented the exhumation of the decaying corpse of France's Alexandre Stavsky, while another showed several members of a San Diego dirigible landing crew falling to their deaths ("Particularly explicit telephoto shots showed the bouncing of the bodies at the impact with the field." [17]). A 1935 Universal newsreel depicting the execution of a Cuban rebel politely warned its audience, "If you do not care to look death in the face, PLEASE CLOSE YOUR EYES," before showing Jose Costiello y Puentes "falling in a pool of blood, his head and chest torn by the rifle bullets." [18]

In one of many demonstrations of the topical public health fear of imagery impacting negatively on the virility of the nation, Mrs. Doris Preisler sued Universal Newsreel and the Pantages theater chain for $4.15 million on the grounds that she miscarried as a result of being shown newsreel images of "Baby Face" Nelson's corpse. But a California jury ruled in the studio's favor. Judge Joseph Sprouls stated, "I consider the service that the newsreels gave the public of great benefit in showing the inevitable end for gangsters who try to evade the law, and for showing proof that crime does not pay." [19]

The studios may have had the power of the courts behind them, but they shriveled in the shadow of greater powers: the Legion of Decency, the PCA and other vocal pro-regulatory groups, which now lumped even factual, documentary footage under the umbrella of "entertainment" with no claim to protection by law. In an editorial entitled "News and Corpses," Terry Ramsay of *Motion Picture Herald* (which was published by Code co-author Martin Quigley), wrote:

> The newsreel ought to be an entertaining and amusing derivative... neither a corpus delecti nor the making of it are considered by any large portion of the public to be entertainment... Skull and reptiles may be facts; they may even be news; but they are not entertainment for persons of sound mind. The fact that they may get attention, that they may create sensations of a sort, does not make them proper screen merchandise. [20]

Though the Hollywood establishment frowned on the exploitation of true-life criminality, it sought to capitalize on the popular thirst for thuggery. Taking the increasingly more reputable tack of cloaking vice in morality, Hollywood gave its characters fictitious identities although they were often based on actual personages and events. The best example is William Keighley's *G—Men* (1935), which recreated the 1933 Kansas City Massacre and turned the Little Bohemia fiasco of 1934 (in which an agent and a civilian were killed in an unsuccessful attempt to capture John Dillinger, "Baby Face" Nelson and a cabin of other felons) into an FBI victory. The major studios were eager to respond to the public's fascination with gangsters but they did so with whitewashed, melodramatic renditions of American crime—just as the "sex" they packaged bore little resemblance to physical intercourse and authentic courtship. Quigley wrote, regarding a dis-

Ted Toddy's *Killers All* featured a lavish lobby display ($25,000 worth, the film claims), live lecturer and a drug-scare film tossed in for good measure.

play focusing on Dillinger's 1934 sidewalk execution: "All the public needs of Dillinger now is a record in a card file, no 'showmanship.'"[21]

Once the Production Code Authority tightened restrictions on Hollywood's infatuation with the criminal, this taboo topic (like illicit sex, drug use and social disease) fell to the exploiteers, who descended upon it with a ravenous vengeance.

Not merely the province of men who make their living from sensational footage, the recording of tragedy has enjoyed a long tradition with ordinary citizens with a movie camera doing its bit for public enlightenment, from Zapruder to Rodney King. *The Vanishing Gangster* (1936, Texas Roadshow Co.) has footage "taken on the spot by an amateur photographer, five minutes after the shooting" of Bonnie and Clyde. In 1952, portions of the film were integrated into a true-crime documentary entitled *Dealers in Death*. The title was borrowed in 1984 for a similar found-footage documentary assembled by John McNaughton (who would later direct *Henry, Portrait of a Serial Killer*) for MPI Home Video.

Dealers in Death is pieced together from a variety of sources (indicated by the intercutting of two different narration tracks) but, like so many exploitation films, has moments of haunting beauty. A staged scene in which Bonnie and Clyde murder two highway patrolmen in Grapevine, Texas is presented in a single take. Lasting 55 seconds, the wide, stationary shot stages the action in the foreground (at a diagonal) while beyond stretch acres of

John Dillinger

Clyde Barrow

unplanted fields, a weathered barbed-wire fence and a lonely barn. In its narrative simplicity and formal beauty it recalls the painterly compositions of certain Lumière films, only witnessed through a lens darkly.

In a preamble to Parker and Barrow's demise, the image is masked on the sides to focus the viewer's attention on a narrow vertical slot within which an unpaved country road wriggles toward the horizon. Lying in wait for the fugitives is a group of non-actors who hunker within a cluster of roadside foliage. Speaking with authentic Texas accents, they (rather convincingly) murmur among themselves while the car approaches, trying to identify the vehicle, psyching themselves up for the moment when they open fire on the bandits—and open fire they do, unloading their rifles of live ordnance for the exploiteer's gratification.

At other times, *Dealers in Death/The Vanishing Gangster* was less imaginative, padding its length with a prolonged montage of newspaper headlines, a technique that allowed them to cover a diversity of stories without the expense of filming reenactments or locating stock footage, all the while underscoring the film's stylistic debt to newsprint.

Like *The March of Crime, American Gang Busters* (1940, Times Pictures) was patched together from old footage, photographs and a few reenactments, and backed with a new soundtrack. Produced, edited and presumably written by a Captain A.F. Dion, *American Gang Busters* was the contribution of a lawman who, like Sonney, retired from the force for a career in show business. Reviews complained about "the sadly deficient condition of the print" upon its New York premiere.[22]

Considering the exploiteers' proficiency at sidestepping authority and a variety of small-time cons, one might expect the exploitation documentary to offer an unconventional, partially sympathetic view of the American bandit. Surprisingly, this is not the case. If anything, the true-crime films were more staunchly condemning of Depression-era gangsters, kidnappers and murderers than was Hollywood (which occasionally allowed them some sympathy and the opportunity for last-reel redemption). The exploitation documentary offered pure vitriol.

"From the homely shelter of this farm," intones the narrator of *Dealers in Death/ The Vanishing Gangster*, "John Dillinger left to become the menace any officer would be justified in killing like a mad dog. A criminal and a fool, for John Dillinger is not smart, only a fool that thinks that crime pays... John should have learned that simple truth in the Friends Church where he went as a boy, but he was too dumb." The film gloats at the sight of "Pretty Boy" Floyd's naked corpse in the morgue, and even carries its cameras to Bonnie Parker's burial to show grieving relatives and to witness the lowering of her casket into the earth.

If the badge of authenticity served as a shield to protect exploiteers from censorship, the chink in this armor was often the wholly concocted "supplemental" footage staged by the filmmaker for the production.

Censors in Memphis, Tennessee approved the film *Ingagi* in 1930, then suddenly reversed their decision on the day it was scheduled to open ("with hundreds of people lined up at the box office"), declaring the film could only be shown if all the "faked" scenes were deleted ("virtually a 'close' order" according to *Variety*).[23] Conrad F. Rose, representing Congo Pictures, Ltd., successfully petitioned the Superior Court of Illinois to overrule the ban of the censors and outcry of the African-American community (who objected mainly to the scenes showing a gorilla living with a native woman[24]), but the victory was only temporary, as the Court heeded the censor board's assertion that they "passed the picture because they believed it was scientific material but later learned of the objectionable passages concerning Negro women and apes."[25]

Two years later, the *Ingagi* debate was put to rest when the Federal Trade Commission closely examined the film and issued a cease and desist order to the distributors. The commission determined that Sir Hubert Winstead, F.A.S., F.R.G.S. and Captain Daniel Swayne, who led the expedition, were fictitious characters; that much of the wildlife was filmed at a Los Angeles zoo; that the film's gorillas were in actuality "human beings dressed in animal skins"; that the pygmies were "colored children from five to 10 years of age, living in Los Angeles"; that a lion which purportedly kills a cameraman on-screen was a trained animal "often used in motion pictures"; that the "Tortadillo" (the strange new species discovered by the filmmakers) "was a turtle with wings, scales and a long tail glued on it"; finally, that the word "Ingagi" did not mean "gorilla" in an African tongue, but was concocted (like everything else) by the filmmakers.[26]

The age-old sexual tension between gorillas and women was the conflict that fueled many an exploitation documentary (and many a Hollywood jungle picture as well).

Ingagi was by no means the only jungle film to include unauthentic footage. Millicent Esper recalls being rather traumatized when, as a young girl, she quietly strolled over to the set as dad was filming the butchering of a pig for *Curse of the Ubangi*: "He

Though it addressed the peculiar topic of "monkey worship," in southeast Asia, and boasted a cast of California African-Americans, bestiality was the central concern of the anachronistic *Forbidden Adventure*.

took a hammer and (whack). What they were going to film was cutting the head off and opening the head and taking the brain out. Dad didn't know I was there. I didn't like the animals dying." [27]

When *Forbidden Adventure* was submitted to the New York Censor Board, its producers classified it as a travelogue, yet it still fell under close scrutiny. The authentic documentary footage of the ruins of the lost kingdom of Angkor (situated deep in the jungles of French Indochina) was not considered objectionable, but the censors demanded cuts in the many embellishments made by the producers.

The true production history of *Forbidden Adventure* is unclear. It definitely began as a serious record of a 1912 photographic expedition into the southeast Asian city known as Angkor. Apparently producers Henry Warner and Roy Purdon acquired the footage from the Harvard University explorers and expanded it into a feature, adding an introduction and narration by former silent-movie actor Wilfred Lucas, supplementing the original material with shots of explorers in false beards cutting their way through the jungle.

In order to make the film more properly exploitable, Roy Reid of Roadshow Attractions spiced it up with the subplot of monkey-worship love rites and glimpses of unadorned flesh. It was apparently at this point that the title changed from *Angkor* to *Forbidden Adventure*. Reid later explained that the "native" women were rented from a Selma Avenue whorehouse and paid $10 apiece to carry the white hunters' gear through the Topanga Canyon. [28] In a peculiar post-production process, much of the nudity was artfully concealed by the superimposition of opaque silhouettes in the shape of leafy foliage, though a portion of the image was always left unobstructed for the benefit of the diligent viewer. Marshall Gordon, who directed some of the retakes, engineered the brothel transaction, and brought the production in for approximately $11,000 ($2,500 more than had been anticipated). Reid estimated the film's total grosses at $200,000, which is a fairly safe figure. An endorsement from the Los Angeles Adventurers' Club was used to add a little anthropological clout to the seedy proceedings (which it needed, since the African-American cargo-bearers are more in keeping with jungle-movie tradition than the ethnography of Cambodia).

The New York censors targeted those scenes "where breasts are unduly exposed"[29] and also demanded revisions in the narration track and the manner in which the film was advertised.

One of the key criticisms of *Forbidden Adventure* (and *Ingagi*) was the suggestion of bestiality... more specifically, that the mating of women and gorillas produced what we refer to as the missing link. The centrality of the threat (or promise) of bestiality was a suspense-generating device integral to the drama of a jungle film, a device later taken up by straight B pictures, such as Adrian Weiss's 1958 film *The Bride and the Beast*, not surprisingly, written by exploitation veteran Edward D. Wood, Jr. and shot by Roland Price, who lensed Esper's *How to Undress*. Even studio pictures such as

A fancy costume does little to legitimize the taboo themes explored in *Forbidd* (1937).

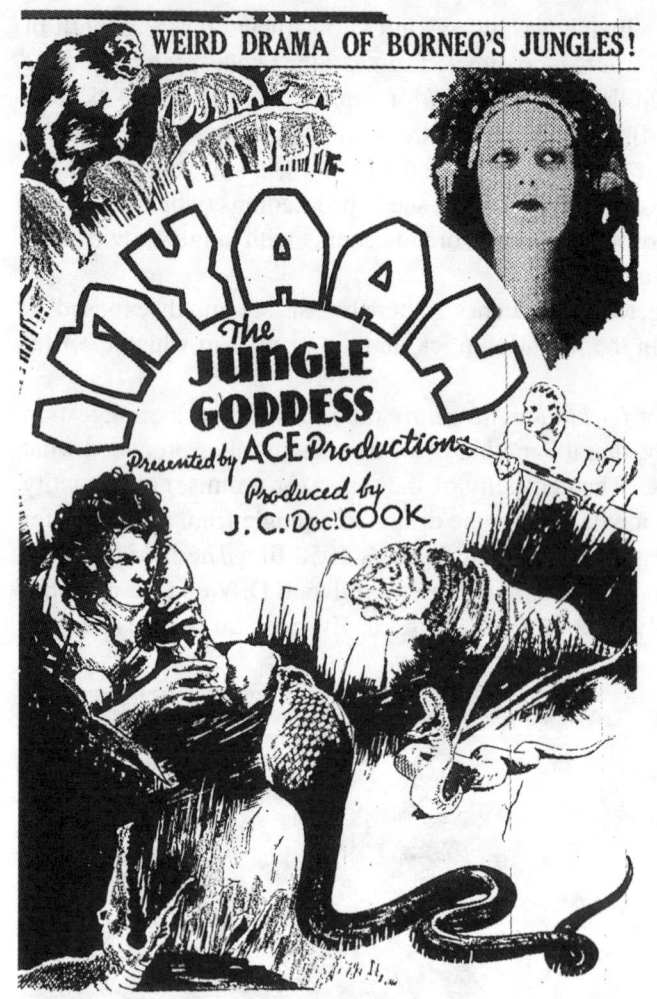

Before being repackaged as an exploitation film, *Inyaah the Jungle Goddess* was just another beast-meets-beauty jungle picture.

King Kong and *Murders in the Rue Morgue* rely upon the fear of women's violation at the hand of an ape for the generation of suspense.

The titillating moral depravity of the uncivilized tribe was a major selling point in the exploitation documentary and the sensational superlatives were applied to films regardless of their authenticity. Originally produced in 1928 by Edward A. Salisbury, from footage shot by Merian C. Cooper and Ernest Schoedsack (the producers of *Chang*, *Grass* and *King Kong*), and released under the title *Gow the Head Hunter*, the film resurfaced in 1931 as *Gow the Killer* (and later as *Cannibal Island*) and played for years as an exploitation film, with such misleading sell lines as "Blood-Chilling Orgies," "Virgin Savagery," "Where Wives Live With Pigs and Men Eat Their Mothers-In-Law."

Karamoja (aka *Wang Wang*), a specimen of substantial ethnographic filmmaking, was hyped with the lines, "They Wear Only the Wind and Live on Blood and Beer." Occasionally, inoffensive films were acquired by cunning exploiteers and given a sensational sell—films such as Harry Schenck's *Beyond Bengal* (1933).

Other exploitation jungle pictures include 1954's *Mau Mau*, composed of equal parts authentic and staged scenes, and the wholly faked pictures *Love Wanga* (aka *Ouanga*, 1935 and, *Bowanga! Bowanga!* (1941). Babb endowed native depravity with a literary twist in *Kipling's Women* (ca. 1957). Jungle shorts were often used to round out a bill, with such titles as *African Frenzy*, *Beasts of the Jungle* and *Jaws of the Jungle* (the content of which, more often than not, was rather innocuous).

One of the most peculiar pieces of exploitation exotica was *The Lash of the Penitentes* which chose as its subject a masochistic religious sect practicing in New Mexico in the 1930s. Appropriately enough, *The Lash* traveled an uncommonly rocky path to fruition and exemplifies the ragtag manner in which the exploitation industry often functioned. The saga began innocently enough in 1935, when self-proclaimed "Vagabond Cameraman" Roland Price captured documentary images of the self-flagellating, cross-toting worshipers and sold the footage along with a story treatment to Extraordinary Films, which intended to package the material as a novelty travelogue/melodrama and which pre-sold the distribution rights to First Division. Unfortunately, Extraordinary was not able to complete the film and, for a fee of $4,000, sublicensed the 18,000 feet of raw negative to the Intercontinent Film Corporation for production and distribution. Perhaps uncertain of how to package this potentially sacrilegious footage, Intercontinent sat on the film for almost a year, until the hand of fate rendered Price's oddball travelogue exploitation gold.

On February 6, 1936, magazine journalist Carl Taylor was killed while investigating the Penitente cult, and producer Harry J. Revier (of The Stewart Productions, Inc.) realized he had access to the clay from which the next off-Hollywood sensation could be sculpted: *The Penitente Murder Case*. Eager to capitalize on the publicity, Revier and writer/director Zelma Carroll—in the three weeks following Taylor's suspicious death—sketched out a crude narrative, recruited a cast of bilingual actors (so that English and Spanish versions could be simultaneously filmed) and began shooting at the low-rent Talisman Studios and backlots. On a three-day production schedule, Revier and Carroll accrued enough footage to shape Price's material into a semi-documentary

No longer sold as an investigation into a masochistic religious cult, *The Penitente Murder Case* was packaged and promoted as pure adults-only entertainment.

murder drama. On March 7, a mere month and a day from Taylor's death, at a total cost of $15,000, the film was deemed "ready for release." Though *Penitente* encountered considerable resistance from the Hays Office, which balked at its "scenes of excessive brutality and gruesomeness" and nudity, Revier forged ahead and, in the second week of March, was organizing stage presentations for the film's five roadshow caravans.

After a year of limited distribution, the film experienced a second life when it was foreclosed upon by International Cinema, Inc.,[30] which in turn sold the picture to Mike J. Levinson of Telepictures, who changed the title to the more enticing *The Lash of the Penitentes* (referring primarily to a sequence shot by Revier and Carroll in which the leading lady is stretched on a cross, crucifixion-style, and her bare breasts flogged with a whip). Levinson also replaced Revier's stage show with a lengthy prologue in which a missionary discusses the history of the Penitente Brotherhood, so that the film could be more economically and widely distributed (upping the 43-minute running time to a feature-length 65; of which only about 35 minutes and an explicit preview trailer exist today). No longer did the film need the publicity surrounding Carl Taylor's death. Thanks to a hefty dose of lurid salesmanship, *The Lash of the Penitentes* became a sensation of its own. Trade publications pronounced that the film had "heavy exploitation possibilities"[31] and was "sensational, lurid (and) must be sold accordingly."[32]

The sensational aspects of Harry Revier's saga were boiled down to their most exploitable essence—the crack of a whip on naked flesh—and given the simple, sexy new title *The Lash*.

Because the impact of a documentary-based exploitation film could be altered so radically by a change in footage, titling, narration and promotion, a film could be tailored to meet the changing desires of the audience. During World War II, one jungle picture had its title changed to *Stolen Paradise* and became an attack on the Japanese through the simple insertion of a new title scroll:

> Since these pictures were photographed of beautiful Bali—Barbaric Japanese hordes have completely overrun this earthly paradise.
> The Island of Bali has long been known as the last outpost of natural beauty. For decades the kindly Dutch, under whose protectorate Bali had enjoyed fullest freedom, successfully discouraged alien influence—thereby permitting these true children of the sun to continue their unfettered lives of natural simplicity as their forebears had lived for centuries past.

> Since Japan's brutal invasion of this island one can well imagine the fate of these freedom loving people.
> We therefore, present these authentic pictures of the Stolen Paradise—that was, Bali!

From there, the film proceeded in its original form, with no mention of Japanese oppression.

World War II opened up a new exploitation market, albeit a limited one. Any film featuring vicious characterizations of Asians might be repackaged as a war effort film, even if the villains were Japanese in the original.

There were also a few low-budget features which treated wartime alliances, such as the 1942 film *Samurai*, in which an American family's adopted (Japanese) son grows up to become an Axis spy.

Just prior to the war, the trend was toward isolationist documentaries, such as Ed Mapel's *Horrors of War* (which boasted of "vivid battlefront scenes uncensored by war or military authorities," although one reviewer noted that these same scenes "are for the most part from *She Goes to War* and other productions, but all sequences in which leading players might be recognized have been removed."[33]), Samuel Cummins's *War Is a Racket* and Mentone Productions' *World in Revolt*. However, some films of the era, such as *Hitler's Reign of Terror* (1934), called for European intervention well in advance of the Second World War.

Written, produced and narrated by Colonel Albert L. Rule, 1934's *The Death Parade* (aka *When Germany Surrendered*) provides a history of warfare from the ninth century through World War I, concentrating

One-sheet poster from Dwain Esper's legendary war atrocities film in one of its many incarnations. (Courtesy Millicent Esper Wratten)

167

mainly on the brutal details of battle seldom referenced in the history books. After explaining in an opening title scroll that "the greatness of a nation must be measured by its power to protect its people and its honor," Rule offers body counts, explains the origin of the term "basket case" (a soldier who has suffered the loss of his arms and legs) and discusses the strategies of decimating the enemy's ranks.

Most of the footage used in *The Dead March* (1937) was drawn from Fox Movietone Newsreels and the British War Museum, but producer/director and outspoken radio commentator Bud Pollard couldn't resist editorializing and filmed a sequence in which casualties of war from around the world rise from their graves to address the viewer.

Produced by Jack Goldberg's Lincoln Productions, which specialized in compilation films for all-black audiences, *The Unknown Soldier Speaks*—released in 1934—offered glimpses of military life narrated by the spirit of the unknown soldier, and was screened in a version for African-American audiences and a revised edition for Caucasian theaters. That same year saw the release of five other war-related documentaries, including *Shame of a Nation*, *War's End* and *Dealers in Death* (not to be confused with the exploitation gangster "newsreel" of the same name).

Following the war, the exploiteer cashed in on the public's curiosity about war atrocities, the best-known example being Kroger Babb's *Halfway to Hell*, which provided many Americans with their first glimpse into the Nazi concentration camps, as did Dwain Esper's patchwork saga *Hitler's Strange Love Life* (later retitled *Conform or Die*, *Mussolini Speaks* and *Day of the Despot*, and re-edited to include the atrocities of Mussolini and Stalin).

But the true-life qualities of exploitation are not limited to the documentaries. The sex hygiene film and drug scare picture are just as reliant on a gritty sense of reality in generating emotional responses. It is because the production values are so poor, the on-screen "talent" so ordinary that the common exploitation film transcends mere schlock. The "quotidian reality" described in Chapter One beckons the viewer to excuse the hackneyed machinations of plot and occasional stabs at artistic pretense and heed the messages of the film. The use of actual authority figures to introduce the stories (as in the silent *Road to Ruin*, *Forbidden Adventure* and the oft-cited crime- and disease-fighting government agencies in opening title scrolls) is one of the more conscious transpositions of fact and fiction.

Just as the exploitation film is clearly visible beneath the factual surface of the documentary shocker, so can one see the documentary lurking about the edges of every typical exploitation film.

The uncanniness of exploitation, its disquieting effect, can be attributed to the uncertainty of its format as it casually drifts from the melodrama and thriller to its crude documentarian impulse. *Mom and Dad* is such an effective film because the relatively high production values of the narrative segments and the harsh realism of the medical footage make the collision of Hollywood melodrama and tabloid reality all the more combustive. Describing the Universal horror films of the 1930s, Denis Gifford succinctly characterizes the place where "horror" has traditionally dwelled in Hollywood's version of the world:

> The settings were interchangeable, the ambiance unchangeable... It gave the great films a continuity that was comforting to come back to... Familiar faces, fa-

miliar places: a sort of security in a world of fear... The impossible took place in a tight false world of studio-built landscape, where every tree was carefully gnarled in expressionistic fright, every house cunningly gabled in Gothic mystery, every shadow beautifully lit into lurking terror; and where every actor was caught in the closing ring of horrors, untouched by the possibility of a normal world beyond. [34]

With its hyper-real locations and actors, exploitation moves the horrific and exotic into our own backyards, into the pleasant facade of sun-drenched California suburbs and stucco cottages, creating a frisson of recognition: that this is *our* world where evil dwells. These films suggest that disease or dishonor might easily originate from the best of families as a consequence of shoddy education or one wrong turn on life's highway. These films were ahead of their time for removing monstrosity from the castles of Transylvania and the cathedrals of Paris to the house just down the road. In exploitation Frankenstein and Dracula were supplanted by modern villains: back-alley abortionists, dipsomaniac mothers and malt shop dope dealers who suggested the very modern aim of exploitation: to locate through a vivid, documentary reality an insidious evil arising from *within* society rather than outside it.

One of the most disconcerting aspects of exploitation's genre-blending occurs when documentary (often of a gruesomely authentic nature) elements collide with hackneyed, seemingly predictable fiction, an aspect of Dwain Esper's *Maniac* that has made it such a popular cult film.

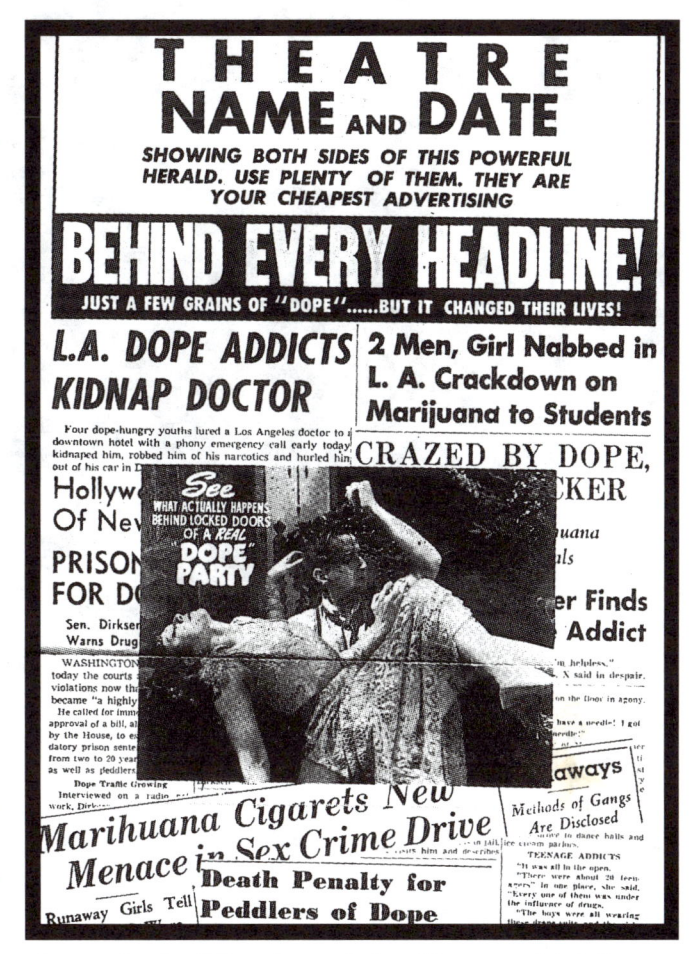

A scrapbook of drug-hysteria headlines provided the perfect background for this promotional piece for Dwain Esper's *Narcotic*.

Though the film is technically crude and discontinuous, it possesses a grittiness—a frightening veracity that comes through partly on the level of *mise en scéne*. When

The psychotic Buckley (Ted Edwards) prepares to ravage Alice Maxwell (Theo Ramsey) in a publicity shot from *Maniac* **(1934). (Ronald V. Borst/Hollywood Movie Posters)**

Maxwell, the lunatic assistant to mad re-animator Meirschultz, attempts to steal a corpse from an undertaker's shop, the body lies in an actual coffin, not a cheaply constructed prop, and a number of Meirschultz's instruments appear to be tools for embalming. Esper seems to have borrowed these props from an actual funeral home, and a clue is perhaps provided by the script's specification that one scene is to be shot at "Robinson's mortuary on Washington Street" (though the shot indicated is not in the finished picture).

To add to the disconcerting, ordinary menace of Esper's film, Meirschultz's lab is situated in a Hollywood bungalow rather than a Gothic castle or spacious white-tiled surgical theater. It is in keeping with what we know of the banality of evil today, that a truly mad scientist *would* be working out of a spare room in his small Los Angeles home. Less atmospheric, perhaps, but—bearing in mind that history's greatest serial killers were almost always suburbanites—it makes the viewer question his or her assumptions about where evil lurks and the false Hollywood convention that it is always somewhere safely remote. In *Maniac*, the innocent victims make no voyage into shadowy hinterlands to find death; it lives down the block from them. The horror lies not only in the basement of a demented scientist, but also in the backyard of an ambitious, cost-conscious furrier breeding domestic tabby cats for their coats in a bizarre twist on the kind of humble, pathetic entrepreneurialism seen in the signs for rabbits and puppies passed on country roads.

Probably more for budgetary reasons than philosophical ones, Esper emphasizes this geographical and cultural proximity of evil to the viewer with scenes shot on public streets, in and about Meirschultz's ordinary American neighborhood. This horror-next-door feeling is underscored by a naturalistic, almost documentary-like scene in which the detective questions a local housewife, who dismisses her neighbor Meirschultz's weirdness with a shrug and a bit of unprompted, spontaneous moralizing (the Depression-era equivalent to modern-day TV news interviewing the unsuspecting neighbors of a mass murderer). The snatch of conversation demonstrates Hildagarde's gift for penning intentionally semi-literate dialogue (elsewhere in Hollywood spoken only by hillbillies and African Americans): "To my notion, those that monkeys with what they got no business to gets queer sooner or later." This immortal line is spoken by Marion Blackton, daughter of J. Stuart Blackton—one of the pioneers of the projected image, who had by then fallen on hard times along with the rest of the country. Marion's brother J. Stuart Blackton, Jr. served as *Maniac*'s assistant director. One of the great blind spots in film history is never knowing what the influential inventor thought of his children working with the cinema's most disgraceful heretic.

Everything about *Maniac* is polluted with morbidity, most often because of the unwholesome collision of death and humor. The film's most chilling scene is one that plays on the sense of realism the film evokes: A conversation between two morgue attendants as they watch Maxwell and Meirschultz trying to resuscitate the recently deceased Maria Altura (again, no actress credited) is one of the film's most chilling in its raw authenticity. Meant to be enjoyed as comedy, the exchange is made terrifying by the amateurs who stumble through their lines, gazing into the lens with lascivious stares, making the hill men in *Deliverance* look like a couple of altar boys. These two men literally express an undercurrent that runs throughout *Maniac*—that ours is a world filled with disintegration and death—as they load a particularly heavy corpse into a box.

> First Embalmer: These stiffs is gettin' heavier and more of 'em every day.
> Second Embalmer: Between the gangsters and the auto drivers, we won't need another war to carry off the population.
> First Embalmer: You didn't even mention... (nervous twitch) the suicides.

Their morgue humor is as believable as it is distasteful. As they watch Meirschultz massage life into a young blonde suicide victim... the First Embalmer says, "Say, didya notice the *beaut* that came in today?" Then he adds with a lecherous grin, "She's the one that's got the coroner doing night work."

By far, the necrophilic comedy duo's most disturbing moment comes at the end of the scene. The First Embalmer, looking at the bearded Meirschultz, is supposed to say, "I wonder who that old Santy Claus is," but before he can finish the sentence, his words deteriorate into wheezing laughter and he is joined by the forced chuckles of his disheveled, toothless partner, who wipes his sweaty palms on his pants as if aroused by the spectacle of Ms. Altura's midnight treatment. Whether by accident or by design (and it really doesn't matter which), Esper concocted an epiphanic moment of profound eeriness, and it's doubtful that any of the masters of makeup could have conjured with their tools such disturbing visions of everyday horror.

When, by the mid-1950s, the shadow of censorship became less threatening to the independent filmmaker, there evolved a change in tone in the exploitation film. As exploiteers liberated themselves from the necessity of grounding salacious stories in issues of social welfare, their films gravitated toward pure fantasy, at the expense of this ethereal quality that had for more than two decades been one of their most unique distinguishing features. As this crudely mesmerizing, real-life quality began to ebb, exploitation made the transition to unqualified and unapologetic sexploitation.

And the exploiteers' death knell began to sound.

While it appears to be an unadulterated "nudie cutie," J.D. Kendis' *Secrets of a Model* (1940) still subscribed to many of the conventions of the traditional exploitation film.

Chapter Eight

SOFT-CORE AND HARD-SELL

> Porno is the end of exploitation and it will be the end of all of us.
> —David F. Friedman [1]

No matter which pressing social issue was being explored on-screen, one unchanging element remained at the core of every exploitation film: sex.

Whether writ large and punctuated with exclamation points or more subtly woven into the fabric of the film, sex was the ultimate mystery which lured the unenlightened into the darkness of the theater.

Though "dirty pictures" have been around since the French postcards of the 19th-century, the photographic representation of sex didn't bubble its way up into the mainstream until exploitation offered its democratic brand of sexual enlightenment for audiences of men *and* **women.**

Before exploitation, pornography was a closeted affair, from which according to Walter Kendrick in *The Secret Museum: Pornography in Modern Culture*: "women, children, and the poor of both sexes and all ages were excluded" much like the exploitation film audience deemed ill-equipped to handle it.

For decades, cinematic depictions of sex were relegated to the medical community and fraternity houses or men's club "smokers" where the all male audience of the 1910s and 1920s made sex films an elite pursuit. Stag films like *A Country Stud Horse* (1920) or one of the earliest X-rated films, *A Free Ride* (aka *A Grass Sandwich*, roughly dated between 1917-1918) offered clinical closeups of the sexual organs, and every sexual novelty from fellatio to penetration, often served up in a highly nonlinear, shock-oriented format that foreshadowed the sexual jolts of exploitation.

Exploitation was a 20th-century answer to a timeless desire: to see extremes of human behavior in raw, authentic detail. It succeeded so grandly because it offered vice in a transportable format without the expense and bother of real burlesque dancers or carnival freaks. "A movie, the whole thing is in a can, it comes to you, you can run it as many times as you want, it doesn't talk back, it doesn't need any money," affirms exploitation's official spokesman David Friedman, illustrating the pragmatic, independence-dictated code of the exploiteer. [2]

But the sex which exploitation sold was not the liberated, wanton brand which is more freely peddled today. Faced with a battlefield of boundaries, sex had to be slightly reshaped (one might even say molested) in order to reach the marketplace without interference.

Since sex—especially the non-reproductive recreational variety—could not be glorified, exploiteers cloaked it in the usual shroud of enlightenment, linking it to moralistic, cautionary tales about the pitfalls of sin. Oddly Victorian in their view of sex, these films promised that copulation's only outcome was a trip to the VD ward or a visit to the neighborhood abortionist.

With their bizarre mix of sex and decay, sex and death, sex and dishonor, exploitation films helped to transform sex into something truly monstrous, underlining its association with violence and fear which later adult films of the '50s, '60s and '70s—"roughies," "ghoulies" and S&M hard-core—made their grisly modus operandi.

But always in a liminal zone, somewhere between Hollywood and hard-core, exploitation could represent the worst of sex, and also the best. Not always exploitive and pornographic, exploitation is often deeply human and compassionate. Many of the films demonstrate a rare empathy for their protagonists, as well as an earnest curiosity about sex that recalls Havelock Ellis' claim, "Sex lies at the root of life, and we can never learn to reverence life until we know how to understand sex."

Mourning their loss of innocence, the black-clad newlyweds (Diane Sinclair, Lyman Williams) face a syphilitic future together in Edgar G. Ulmer's *Damaged Lives*. (Photofest)

Unlike Hollywood films, where narratives seemed to unfold in a fairy-dusted Otherworld, exploitation films dealt with carnal matters on a more realistic, rather than escapist, level. Audiences are connected and implicated in exploitation because the context in which it places sex—alongside syphilis, unwed pregnancy, drug addiction, white slavery and social dishonor—were real-life fears the audience could understand. In exploitation, every incident carries with it the caveat emptor, that if it couldn't happen to you, then it could certainly happen to your daughter, your son, your husband or your wife.

Undeniable in exploitation's repertoire is the horror film convention of suspense: the anticipation of what horror or pleasure may be revealed. Exploitation may in fact have as much in common with the horror film as it does with pornography, using elements of both to suggest our bodies are monstrous and capable of undergoing cataclysmic, terrifying changes beyond our control, as exploitation's gruesome images of decayed bodies graphically demonstrate. Films like *Sex Madness* and *Damaged Goods* make the body the linchpin and tension-generating center of their stories. In *Sex Madness*, a mother passes syphilis on to her baby and in *Damaged Goods*, a father transmits VD to both his wife and newborn child. The perfusion of the disease becomes like the spreading contamination of "pod people" in the 1956 science fiction thriller *Invasion of the Body Snatchers*. We watch in horror as our own fears of losing control of our bodies, or having our bloodstreams polluted, are given disturbing visual expression.

In its often profoundly creepy meld of sex, death and disease, exploitation seemed to echo the puritanical bent of an America who viewed the body and its functions as a dirty secret mirroring the very forces that attempted to suppress it.

Exploitation was especially censorable because so much of its sexual interplay was not aimed at reproduction. The short-term "romances" of exploitation are far removed from the tidy heterosexual courtships and fluid-free final kisses of the Classical Hollywood Cinema.

The 1942 shocker about kiddie marriage, *Child Bride,* is a case in point. A disconcerting mix of titillation and cautionary tale, *Child Bride* is the twisted saga of a little girl, Jennie, threatened with adult intercourse with a man twice her age under the sanction of marriage. Like most of exploitation, *Child Bride*'s universe is steeped in sexuality.

Little Jennie, the blossoming adolescent in *Child Bride,* is the shadow twin of Judy Garland (whose breasts were bound tightly underneath her *Wizard of Oz* costume) and the ebullient, precocious miniature love object Shirley Temple. Where Garland and Temple are sensuality made covert, Jennie is openly sexual because her body is shamelessly bared to the viewer. As is so often the case with exploitation, these films made manifest the latent obsessions of Hollywood for teenage and adolescent coquettes. *Child*

The strip poker sequence was a popular fixture in exploitation (as in *Road to Ruin*). (Photofest)

175

In *Child Bride*, the nature of "throbbing drama" is purely sexual.

Bride is a more frank and also more disturbing picture because it makes few bones about the sexual appeal children hold for some men. Unlike Temple or Garland, Jennie is presented as a sex object plain and simple, with no cute little jig or sausage curls to convince us of the innocence of our desire in watching frolicking, adorable femininity. Though *Child Bride* goes to great lengths to suggest Jennie is still a child who excels at school and helps her parents with chores, this gloss of innocence is as false as the cheerleader or nurse's uniforms in contemporary pornography, something that makes the defilement of innocence all the more tantalizing.

Exploitation is a pulp novel vision of American life and traffics in the same leitmotifs of innocence assailed, femmes fatales, mustache-twirling fiends and morally corrosive sex. Its heroines often sport the angora and satin slipcovers of a sensuality worn on the skin's surface like a badge of honor—or shame. Recalling the crude, inflammatory covers of magazines like *Spicy Detective* and *Weird Tales*, exploitation plays into grimy, all-American prejudices about unshaven men lurking in dark alleyways and unscrupulous abortionists wielding bacteria-covered instruments. While true crime stories offered a glimpse into hidden criminal worlds, the sex-oriented exploitation films offered a peek into the tantalizing, hidden mysteries of the human body.

In keeping with the Victorian sensibility that gives pornography its special charge, exploitation films deal in extremes of untarnished good and scum-of-the-earth evil. Girls kidnapped into sexual slavery, women compromised in countless, lurid ways, the prurience of exploitation is intensified by the purity of its victims. In *Slaves in Bondage*, the virginal Mary Lou is abducted while walking home from church and threatened with extradition to a notorious roadhouse/brothel known as Berrywood, where other formerly innocent girls are reduced to nonplused molls lounging around in their skivvies, manhandled, *broken* by thuggish pimps. Exploitation assumes there are ultimates in virtue and vice, and that once one has been too thoroughly indoctrinated into the latter, there's no turning back.

For the women in exploitation, virginity is their most profound and guarded resource. Possession of it is possession of one's self—to lose it is to lose oneself, in dishonor and disgrace, to become nameless, faceless, one lost soul among many others.

Just as tuberculosis plagued 19th-century heroines, like *La Traviata*'s Violetta and *La Boheme*'s Mimi, so too venereal disease and sexual dishonor maimed and consumed the exploitation heroine in pathetic melodramatic suffering. In exploitation, venereal disease carries the stigma of dirt, poverty and sexual dishonor that tuberculosis carried in the late 19th and early 20th centuries, serving as a centrifuge for spinning out good from bad. The taint of VD was one way in an increasingly medical-oriented society, that honor was being measured. And exploitation, being a literal and visual-minded forum, took advantage of this very shocking way of presenting evidence of naughtiness.

By the same token, the high price placed on virtue means saving it is often the exploitation film's most thrilling, heart-pounding chase, as good girls cling desperately to a shred of chiffon and their precarious chastity, threatened with the brothel or rape. Whether it's the surgeon's knife hovering over a girl's mons veneris in *Tomorrow's Children* or the horrifying honeymoon of *Child Bride*, the job of saving women's virtue is always a race against time in some sense, when one considers the omnipresent threat of sexual dishonor. Even when good girls are rescued from white slavery's big house, there remain the girls-gone-bad who are beyond redemption, reminding the viewer of the permanent perils of sin. Salvation comes too late to Ann Dixon in *Road to Ruin*. After her fall from grace into premarital sex, pregnancy, prostitution and abortion, she is branded a "sex delinquent" by the juvenile court. A cure for her VD can't change the mark of disrepute that she is forced to wear. With a downfall this tawdry, anything less than death would merely be prolonging the punishment and pain. Ann fulfills her destiny with a death that is graceful and exquisite—the most that a fallen woman can hope for.

In *Slaves in Bondage* a newly recruited whore, transformed from a sweetly modest country girl into a platinum-rinsed, silk-clad hussy out of a Hollywood golddigger melodrama, still possesses an understanding of the visible difference between right and wrong and tells another tawdry fashion plate upon first glimpse of Mary Lou, "You can tell, just by looking at her she's a good girl." Mary Lou stands between these two figures of sullied and jaded vampery like

In a piece of poster art that profoundly encapsulates the exploitation formula of sex appeal, a woman shamefully hides her face and breasts while her body is immodestly revealed.

a fought-over rag doll as the other asks, "Well what are *we*?" But no answer is necessary: Once degraded, any girl with hopes of surgically reattaching her character is sorely mistaken. We can easily measure the dividing line between good girl and bad in the swirl of fabric on naked hips, the knowing expression, the unrestrained bosom and insouciance that distinguishes "bad." The men who pay for their services are less easily knowable.

The moral standard for men is generally more relaxed. A glimpse of two "Johns" at the Berrywood brothel is, rather than an indictment of their characters, a moment of comic relief. Two drunk, overweight middle-aged men, one intoxicated apparently to the point of retardation, stand at the bar and insult the "help." "May I call you Miss, or am I too late?" the less drunk Lothario asks a passing blonde, who smiles dimly, like the butt of a tired burlesque joke. The prankster proceeds to mix a "cocktail" of straight liquor in his companion's mouth, shaking his head to stir, indicating the vaudevillian spirit of such comic asides. The men's presence in the brothel is excused in jest, in their carefree, vaguely moronic repartee. They are wiser than the women because they make the jokes at their expense and are only visiting for a time, passing through. It is a man's prerogative and natural instinct to have a good time, but a woman's downfall to be the entertainment.

The "Johns" in these dramas are by and large phantoms—pushed aside for the central drama of how the women become whores, disease-carriers or sex slaves. Men are never degraded in the same manner because in Western culture a man's body cannot be sexually defiled, since it has no inherent physical virtue to protect (though corruption through drug abuse is another matter entirely, as shown in *Narcotic* and *Reefer Madness*). When, in the case of male-centered dramas like *Damaged Lives* and *No Greater Sin*, the husband carries the syphilis germs, suspense derives from when and how he will transmit them to his wife, and then, his unborn child. The real travesty is always the contamination of innocence as represented by the virtuous wife and mother.

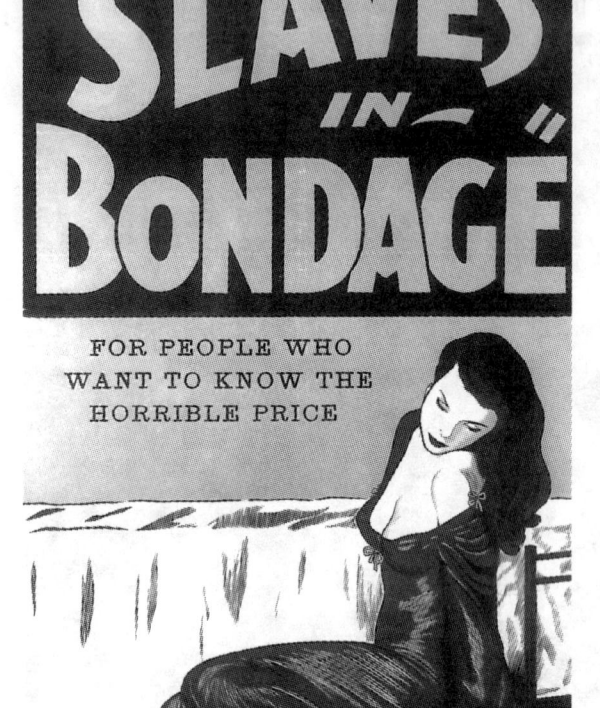

Bringing to mind the white slavery exposes of the mid-1910s, *Slaves in Bondage* played upon the same widespread fears of corrupted innocence.

Demonstrating the almost exclusive association of sin with women, in *Honky Tonk Girl*, it is the hitchhiking prostitutes who carry sin's burden squarely on their shoulders. The men who pluck them from the roadside in their pickups and coupes, lured with their road culture come-on "Going my way, Mister?" and lusciously arched thumb are merely succumbing to sin freely given.

Woman, as represented in exploitation, is in a precarious state, always on the verge of degradation and struggling toward a respectability which can be jeopardized through one bad decision. Exploitation reminds us of an almost vanished sense of morality, where good and bad were truly divided, where a girl's reputation was all she had, and one mistake could alter the course of her life. In *Cocaine Fiends*, a country girl's chance encounter with a city slicker begins a rapid downward spiral into cocaine addiction and prostitution. In *Guilty Parents*, Helen's induction into her high school pals' drinking club is the initial toppled domino which sets off a chain reaction including pregnancy, murder, attempted suicide and her pimping of other women. Femininity is a condition—a malignant growth prone to sudden, horrible eruption—in exploitation, which threatens to lead the protagonist into disgrace and dishonor if not carefully controlled.

As in contemporary pornography, exploitation's narrative action is largely a kind of filler to get the characters from place to place, that "place" being where the clothes come off. Expectation is built up around how much of and when the female characters will be revealed. Viewers are encouraged to take the objective gaze of science in looking at the female body as anatomical subject. Exploitation thus set a precedent for the scientific hard sell of Times Square porn during the '60s when Swedish sex films were advertised as educational marital aids to cloak their prurient appeal. Marrying the objectification of women in early porn with the objectification of the freak by the medical community, exploitation forged the female body as the latest sexual curiosity.

It goes without saying in the changeable, diverse substratum of exploitation, that the degree to which women are made into sex objects varies from film to film. Some films show "a lot," some only a little. Some exploitation focuses exclusively on the physical wonders of the female landscape, while others are more democratic, offering

A young married woman chooses suicide as a means of escaping the shame of venereal disease in *Damaged Lives*. (Photofest)

medicalized glimpses of both male and female bodies with little sexual content, as in Edgar G. Ulmer's *Damaged Lives*. In *Damaged Lives* a wealthy young businessman afflicted with syphilis is given the conventional Grand Tour of the VD ward—a horrific cabinet of curiosities where, in exploitation's most democratic tradition, male and female bodies are given equal play.

But whether viewers are rewarded with or denied what they came to see, the anticipation of glimpsing the taboo is built up irregardless by advertising and the salacious aura of exploitation, as in the randy come-on for *Guilty Parents* promising, "Beautiful young girls bartered like cattle and sacrificed on the altar of lust," and poster art featuring women in tantalizing degrees of degradation and undress.

The interplay of revelation and concealment in exploitation suggests the comparable rhythm of striptease. Like pornography and striptease, exploitation operates from the premise, that while there are degrees in what may or may not be shown, women are essentially sexual beings, who will reveal their nature if given the chance.

Recognizing the value of a little creative costuming over outright naked displays, exploitation perfected a kind of striptease aesthetic, of partial-revelation and maximum suggestion. Ads for the films capitalized on this idea of glimpsed nudity which may or may not be seen, depending on whether or not the print had been scissored by state censor boards in the past. A poster for *Cocaine* (1939) is typical for highlighting sexual provocation rather than the subject at hand, by displaying a drawing of a woman reclining on a bed in a slip that is short enough to reveal her naked thighs. Similarly, a poster for *Marihuana* featured, not the drug the title promised, but actresses hiking their dresses up above their knees to expose a tantalizing column of leg and stockings. One woman cradles a man's head to her breast, while another lifts her dress in order to lean over the reclining couple.

As in the freak show, display is of supreme importance in the exploitation film as female characters lift their skirts or remove their dresses in an elaborate striptease of sexual difference. The complicated revelation and display of the body in exploitation's

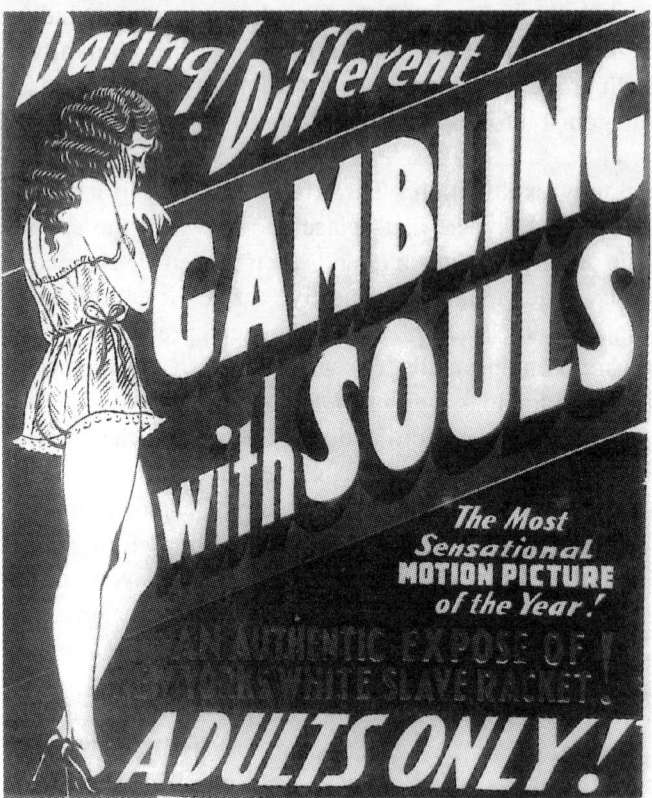

The subject matter of a film was often rendered irrelevant by saucy poster artwork, as with this window card for *Gambling with Souls*.

often fragmented closeups—featuring body parts rather than full physiques—resembles the photographs of "freaks" similarly posed with skirts lifted or shirts opened to reveal the seed of their difference. The provocative, gradual display of John Merrick, the Elephant Man, with successive garments cast aside to expose more and more of his flesh, is revisited in the similar slow revelation of bodies in exploitation and the shared mix of sexual titillation and presentation of the taboo.

Actual striptease is also a sub-genre of exploitation and was often incorporated into the films, in the numerous burlesque shorts of black women, white women or twins (like the specialty acts of the freak show, divided by color or gimmick). These women performed for the camera in the square-ups which awaited viewers patient enough to wade through exploitation's main feature or which would be thrown on to appease an audience disappointed by what had been offered in the feature. With titles such as *Doris Ake Presenting Her Pearl Harbor Hula* and *Mildred and Bow: The Quality Sisters in Boogie Woogie*, these striptease and burlesque dance shorts offered an advantage over the stagebound vaudeville and burlesque displays of dancing, cavorting cuties. The camera's freedom to roam and assume the most advantageous perspective, meant the increased spectatorial pleasure of a closeup to isolate the gyrating lower body of Doris Ake, Rita Zane in her "Peacock Promenade," Betty Ware in "Evening at the Gaiety" or the cavalcade of group striptease shot from a gratuitous below-the-neck angle in *What Happened to Tom in the Ladies Gym*. Though relatively tame by today's standards, burlesque films offer a glimpse at the sexual preoccupations of another age, with their frequently censored bellybuttons and coquettish revelation and concealment of the dancer's body with feathers or soap bubbles. Though what they often ended up revealing was minimal—nipples covered by pasties, and pubic hair by a substantial bikini bottom—their very foundation, rigged to tease and turn on a male audience, was nearly titillation enough.

Like the freak show, the burlesque theater also suffered a decline after 1930,[3] providing the exploitation industry with another torch to carry. Integrating burlesque's conventions, exploitation gave motion picture audiences yet another privileged view of the illicit but in a far more accessible and easily transported form—the film can.

Just as the freak show moved from a popular amusement in its heyday, to a lower class vice in the traveling carnival circuit, burlesque's fall from grace came with a "bourgeoisification" of the entertainment industry. Burlesque's fall from respectability

Before making the transition to unabashed sex films, the exploitation industry produced a series of filmed burlesque such as *The Good Old Days of Burlesk*.

181

The theatricality of burlesque made its display of the female body somehow justifiable, and was used as a legitimizing device by many an exploiteer. As this *Hollywood Burlesque* stil shows. (Photofest)

also meant its exclusion from middle-class promotional venues—like the newspaper—and an increased reliance on posters and ads to trumpet its arrival. As the popularity of burlesque dwindled, there came a change in the dancer's performance style. The finesse, skill and empowerment of burlesque's female performer gave way to the mute cooch dancer and subsequent striptease artists whose performance was founded more on blatant, unartistic sexual exhibition.

Increasingly, a dancer's "voice" was reduced literally and figuratively as she became merely a sexual spectacle, and often the butt of jokes in comic routines previously predicated on female involvement—now performed solely by men. The dancer's newfound silence was a crucial element in stripping the sexually displayed woman of her power, a feature also seen in the conventions of exploitation.

But not all of exploitation offers such a direct translation of the burlesque striptease to the film loop. Much of exploitation changes the nature of striptease and burlesque, with its sweetly smiling or teasing revelation turning into scenarios of degradation in which women offer their bodies for view surreptitiously and shamefully. Their averted eyes or turned backs indicate embarrassment or refusal to collude in a sexual act. This, coupled with a pathetic female exhibitionism, suggests their sole worth is in what these actresses can show of their bodies, like the kewpie-faced brunette giving it up to the camera in the abortion expose *Race Suicide*.

A well-acted, quickly paced melodrama of the police and coroner's attempts to shut down an illegal abortion racket, *Race Suicide* offers numerous interludes of female striptease to spice up its storyline. In addition to a randy nightclub songstress, a fantasy interlude of women undressing for the camera, and a striptease behind a backlit bedroom screen, *Race Suicide* offers a candid look inside the abortionist's inner sanctum. In the offices of Drs. Van Helsen and Botts, a young brunette undresses in preparation for her examination. The licentiousness and raw shock of her strip is increased by the sleazy connotations of the abortionist's illegal operating room where she disrobes. In one of the amusing, vaguely eerie overlaps that makes exploitation so uniquely surreal, the nurse who assists the girl is Florence Dudley (aka Belle Harris), the brothel madam in *Slaves in Bondage*, adding yet another uncanny sexual element to the scene. The girl turns her back to the camera as she shucks off her dress and camisole in an unusually frank and prolonged display even for the exploitation film. That this sexual thrill is delivered in narrative terms by a girl "in trouble" and about to undergo a D&C melds in the exploitation tradition, the association of sex and sin.

Such moments epitomize the disquieting, creepy quality of exploitation and give some indication of the unhealthiness censors objected to in these admittedly disturbing films, with their coupling of medicine and titillation.

Of the two kinds of sexual revelation in the exploitation film: the burlesque-styled striptease where the performer makes the sexual meaning of her act straightforward; and the sly, secret "captured" disrobing and medical footage, the latter is the most intriguing and complex for its disingenuous suggestion that no sexual meaning is intended. In such scenes the women are supposed to be caught unaware—though they often directly acknowledge the camera by contorting their bodies to give us the best view, in the tradition of early film pornography like *The Virgin With the Hot Pants*. Both aspects of sexual titillation can be linked to a long tradition of pornography, and a history of looking at the female body as a dirty little secret revealed "reluctantly" to the male audience.

The seductive unveiling of the flesh, traditionally associated with the Biblical temptress Salomé, and later made into an industry with burlesque, also has a long history in the representation of medicine. As scholars such as Elaine Showalter and Thomas Laqueur have noted in their historical studies of sexual representation, the scientific and medical depiction of the female body has often borne a close resemblance to the depiction of the female body in striptease, as in the statue *La Nature se devoilant devant la science* by Louis Ernest Barrias, exhibited

Life itself seemed a little more raw in the city from which the nation's fantasies sprang.

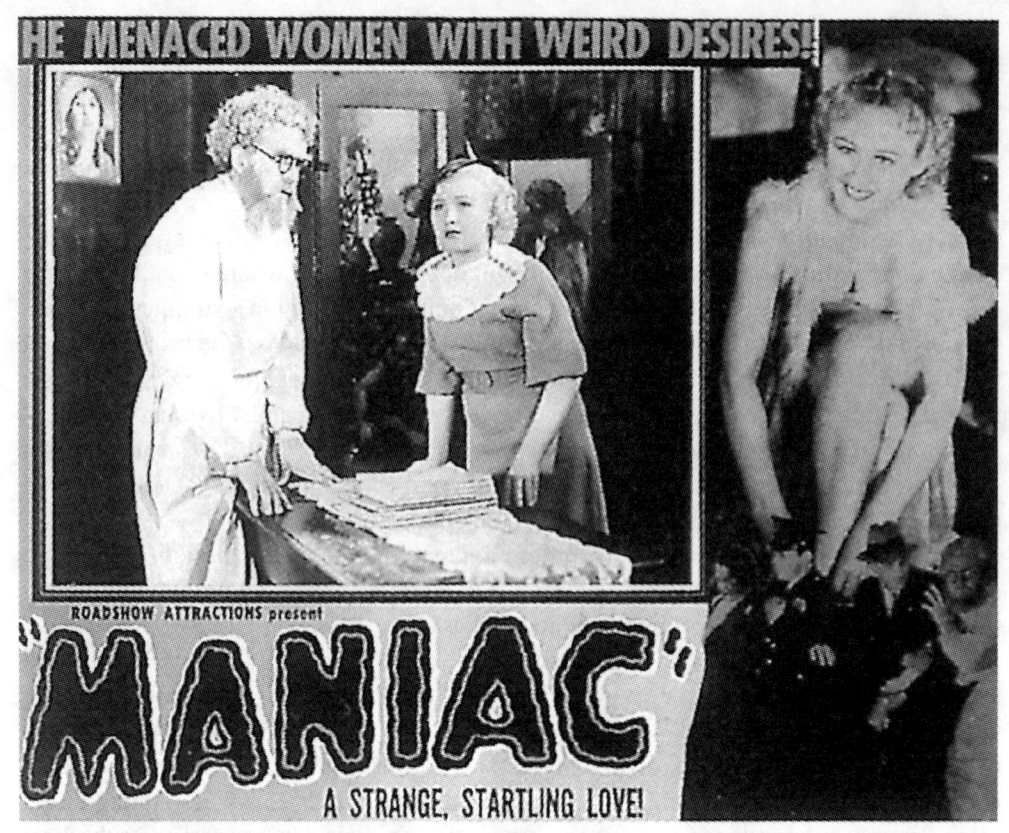

A scientist's assistant (Bill Woods) wrestles with the moral implications of desire on the exam table in Dwain Esper's *Maniac*. **(Ronald V. Borst/Hollywood Movie Posters)**

in Paris in 1895. A metaphor for the ostensible "educational" aims of medicine, "Nature Unveiling Herself Before Science," depicts a woman, eyes downcast, pulling back her gown to reveal her naked body, delivering a striptease which serves greater medical inquiry and knowledge.[4] *La Nature* demonstrates that science was not immune from feelings of shame and guilt associated with looking at the body, and therefore romanticized its noble calling—and passed the buck—in artwork and illustrations where women freely display their bodies. As in exploitation, some of the guilt associated with looking is removed when the subject participates or allows us to look at her body.

Shades of a "scientific" revelation of female nudity resurface in the exploitation instructional *How To Undress*, which derives its lascivious thrill from the women it shows colluding in the audience's voyeurism. Directed by exploitation maverick Dwain Esper and written by his wife Hildagarde, *How to Undress* is a paradigmatic example of a supposedly open, yet actually guarded sexual display which took center stage in exploitation. Although the male narrator of *How To Undress* tells the viewer that the two women we "surreptitiously" watch undress are unaware of our presence, the provocative over-the-shoulder glances Elaine Barrie Barrymore gives the camera, and her carefully posed body which both hides and reveals, indicate otherwise.

How To Undress offers not only the spectacle of striptease, but an instructive peek into the private sphere of the woman's bedroom, with traces of a scientific or educational motivation. As with many exploitation films, *Undress* provides a glimpse into a secret female world of rented apartments and backstage dressing rooms where women let their guard down, and, in anthropological fashion, their rituals and natural behavior can be observed. And just as Hollywood created a fiction of what life should look like, sending impressionable consumers to department stores to buy a dress or hat that would gain them access to the fantasy, exploitation presented an artificial, often ridiculous impression of sexual "reality."

Like *How To Undress*, Esper's Grand Guignol horror film *Maniac* offers its audience a peek into the mysterious, veiled female universe. A jarring nonsequitur inserted in Esper's laboratory-thriller for the usual purpose of arousal, *Maniac* features the kind of naughty tableau of lounging hotsy-totsies that exploitation made into an art form. In a busy communal apartment, roommates loll about in their underwear, bathe, gossip, use a vibrating exercise belt, dance and in every way maximize the display of their bodies while indicating in this secret look inside their domain their "true,"—which boils down to their *sexual*—nature. By pulling back the veil on a formerly hidden world, exploitation films like *Maniac* not only give the viewer a picture of the woman Hollywood denies, but a purportedly "real" look at Everywoman.

The exploitation cinema's collapsing of carnival and cinema to encourage a certain kind of looking at the female body is also apparent in the genre's visual conventions. While the abundance of long-shot compositions in exploitation films is both a holdover from early cinema techniques and a budgetary constraint (less editing needed, less film used), the lack of closeups also shows a different emphasis of these films. Since there were few real female stars in exploitation, women tended to be archetypal; a random collection of faceless T&A. Whereas the Hollywood closeup emphasizes psychological and emotional relationships between characters, exploitation is all about the female body presented for maximum sexual exposure, in long-shot. When closeups *are* employed they are often just a means of zeroing in on the sexual geography of legs or breasts, rather than a way to convey expressive meaning in facial closeup. Like the fetish-porn of low-grade magazines like *Juggs* and *Leg Show*, exploitation often presents women broken down to their definitive parts.

Evidence of exploitation's reliance on fetishized body spectacles can be seen in the frequency with which closeups of legs occur in scenes of the dancing girls in *The Pace That Kills* (1928), or other scenes of libidinal drug addicts thrashing about in the throes of sexual ecstasy in *Narcotic*. While Hollywood

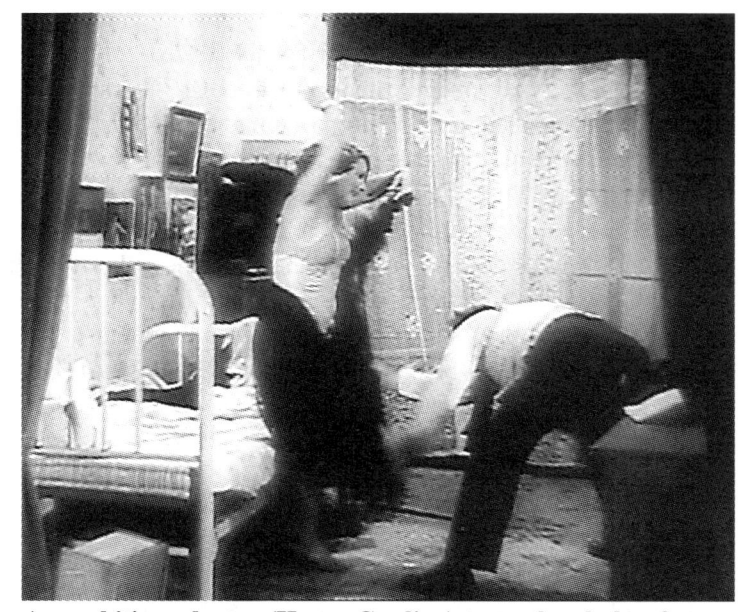

An ambitious doctor (Harry Cording) tears the clothes from a prostitute near the grisly finale of *Narcotic*. (frame enlargement)

A group of schoolgirls bare their legs and expose their souls to corruption in the "petting party" sequence from *Road to Ruin*. (Photofest)

was solidifying the Classical Style—which tended to figure the backlit, soft-focus starlet's face as the archetypal romantic and sexual image—exploitation featured a unique editing strategy in its classic Leg Shot: a woman's legs displayed with skirt raised like a theater curtain opening on the show to herald the view.

When faces, identity and wardrobe become less important, it's amazing to see what takes their place. The degree to which legs are figured as fetish and sexual signifier in these films at times borders on the archaic and ridiculous. Compared to modern pornography, this attention appears almost quaint. But when considered on another level, legs have naughtier connotations. Gateway to a woman's sexual organs, legs are the closest, geographically speaking, filmmakers could get to showing the vagina without resorting to potentially unarousing, murky closeups of childbirth or VD. Such sex-and-medicine shots were tried though on the chance that some palooka in the audience could get a rise out of them.

In *Slaves in Bondage*, Belle Harris surreptitiously auditions young girls under the pretext of legitimate employment at the beauty shop she uses as a front. In a film that, contrary to Hollywood evasion of the subject, explicitly concerns the Depression and its impact, young women parade through Belle's office while she surveys their legs, indicated in a series of point-of-view closeups. Not only measuring the aesthetic appeal of the women's "figures," Belle also looks for signs of an exploitable economic hardship, like the young blond whose torn nylons indicate her desperate economic status. The madam's attention to the girl's legs establishes not only the sexual nature of their work, but it obviously affords the viewer a privileged gander at this provocative hot zone of the female body.

Sexual ecstasy and drug-crazed abandon are therefore represented by the jitterbugging female characters lifting their skirts higher and higher in *Assassin of Youth*. The 1930s teenager's version of dirty dancing, jitterbugging's spastic, grinning mania may look innocent by today's standards, but was as much a kind of public foreplay as any. And certainly enough to set a parent's teeth on edge. The degree to which such wildly expressive, energetic dance is privileged in these films seems to suggest an ecstatic female sexuality conveyed through performance. In *Guilty Parents*, multiple dance scenes overemphasize the female body in all its lusciously mobile glory at nightclub performances and at the dancing school.

The scenes recall the prohibitions of the Motion Picture Production Code:

> Dances of the type known as 'kooch,' or 'Can-Can,' since they violate decency... are wrong. Dances with movements of the breasts, excessive body movement while the feet remain stationary, the so-called 'belly dances'—these dances are immoral, obscene, and hence altogether wrong.

Needless to say, such uninhibited undulations are a staple of the exploitation genre, as integral to the formula as the opening scroll or last-minute happy ending.

When Helen in *Guilty Parents* auditions for a chorus line job, the camera lingers lecherously on the dancers' audition numbers. It is close enough to capture the movement of the dancers' braless figures before cutting to closeups which show the gyrations of their thighs as they dance. Likewise, *Road to Ruin* (1934 version) emphasizes the boundless sexual energy of youth in the "Campus Crawl" number performed by a shimmying teenage girl. Exploitation is rife with such images of sexual delirium and a lax moral environment expressively conveyed via the female body.

In *Assassin of Youth* a drunken teenage party affords the viewer glimpses of young women dancing with skirts raised to reveal garters and a hint of thigh, and in *No Greater Sin* the camera fixates on the twitching posteriors of its roadhouse dancers as they jitterbug the night away. This exposure, so conveniently and seamlessly worked into the narrative, leaves female sexuality looking at once accidental and provocative. Like the patently artificial scenarios of porn, with their lonely, sex-crazed housewives and precociously promiscuous young women, exploitation makes sex look like a jerry-rigged, winking come-on, a joke men are in on, and women pretend to be oblivious of. The female body becomes a complicated site of tease as when "bad girl" Linda's body can be viewed in her diaphanous nightclothes, or "good girl" Joan's figure is outlined against a moonlit sky as she changes out of wet clothing, in direct violation of one tenet of the 1930 Production Code, which warns, "Transparent or translucent materials and silhouette are frequently more suggestive than actual exposure."[5] And how.

Exploitation not only *promised* visceral thrills, it often delivered them in spades, as one audience member at a 1948 showing of *Mom and Dad* recalls. Fifteen-year-old

Clever newsboys capitalize on the crowds surrounding a theater (showing *Sins of Love*) in a photo that captures the grungy reality of a late-night exploitation screening.

August Helms remembers that grown men overcome with revulsion had to be escorted to cots during the venereal disease portion of the film, and that, as the female audience members exited the film, men waiting in line for the Men Only showing met them with catcalls. "Some of the girls seemed embarrassed, not because of the various comments, but by being *seen* leaving...the picture was certainly a visual eye opening." In the eyes of the male spectators, looking at women's bodies could be nauseating or titillating, but it was sure as hell no place for a lady. When it is female bodies being looked at, live women spectators are redundant. The female body, formerly the province of women midwives, healers and attendants, was beginning to seem the stomping ground of doctors in a professional setting, and an audience of men in America's entertainment venues.

As a precursor to hard-core pornography, exploitation was groundbreaking in depicting the female body in a certain way—defining it as a pornographic object, the means for a medical, educational and scientific investigation. While the viewer was encouraged to view the female body in a clinical manner, exploitation also ran counter to the Hollywood and pornographic film by giving audiences information they could use.

Exploitation films seem to mark a pre-porn dilemma in how to reveal the body, often resorting to horrific shocks of disease and birth in order to achieve some essential truth about what Hollywood is hiding. Delving into flesh and blood, these films exhibit a great deal of fear of what lies inside us, and especially what lurks and is incubated inside women. The hidden curse of syphilis or the period-that-never-comes are indications of the covert operations of the female body which bide their time to then spring their surprises on the unsuspecting. Men are knowable, in the exploitation universe—you can read their intentions and moral character in the tilt of their hat or a cocky walk, but women can surprise you, exploitation warns.[6]

A retitled version of Willis Kent's *The Wages of Sin* invites the viewer to take along hard look at this vintage window card.

Exploitation trains the viewer to look at the female body as "parts," prefiguring the fetishistic look of later pornography. It is thus this "bridge" of science, from the freak show to exploitation to pornography, which validates our looking at the body in a certain way while also demanding control of this gaze. Just as Western culture has seen a constant drive toward mapping out the peculiarities and vagaries of sex, exploitation continues the trend, breaking sex and the female body down into images.

Voyeurism—the pleasure derived from looking without being looked at—is the fundamental law of the theater. It is what separates its pleasures from those of any other entertainment form. Until cinema came along, no entertainment form dependent on an audience and a performer offered the novelty of watching women who could not watch back or acknowledge one's presence. Film offered the added surreality of a dark room full of other people silently colluding with your voyeurism. Looking at the nude or partially clad body of a woman without her acknowledgment of that looking has been the crux of modern pornography, and also exploitation—it is what most clearly makes exploitation porn's antecedent.

189

Chapter Nine

OUR SECRET HISTORY

Just as the freak show began its slow fade from popularity and acceptance in the 1930s, exploitation also experienced a gradual demise as a cultural force. By the 1950s, exploitation was suffering its death throes, its real heyday essentially at an end. Those remaining exploiteers who doggedly continued the roadshow tradition had no new educational wares to peddle and were forced to recycle old prints of *Mom and Dad* or *Because of Eve* for the burgeoning drive-in circuit (delivering their lectures via microphone from the concession stand).

An age of on-screen permissiveness was dawning and the cheaply made sexploitation and gore-cinema of the late 1950s and early '60s usurped the once mighty reign of exploitation as America's favorite breaker of taboos. No longer bound by the educational pretense of its predecessor, this new breed of carnal cinema was allowed to dispense with the creaky "moral" tone of classic exploitation, and showed as much nudity as a tissue-thin plot could sustain. Since guilty consciences no longer needed to be assuaged by medical authority, the exploitation conventions of roadshowing films and live lecturers also became unnecessary. The nudie movie business boomed and low-budget sex films were able to find distribution in greater numbers, especially since they no longer required the delicate handling typical of an exploitation roadshow.

With the birth of exploitation's naughty upstart child, sexploitation, there also came a distinct change in the underground cinema's tone. Quaint fears of marijuana's effects and the nightmare outcome of premarital sex shifted with films of the '50s and '60s. These films boasted a harsher, more nihilistic tone, with scenes of rape and gore-drenched violence becoming more prevalent in subterranean fare labeled "roughies" and "ghoulies." The equation of sex with violence that would come to dominate the slasher cinema of the 1970s replaced the relatively carefree cat fights of *Maniac* and *Test Tube Babies*. A genre founded on innuendo and tease was steamrolled by an audacious new age, though as critic David Chute rightly notes of the sexploitation and gore to come, ultimately, "the newer pictures bore because they don't flirt."[1]

This new cycle of sinema was pioneered by former roadshowman David Friedman and a new breed of filmmaker, Herschell Gordon Lewis, whose 1963 *Blood Feast* was one of the definitive shockers of its day, an epically bloody tale of ritual sacrifice and nude women. While Lewis established himself as one of the pioneers of lowbrow gore, "King of the Nudies" Russ Meyer carved his own niche in sleaze circles with a prototypical "nudie-cutie" flick, 1959's *The Immoral Mr. Teas*. Foreshadowing a new breed of sex cinema distinct from classic exploitation, *The Immoral Mr. Teas* featured a glossy, polished surface (indebted to its colossal—in classic exploitation terms—$24,000 budget) and the unapologetic thrill of showing naked women without an educational screen to hide its naughty wares. Such films also had a distinctly saucy, comical, all-American breeziness that countered the peculiar mix of moralizing and thrills that made exploitation so uniquely guilt-ridden.

Cured of their diseases and enlightened as to the workings of the reproductive system, John Parker and Wanda McKay in *Because of Eve*, bid farewell to the age of exploitation.

The floodgates of film filth to come were thus opened as the Golden Era of the exploiteer died. As chronicler of the exploiteer's code, David Friedman in *A Youth in Babylon* noted in typically alliterative, flamboyant carny prose about the dwindling draw of a 1958 run of *Because of Eve*:

> Our shows were beginning to show their age. Customers were being offered more skin on screen than ever before, movies where the showgoer didn't have to endure some 'professor's' preachment and dire warnings of the perils of promiscuity, then be incited to pop for a buck or two for some thin little biology home-study books. (p.214)

As the carnal cinema "progressed" to something less educational and more explicit, the importance of craftiness and creativity in the making and marketing of films steadily diminished. As exploitation evolved—some might say devolved—into sexploitation, the genre lost not only its innocence but also its charm.

In his handbook for aspiring starlets, *Hollywood Rat Race*, Ed Wood Jr. also lamented the arrival of "nudie cuties" in no uncertain terms.

> These particular films have no purpose beyond titillating with sex and the naked female, of course, and it

wouldn't be difficult to determine what kind of person is buying a ticket. There are perverts in all walks of life who can find something in these films. Of course, there are the "sleazy producers" who put out pure, unadulterated crap strictly for this type of demented individual... There is little or no story line, just one weak excuse after another to incident after incident, so the girls take their clothes off in front of the camera... Once you see the film you'll want to vomit.[2]

Self-righteous on the surface, Wood's text is tragically self-loathing when one considers the director's own circumstance at the time, already entrenched in the "nudie cutie" genre. By the time Wood penned this furious indictment he'd already written the atrocious graveyard striptease film *Orgy of the Dead*, and would later script and appear in other, more explicit low-end sex pictures. But there's something *to* Wood's rage at his audience of perverts. While exploitation undoubtedly attracted its share, it was also a disreputable, underground cinema that drew from many walks of life, attracting both men and women, those looking for a little skin and others, looking for a little enlightenment.

Was Ed Wood referring to his 1965 schlock-strip film *Orgy of the Dead* when he said, "Once you see the film you'll want to vomit"?

The fall of regional censorship (and the consequential end of exploitation) was also accelerated by foreign "art films" of the 1950s, whose poster art capitalized on the looser European standards where nudity was concerned, playing up luscious female stars like Sophia Loren, Harriet Andersson and Brigitte Bardot. This rash of foreign imports gave old-time exploitation a run for its money, since these films were sellable as both sophisticated art films and babe-oramas in keeping with the exploitation play-it-both-ways approach. And while exploitation operated in respectability's shadows, the new breed of Euro-titillation was booked into legitimate theaters and often endorsed by mainstream critics rather than by fictitious medical boards and phantom clergymen. Even the wiliest exploiteers could no longer compete with the randy Euro-sinema typified by Bardot's *And God Created Woman*, a film Friedman pinpointed as the C-cup omen of exploitation's doom.

By the 1950s, what could be called the "true" exploitation film was disappearing, its most unique feature—the roadshow—essentially withered away, the golden age of the genre giving way to an uninspired rash of conventional teen melodramas, banal sexploitation and cheapo gore.

In Hollywood, two other factors contributed to the extinction of the exploitation film. One was the Supreme Court's decision to apply the Sherman Anti-Trust Act to motion pictures in 1948. The studios which had formerly controlled all phases of the industry—production, distribution, exhibition—were ordered to stop such complete, unilateral control of the motion picture business. And because the studios were no longer producing enormous amounts of product to fill their own film screens, exhibitors could now choose which features they wanted for their theaters and not have to fill their cinematic dance cards with second-rate B-picture product. Exhibitors increasingly turned to the new crop of independent filmmakers to stock their screens.

The reason behind Hollywood's move away from high-quantity, mid-quality programmers was the bite taken out of the market by television and the geographic dispersion of audiences. With postwar audiences now fleeing urban centers for the suburbs, movie houses were not as accessible as before and could certainly not compete with television, which provided its entertainment for free. Hollywood's ticket sales were declining and the industry fought back by offering blockbuster productions, new technology such as CinemaScope, 3-D and all variety of color processes to distinguish its product. The only other way Hollywood could compete with TV was in offering audiences something they could not get at home, namely adult themes and sexual material.

The definitive blow to Hollywood's Production Code came in the Supreme Court's 1952 decision concerning Roberto Rossellini's Italian film *The Miracle*, blocked by the New York State Board of Censors for its treatment of religious matters. Contrary to prevailing laws which classified film as pure profit-driven entertainment, the Supreme Court (in *Burstyn v. Wilson*) ruled that films are "a significant medium for the commu-

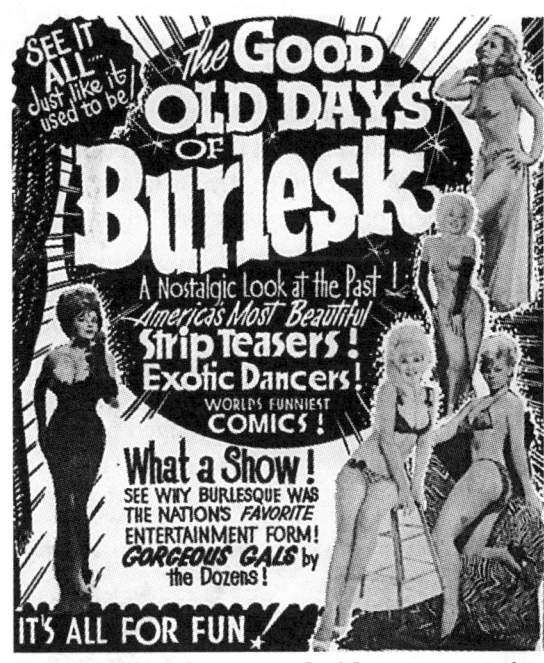

By the 1950s, ads appeared without any mention of pressing social concerns or educational value.

nication of ideas," summarily deflating the balloon of hyperbole and moral crusading that made exploitation films exceptional.

The Supreme Court ruled that movies had the same rights under the First Amendment as other protected forms of speech such as newspapers and magazines, a decision which led to a definitive revision of the Production Code in 1956. Audiences could now enjoy previously forbidden themes and topics only the underground exploitation film could treat in the '30s and '40s. In the 1950s, Hollywood trespassed upon exploitation's terrain with films like the capital punishment shocker *I Want To Live!* and *The Man With the Golden Arm*, a tale of heroin addiction starring Frank Sinatra. And, making their product even more appealing, Hollywood offered these new libidinal, scandalous subjects with its typical high-gloss, big-budget treatment, offering audiences the thrill of favorite stars acting out dramas culled from newspaper headlines and police records as once only unknown actors could. Almost as pleasurable as a real scandal (like the Robert Mitchum pot bust) was watching Susan Hayward or Sinatra or Jack Lemmon reduced to a hardboiled junkie or trembling alcoholic in sordid performances that stoked the two-pronged public lust for celebrities and a glimpse into the darker side of life.

But showmanship cannot be easily vanquished, and the 1950s saw the spirit of exploitation appearing in unusual new forms, like the spook shows which bore a strong resemblance to exploitation. In this tiny subgenre, traveling showmen toured towns with one or two outmoded horror films, and supplemented the double feature with live performances of magic and illusionism. Almost surpassing the already fraudulent hype of many exploitation films, spook shows routinely promised *live* appearances by everyone from Frankenstein and Dracula to the ghost of James Dean (via rubber masks or glow-in-the-dark placards paraded up and down the darkened theaters' aisles). Spook shows raffled off "live babies" (baby chicks, that is) and employed every conceivable form of Barnum-esque trickery to coax audiences into the seats.

Directed by John Waters, a former disciple of exploitation, *Pink Flamingos* embodies much of the excessive punch and gritty charm that made the genre so memorable.

Meanwhile in Hollywood, Columbia Pictures producer William Castle took obvious note of exploitation's potential and adapted similar methods of hype to promote his own series of cornball horror films. Audience polls, inflatable skeletons on strings, electrified seats and insurance policies (against death by fright) are only a few of Castle's innovations that returned to the moviegoing experience the carnivalesque atmosphere of exploitation.

But though the true exploitation film eventually faded away, the contributions of the Golden Age of exploitation cinema to popular culture remain, surfacing sporadically in Tim Burton's bio-pic of visionary (but technically inept) filmmaker Ed Wood, (which was based on Rudolph Grey's *Nightmare of Ecstasy,* a far more compelling survey of the cinematic madman's career). The genre's remnants can also be found in less obvious places such as the campy, irony-laden exploitation retreads of John Waters (whose scratch-and-sniff *Polyester* paid homage to the florid gimmickry of William Castle) and in more serious homages to exploitation seen in David Lynch's postmodern morality tales.

Though he has not discussed the influence of the exploitation film upon his work, the genre is clearly reflected in the road-to-ruin plots of *Blue Velvet* and Lynch's *Twin Peaks* TV series. Linked to the Depression-era fables of wholesome American kids drawn by their own curiosity down a path of sexual peril, Lynch's films feature exploitation extremes like the ultra-wholesome Jeffrey Beaumont (Kyle MacLachlan) and Sandy Williams (Laura Dern) of *Blue Velvet*, who cross over to the wrong side of the tracks and are physically and psychologically ravaged by the contemporary incarnation of exploitation's white slavers and dope dealers, Frank Booth (Dennis Hopper). The predicament of a respectable and happily married father coming face-to-face with his seemingly innocent daughter who is secretly working as a prostitute occurs in the 1928 version of *Road to Ruin* and twice in Lynch's work (*Twin Peaks* and *Twin Peaks: Fire Walk With Me*). Less specifically, Lynch's films embrace the artificiality of the exploitation film, its tendency toward excess, its use of saccharine sentimentality and all-American iconography, not to mention the wonders and horrors of medical technology (*The Elephant Man*, the father's hospital room in *Blue Velvet*, the abortion in *Wild at Heart* and the dental hygiene tableaux that appear in *Images*, Lynch's book of photography).

Lynch's TV series (*Twin Peaks*) and movie (*Twin Peaks: Fire Walk With Me*) storylines were prototypical exploitation, with their tales of innocent high school girls corrupted by overage drug dealers and pimps at the Roadhouse, a remote center of illicit activity clearly referencing the classic exploitation dens of iniquity. While Lynch's Roadhouse featured a swinger's club in its bowels, his *Twin Peaks* brothel, One-Eyed Jack's, recruited its high school prostitutes from the local department store, like the manicurist shop in *Slaves in Bondage* which also lured gullible smalltown girls into a netherworld of prostitution.

Other films, like the 1975 exploitation parody *The Rocky Horror Picture Show* also reference those long-ago tales of sexual degradation. Featuring a medical lecture by a pompous-but-clueless Dr. Know It All, Everett Scott, *The Rocky Horror Picture Show* centered upon a typically clean-cut pair of sweethearts, Brad Majors (Barry Bostwick) and Janet Weiss (Susan Sarandon). Brad and Janet's timidity mimes the Squaresville blundering of exploitation's teenyboppers, provoking their own degradation by transsexual Dr. Frank-N-Furter in *Rocky*'s savvy tongue-in-cheek send-up of classic exploitation. The film's cult following, which centered on audience participation, also echoes the exploitation film's fusion of live performance and film and a more elastic relationship between film and audience.

But exploitation's legacy is not restricted to conscious directorial odes to this lost chapter of film history. American culture remains fascinated with the connection between sex and death examined in exploitation's sex hygiene melodramas and true crime documentaries, and anxious to explore the taboo subjects kept hidden from the public. This thirst for the unknown has saturated the lowest and highest reaches of American life, from the visual arts to the tawdry fixations of tabloid TV.

The highbrow reaches of the visual arts and academia have lately shown an interest in exploring the same taboo subjects of death and disease which so fascinated exploitation's producers and audiences. It seems the cultural elite are as prone to ghoulish interest in the great unknowns as the "hayseed" exploitation audiences of the '30s and '40s.

In its tale of strayed sweethearts discovering new worlds of vice and degeneracy, *The Rocky Horror Picture Show* was a true tongue-in-cheek exploitation film, complete with camera address by the eminent Dr. Scott.

The traveling exhibition "Police Pictures: The Photograph as Evidence" curated by San Francisco's Museum of Modern Art (and documented in an accompanying book) featured elaborate charts of criminal features—characteristic noses, eyes, lips, to be used in identifying the criminal visage, in eugenical tradition—as well as crime scene images of murder victims, surveillance photos and a host of photographs which may recontextualize death as socially and historically significant art, but indulge the same curiosity about taboo subjects seen in exploitation.

Photographers like Weegee, Brassai, Diane Arbus and Mathew Brady delivered early dispatches from an unseen world of deformed bodies, suicide and grisly battlefields, but current photographers like Joel-Peter Witkin and Andres Serrano have reverted to this still provocative subject matter. Famous for his publicly condemned "blasphemous" image "Piss Christ," Serrano has recently documented various global sexual practices in his photographic survey, "A History of Sex" and dead bodies in his hypnotically beautiful series of color photographs "The Morgue." Serrano's work recalls the syphilis-ravaged bodies and graphic scalpel incision of a cesarean section in early exploitation which was so unimaginatively replaced by the T&A centered sexploitation. Though such artists do not specifically reference exploitation films, they show the continued cultural interest in the themes exploitation films explored: the same fascination with bodily functions hidden by a modern culture that denies the bloody reality of death and birth.

The 1973 book that signaled a new interest in the country's secret history, Michael Lesy's *Wisconsin Death Trip*, about the hidden stories of disease, murder and suicide operating beneath the surface of a turn-of-the century Wisconsin town, inaugurated a trickle of examinations of the taboo. Recently that trickle has evolved into a pre-millennial torrent. Books such as *Death Scenes: A Homicide Detective's Scrapbook*, *Looking at Death* and *Death in Paradise: An Illustrated History of the Los Angeles County Department of Coroner* revisit the visual outrages of the "March of Crime" documentaries and exploitation lobby displays of death cars, mummies and drug paraphernalia. A rash of books have also resuscitated exploitation's curiosity about the body, from Luc Sante's haunting collection of black-and-white photographs of 1910s crime scenes, *Evidence*, to the pioneering work of medical archivist Stanley B. Burns, who documents the medical community's often prurient, sexual obsession with photographically representing its patients' bodies.

But hardly restricted to academic theorizing of "the body" and subcultural interest in grisly, truthful antidotes to America's white-washed past, even a more middlebrow and middle-of-the-road public soaks up the same viscera-fascination nightly on television programs such as *America's Most Wanted, Rescue 911* and *Unsolved Mysteries,* in serial killer true crime novels, *National Enquirer* headlines and *Faces of Death* videos. Faux news programs like *Hard Copy*, talk shows, or A&E *Biography* with their pretense of enlightening the public and their pandering treatments of the most grotesque subject matter can make early exploitation look tasteful by comparison.

The "voices of authority" represented by William Shatner in *Rescue 911* and Robert Stack in *Unsolved Mysteries* are also clearly indebted to exploitation's "experts" who temper unpleasant subject matter, acting as buffers between often disturbing content and the audience, and give a gloss of high purpose to the most profane or shocking subject matter.

The same sense of a culture re-examining its relationship to mortality and morality which accompanied the turn of the century has characterized the pre-millennial decades. Though exploitation is a long gone, forgotten chapter in film history, its influence lingers. Exploitation's visualization of fears and desires continues in a culture searching for the leavings of its secret history. Twentieth-century reservations about industrialization and a desire to see the hidden realities erased with progress have only magnified in our own increasingly alienated, technologically buffered age. As the mechanics of life and death become more and more mysterious we recognize how a society supposedly saturated with information is, in fact, chronically naive.

As we forage for the forbidden in video stores, on television and in true crime paperbacks—we continue to spiritually occupy those 25-cent seats in the dingy exploitation main street theater. We grapple with our own guilt, and struggle to understand the world and discover its mystifying secrets.

The same human desire for carnal knowledge commemorated in the original folklore of the human race, Genesis, is the same desire that sparked the corruption of all the innumerable Bobs and Sallys of exploitation legend—the same shameful curiosity that sends us even today tiptoeing into the shadows for a glimpse of the taboo... and a taste of tantalizingly forbidden fruit.

NOTES

Introduction
[1] Margolies, John and Gwathmey, Emily. *Ticket to Paradise: American Movie Theaters and How We Had Fun*. Boston: Little, Brown and Co., 1991. p. 100

Chapter 1
[1] *Motion Picture Herald*. May 5, 1934. p. 57.
[2] *Motion Picture Herald*. June 30, 1934. p. 72.
[3] Hamilton, Denise. "Actress Recalls Days of 'Reefer Madness.'" *Los Angeles Times*. February 12, 1987. p. 30.
[4] Interview with Shan Sayles, November 5, 1992.
[5] Grey, Rudolph. "Umberto Scali Lives!!! The Timothy Farrell Interview." *Psychotronic*. Winter 1992/93. pp. 22-23.
[6] Ibid. p. 25.
[7] Spoken in Rogers' 1934 address to a convention of the Motion Picture Theatre Owners. Quoted in Hays, Will. *The Memoirs of Will H. Hays*. New York: Doubleday and Co., Inc., 1955. p. 452.
[8] *Motion Picture Herald*. June 30, 1934. p. 72.

Chapter 2
[1] *New York World*, May 28, 1895, p. 30.
[2] These same topics resurfaced in later exploitation films such as *Test Tube Babies, Pin Down Girl* and *Maniac* (catfights), *Secrets of a Model* (artists' models) and *The Violent Years* (armed women).
[3] Searchlight Theater program reproduced in Musser, Charles. *The Emergence of Cinema: The American Screen to 1907*. Berkeley: University of California Press, 1990. p. 302.
[4] Musser, pp. 467-468.
[5] Ramsaye, Terry. *A Million and One Nights*. New York: Touchstone, 1986. p. 474.
[6] *Moving Picture World*. December 21, 1907.
[7] Brownlow, Kevin. *Behind the Mask of Innocence*. New York: Knopf, 1990. p. 61.
[8] *Variety*. March 30, 1917. pp. 27-28.
[9] "The Cocaine Traffic." *Variety*. February 27, 1914. p. 23.
[10] *Variety*. October 1, 1915.
[11] "'Sex' Film Mgr. Fined On Obscene Book Charge." *Variety*. March 14, 1928. p. 5.
[12] New York State license records. Incidentally, Willis Kent borrowed the popular "Octopus" metaphor for *The Pace That Kills* (1928), which features a menacing painting of the creature beneath the film's opening credits.
[13] "Birth Control Pictures." *Harrison's Reports*. March 2, 1929.

Chapter 3
[1] "Dan Sonney: Last of the 40 Thieves." *Cult Movies*. No. 12. 1994. pp. 25, 27.
[2] *Variety*. December 19, 1935.
[3] Interview with Bobby Glendon, June 8, 1997.
[4] Gomery, Douglas. *The Hollywood Studio System*. New York: St. Martin's Press, 1986. p. 2.
[5] Congressional Record, Senate. February 23, 1932. p. 4496.
[6] *Motion Picture Herald*. December 29, 1934. p. 71.
[7] *Motion Picture Herald*. July 7, 1934. p. 61.
[8] *Motion Picture Herald*. June 23, 1934. p. 131.
[9] *Motion Picture Herald*. June 23, 1934. p. 134.
[10] "Will Hays Making Moral Code 100% Effective; Curbing 'Dirt' By Sexy Indie-Legit Producers." *Variety*. August 27, 1930. pp. 25, 58.
[11] Steinberg, Cobbett (ed.) "The 1930 Production Code." *Reel Facts*. New York: Vintage, 1982. pp. 392-393.
[12] Lorentz, Pare. *FDR's Moviemaker*. Reno: University of Nevada Press, 1992. pp. 21-22.
[13] Congressional Record, Senate. February 23, 1932. p. 4494.
[14] "Sinful Girls Lead in 1931." *Variety*. December 29, 1931.
[15] Hays, Will. *The Memoirs of Will Hays*. New York: Doubleday and Co., Inc., 1955. p. 437.
[16] Irving Briskin to Joseph Breen. December 16, 1938. Margaret Herrick Library, the Academy of Motion Picture Arts and Sciences (AMPAS).
[17] Joseph Breen to Irving Briskin. December 17, 1938. AMPAS.
[18] Irving Briskin to Joseph Breen. December 20, 1938. AMPAS.
[19] Joseph Breen to Sam Katzman. March 21, 1938. AMPAS.
[20] Production Code Administration to Ray Friedgen. August 28, 1943. AMPAS.
[21] C.C. Pettijohn, Film Boards of Trade, to Secretaries of all Film Boards of Trade. Undated. AMPAS.

22 De Grazia, Edward and Newman, Roger K. *Banned Films: Movies, Censors and the First Amendment.* New York: R.R. Bowker Company, 1982. p.252.
23 Ibid. p. 216.
24 *Elysia* pressbook. AMPAS.
25 "Patrons Vote on Banned 'Ingagi.'" *Variety.* August 13, 1930. p. 19.
26 "Sex Perversion Film." Memo for Files. November 29, 1939. AMPAS.
27 Joseph Breen to James Wingate. May 9, 1938. AMPAS.
28 "In the matter of the Proceeding for the Revocation of the License issued on the Picture 'Forbidden Adventure.'" September 11, 1940. Motion Picture Division, Department of Education, State of New York (New York Censor Board, [NYCB]).
29 Irwin Esmond to Roadshow Attractions, Warner-Purdon Productions, Mapel Attractions. March 26, 1938. NYCB.
30 Interview with Dwain Esper conducted by Mark Woods, Jr. Used with permission.

Chapter 4

1 "Something for the Soul," *Time.* April 18, 1949.
2 Brownlow, p.xvii.
3 Allen, Frederick Lewis. *Since Yesterday: The 1930s in America.* New York: Perennial, 1940. p. 107.
4 Croce, Arlene. *The New Yorker.* May 8, 1995.
5 Dennis, James M. *Grant Wood: A Study in American Art and Culture.* Columbia: University of Missouri Press, 1986. p.10.
6 Ibid. p.10.
7 Greif, Martin. *Depression Modern: The Thirties Style in America.* New York: Universe Books, 1975. p.32.
8 Burns, Stanley B. *Sleeping Beauty: Memorial Photography in America.* Twelvetrees Press, 1990.
9 Steinberg, p. 393.
10 Foucault, Michel. *The History of Sexuality, I.* New York: Vintage Books, 1978. p. 146.
11 Laqueur, Thomas. *Making Sex: Body and Gender From the Greeks to Freud.* Cambridge: Harvard University Press, 1990. p. 233.
12 De Grazia and Newman, p. 252.
13 Schaller, Michael. "The Federal Prohibition of Marijuana," *Journal of Social History* 4 (1970-71): 63-64.
14 Allen, *Since Yesterday*, p. 84.
15 The introductory text is attributed to "Wm. S. Sadler, of Chicago Institute of Research and Diagnosis."
16 *Harrison's Reports.* July 21, 1934.
17 Section III of the Production Code, drafted in 1930, as reproduced in Steinberg, p. 392.
18 Ludmerer, Kenneth M. *Genetics and American Society.* Baltimore: Johns Hopkins University Press, 1972.
19 Committee of the American Neurological Association. *Eugenical Sterilization.* New York: Macmillan, 1936.
20 Bergman, Andrew. *We're in the Money: Depression America and Its Films.* New York: Harper Colophon Books, 1971. p. 18.
21 Because of the chaotic business of exploitation production and distribution, film dates cannot always be definitively claimed. However, copyright dates on films or review dates have been used when they appear.
22 Jacobs, Lea. "Reformers and Spectators: The Film Education Movement in the Thirties," *Camera Obscura* 22 (January 1990): p. 29.
23 Brantlinger, Patrick. *Bread and Circuses: Theories of Mass Culture as Social Decay.* Ithaca: Cornell University Press, 1984. p. 23.
24 Cooper, Courtney Ryley. *Here's To Crime.* New York: Little, Brown and Company, 1937. pp. 190-91.
25 Blumer, Herbert. *Movies, Delinquency, and Crime.* New York: The MacMillan Company, 1933. p. 118.
26 Ibid. p. 118.
27 Ibid. pp. 118-119.
28 Ibid. p. 74.
29 Interview with Hildagarde Esper, November 3, 1988 by Eric Schaefer. Used with permission.
30 Dye, Nancy Schrom. "The Medicalization of Birth," *The American Way of Birth.* Philadelphia: Temple University Press, 1986. pp. 42-43.
31 Duffy, John. *The Sanitarians: A History of American Public Health.* Urbana: University of Illinois Press, 1990. p. 256.
32 Ibid. p. 265.
33 Ray, Joyce M. and Gosling, F.G. "American Physicians and Birth Control, 1936-1947," *Journal of Social History* (Spring 1985): p. 407.
34 Musto, David F. *The American Disease: Origins of Narcotic Control.* New Haven: Yale University Press, 1973. p. 223.

Chapter 5

[1] Quoted in website devoted to June (Ormond) Carr (http://www.jtr.com/junecarr), July 28, 1997.
[2] Mrs. James Looram to Harry Blair, Grand National Films, June 4, 1937. AMPAS.
[3] Mrs. James Looram to Harry Blair, June 16, 1937. AMPAS.
[4] "At the Criterion." *The New York Times*. July 16, 1938. p. 7.
[5] Patrick Carlyle to Joseph Breen, September 18, 1936. AMPAS.
[6] Hobart Glassey, The Fraternity Elysia, to Joseph I. Breen, June 15, 1936. AMPAS.
[7] *Sex and Buttered Popcorn* (videocassette). Kit Parker Films. 1989.
[8] "Dan Sonney." *Cult Movies*. p. 25.
[9] Friedman, David F. with De Nevi, Don. *A Youth in Babylon: Confessions of a Trash-Film King*. Buffalo: Prometheus Books, 1990. pp.59-60.
[10] Ibid. p. 119.
[11] Duncan, David D. and Ridley, Jim. "The Ormonds." *Psychotronic*. Number ——. p. 51.
[12] http://www.jtr.com/junecarr.
[13] Friedman. p. 35.
[14] Turan, Kenneth. "'You've Got To Tell'em To Sell'em,' Said Kroger Babb, and Did He Sell'em," *The Washington Post*. August 1, 1977. p. B3.
[15] "Something for the Soul," *Time*. April 18, 1949.
[16] Interview with David F. Friedman.
[17] Turan. p. B3.
[18] "Charge 'Fraud' in Hallmark 'Beauty' Prod'n," *Daily Variety*. July 28, 1953.
[19] News clippings. Kroger Babb File, AMPAS.
[20] "Bryan Foy, 82, Rajah Of 'B' Pics," *Variety*. April 27, 1977.
[21] Interview with Edgar G. Ulmer by Peter Bogdanovich. *Kings of the Bs*. New York: E.P. Dutton & Co., 1975. pp. 386-387. An article in the March 31, 1933 issue of *Film Daily* lists the producer as Maxwell Cohn and reports that it was photographed at the Western Service Studios.
[22] Friedman. p. 311.
[23] "S.S. Millard Arrested," *Variety*. March 28, 1928. p. 10.
[24] "Salacious Billing for 'Is Your Daughter Safe?'" *Variety*. May 11, 1927. p. 5.

Chapter 6

[1] *The Nation*. March 19, 1908.
[2] *Harrison's Reports*. July 16, 1932. p. 114.
[3] Mark Woods Sr. to Bret Wood.
[4] Ibid. p.289.
[5] *Variety*. June 23, 1937.
[6] Generally a fraudulent medical expert. In the case of *Mom and Dad*, numerous lecturers toured simultaneously under the common identity of "Elliot Forbes."
[7] *Variety*. May 4, 1938. Interestingly, the *Variety* ad also betrays a class bias in its description of the gullible audience as "peasants."
[8] Ibid. p. 62.
[9] *Highway Hell* was one of the film's alternate titles.
[10] Robert C. Allen, p. 230.
[11] Mannix, *Freaks: We Who Are Not As Others*, p.49.
[12] Allen, Robert C. *Horrible Prettiness: Burlesque and American Culture*. Chapel Hill: University of North Carolina Press, 1991. p.236.
[13] *American Journal of Clinical Pathology*, Volume V, No. 1, January 1935.
[14] Bogdan. p. 64.
[15] De Grazia and Newman. p. 218.
[16] Ibid. p. 229.

Chapter 7

[1] State of New York Education Department, Motion Picture Division to Classic Pictures, Inc. April 9, 1946. NYCB.
[2] "Publix Testing Nudist Film," *Film Daily*. January 13, 1933 p. 2.
[3] *Film Daily*. February 25, 1933. p. 2.
[4] Friedman. p. 91.
[5] Frank B. Dermody to Irwin Esmond, director. March 29, 1938. NYCB.
[6] Interview with Millicent Esper.
[7] "Electric Chair Ballyhoo for Hickman 'Special' Killed It," *Variety*. February 15, 1928. p. 8.

8 Ibid.
9 "Minn. Barred Hickman Film," *Variety.* February 1, 1928. p. 5.
10 Friedman. p. 178.
11 "Films Enlisted to Track Down Slayer in Detroit," *Motion Picture Herald.* March 30, 1935. p. 18.
12 Krosnick, David A. "Movietone Goes to Court," *The Survey.* December 1, 1929. pp. 290-291.
13 Interview with David F. Friedman.
14 "Dan Sonney." *Cult Movies.* p. 25.
15 Interview with David F. Friedman.
16 Interview with Millicent Esper.
17 Ramsaye, Terry. "News and Corpses," *Motion Picture Herald.* September 1, 1934.
18 "Execution in Newsreel Delivered With 'See-It-Or-Don't' Warning," *Motion Picture Herald.* May 18, 1935. p.
19 "Newsreels Not Liable for Picture Shocks," *Motion Picture Herald.* March 30, 1935. p. 18.
20 Ramsaye. "News and Corpses."
21 *Motion Picture Herald.* September 7, 1935. p. 7.
22 *Variety.* March 27, 1940.
23 "After Okaying 'Ingagi' Censors Change Minds," *Variety.* August 20, 1930. p. 5.
24 "Censor's New Stunt; Make Cuts Months After Giving Okay," *Variety.* October 29, 1930. p. 12.
25 "Permit Revoked on 'Ingagi' in Censors' Victory—Sets Precedent," *Variety.* January 7, 1931. p. 5.
26 Burt, Francis L. "Officially 'Fake' Now," *Motion Picture Herald.* May 13, 1933. p. 14.
27 Interview with Millicent Esper.
28 Teitel, Chuck. "Film-Flam Man," *Los Angeles.* May 1989.
29 "Eliminations Directed To Be Made in 'Angkor.'" Clipping, NYCB.
30 Due to sketchy reportage in the trade magazines, the exact path of ownership of *The Penitente Murder Case* is difficult to trace. International Cinema and Intercontinent Film may be one and the same, but if one assumes all the reports to be accurate, the Penitente footage passed through at least five companies within a period of two years: Extraordinary, Intercontinent, Stewart, International and Telepictures.
31 *Film Daily.* March 10, 1937. p. 8.
32 *The New York State Exhibitor.* March 15, 1937. p. 36.
33 *Motion Picture Herald.* February 17, 1940. p. 41.
34 Gifford, Denis. *A Pictorial History of Horror Movies.* London: Hamlyn, 1973. p. 192.

Chapter 8

1 Chute, David. "Exploitation! The Midsection That Wouldn't Die," *Film Comment.* July/August 1996.
2 Ibid.
3 Allen, Robert. *Horrible Prettiness: Burlesque and American Culture.* Chapel Hill: University of North Carolina Press, 1991. p. 197.
4 Showalter, Elaine. *Sexual Anarchy: Gender and Culture At The Fin De Siecle.* New York: Penguin Books, 1990. p. 145.
5 Steinberg. p. 396.
6

Chapter 9

1 Chute.
2 Wood, Ed Jr. *Hollywood Rat Race.* New York: Four Walls Eight Windows, 1998. pp. 109, 111.

FILMOGRAPHY

ASSASSIN OF YOUTH
1937   BCM Productions   B&W
Producer: Leo J. McCarthy, Associate Producer: Charles A. Browne, Director: Elmer Clifton, Screenplay: Browne and Clifton, Story: Clifton and McCarthy, Cinematography: Edward Linden, Editor: Rose Loewinger, Sound: Corson Jowett, Music Supervisor: Abe Meyer.
With Luana Walters, Arthur Gardner, Dorothy Short, Earl Dwire, Fern Emmett.

Plot synopsis: A newspaper reporter goes undercover in a small town to follow up on the story of a grandmother killed by marihuana-crazed youths in a car accident. The grandmother has promised to leave her granddaughter all her money if she stays "good." But Joan's marihuana-dealing cousin Linda and her boyfriend are determined to make Joan bad and thus acquire the fortune. Joan's sister, meanwhile, has become a drug addict and psychotic. The reporter saves Joan's reputation by revealing the evil plot in a last-minute courtroom testimony.

BACK TO THE SUN
1933   Josmin Productions, Inc.   B&W
Screenplay: Vincent Valentini, Cinematography: Sam Rosen, Sound: Murray Dichter.

Synopsis: This thoughtful examination of global nudism focuses on African natives, a harem-like Middle Eastern bar, artist's models, Apache dancers and a nudist colony.

BECAUSE OF EVE: The Story of Life
International Pictures Inc.   B&W
Director: Howard Bretherton, Screenplay: Larry Allen, Walter A. Lawrence, Cinematography: Arthur Martinelli, Elmer Moss, Editor: Dede Allen.
With Joseph Crehan, Wanda McKay, Robert Leaver.

Plot synopsis: When Bob and Sally visit a doctor before marriage, each learns of the other's dark sexual secret: Bob has previously had a venereal disease and Sally has already had a child. The good doctor quiets their fears and patches the relationship by showing them a couple of reels of informative and explicit educational films.

BIRTH OF A BABY
The American Committee on Maternal Welfare, Inc.
72 min.   B&W
Producer: Jack Skirball, Director: A.E. Christie, Screenplay: Burke Symon, Arthur Jarrett, Cinematography: George Webber, Editor: Sam Citron.
With: Eleanor King, Richard Gordon, Ruth Matteson, Josephine Dunn, William Post Jr.

Plot synopsis: A young married woman expresses interest in greater knowledge of the body's functions, so throughout her pregnancy she is offered detailed information by her doctor. The film climaxes with Mary's at-home birth of a daughter.

BIRTHRIGHT
1951   Classic Pictures Inc.   B&W
Director: Bill Clifford, Screenplay: George C. Stoney, Photo and Assoc. Producer: Ralph A. Woolsey, Assistant Director: Speight Cooper, Editor: Fred Lasse, Sound: Bill Godsey, Musical Director: Louis Applebaum, Music: Lan Adomian. Produced by the Southern Educational Film Service (Athens, Georgia).
With Boyce Brown, Marjory Morris, Paula Haygood, Mr. and Mrs. W.O. Jarrett, Howard Williams, Allie Mae Williams, C.S. Buchanan, Robert Fisher, Claribel Jones R.N., W.T. Gantt Jr., "Jake" Ellerd, Edward Mangum.

Plot synopsis: In this mild government-produced film, a rural farmer and his wife are introduced to the finer points of birth and venereal disease. The film, which includes birth footage, was rendered an exploitation film by a racy ad campaign and the insertion of a bit of footage of a man and woman undressing pre-coitus.

BO-RU THE APE BOY
ca. 1934   Hollywood Producers and Distributors   B&W
Producer: Dwain Esper

Synopsis: This, along with *Curse of the Ubangi* was one of several of Dwain Esper's jungle shorts. While the content of *Bo-Ru* is perfectly tame, the film was made sensational by a lengthy title scroll that speculated about the origins of this half-boy, half-gorilla.

CHAINED FOR LIFE
1951   Classic Pictures, Inc.   B&W
Presented by Renato Spera, Producer: George Moskov, Director: Harry L. Fraser, Screenplay: Nat Tanchuk, Additional Dialogue: Albert de Pina, Based on an Idea by Ross Frisco, Cinematography: Jockey Feindel, Editor: Joe Gluck, Art Director: George Van Matar, Musical Director: Michael Terr, Orig. Music: Henry Vars, Lyrics: George Brown.
With Daisy and Violet Hilton, Mario Laval, Allen Jenkins, Patricia Wright, Alan Keys, Norvel Mitchell.

Plot synopsis: Told in flashback from a murder trial, *Chained for Life* involves a pair of Siamese twins who perform on the music hall stage. Their ambitious manager suggests one of them marry as a publicity stunt. During the course of the staged romance, one of the twins actually falls in love and kills the would-be Romeo when she discovers he has been deceiving her. The trial must determine whether both women should be put to death for one of their crimes.

CHILD BRIDE
1942   Astor Pictures Company (Dallas)   B&W
Producer: Raymond Friedgen, Director: Harry J. Revier, Cinematography: Marcel Picard, Editor: Helen Turner; Musical Director: Felix Mills.
With Shirley Mills, Bob Bollinger, Warner Richmond, Diana Durrell.

Plot synopsis: An innocent and clever mountain girl lives simply with her mother and father, whiling away her days playing with her young boyfriend. One night a local tough who has had his eye on the little girl sees her mother fighting with her drunk husband and almost killing him. He finishes the job and blackmails the mother into letting him wed the little girl in order to keep her out of jail. In a parallel storyline, the local schoolteacher is on a one-woman crusade to rid the community of child marriage, for which she is harassed and physically assaulted by the locals. The little girl eventually marries the older man, but her young boyfriend kills him before the marriage is consummated. In the meantime, the schoolteacher's boyfriend has managed to lobby for a law ending child marriage.

CHILDREN OF LONELINESS (aka THE THIRD SEX)
1937   Jewel Productions, Inc.   B&W
Producer, Screenplay & Director: Richard C. Kahn, Supervisor: George Merrick, Cinematography: Bert Baldridge, Editor: William Ferris, Sound: Cliff Ruberg.
With Dr. S. Dana Hubbard, Wallace Morgan, Luana Walters, Jean Carmen, Sheila Loren, Allan Jarvis, Wayne Lamont, John Elliott.

Plot synopsis: Elinor, a young woman with a sexual fear of men, contemplates welcoming the advances of her female roommate "Bobby." A psychiatrist encourages Elinor to instead marry her co-worker, a football player. "Bobby" reacts violently to the rejection and, after a scuffle with the athlete, is scalded with acid and hit by a passing truck.

CURSE OF THE UBANGI
ca. 1934   Hollywood Producers and Distributors   B&W
Producer: Dwain Esper

Synopsis: This, along with *Bo-Ru the Ape Boy* was one of several of Dwain Esper's jungle shorts. The film was composed primarily of footage from the 1931 film *Ubangi* (presented by William M. Pizor, employing 1924 Congo expedition footage shot by Dr. Louis Neuman and Dr. Jacques Maus), along with some newly filmed material.

DAMAGED GOODS (aka MARRIAGE FORBIDDEN, FORBIDDEN DESIRE)
1937   Criterion Pictures   B&W
Producer: Phil Stone, Associate Producer: Irving Starr, Director: Phil Stone, Screenplay: Joseph Hoffman, Based on the Play by Eugene Brieux, Adaptation by Upton Sinclair, Cinematography: Ira Morgan, Editor: Holbrook N. Todd, Sound: Ferl Redd.
With Pedro de Cordoba, Phyllis Barry, Douglas Walton, Arletta Duncan, Ferdinand Munier.

Plot synopsis: George contracts syphilis from a prostitute at his bachelor party and is told by a quack physician he can be cured in six months. George goes through with his wedding to Henrietta, who passes syphilis on to their infant. A knowledgeable doctor offers a more time-consuming but effective cure.

DAMAGED LIVES
1933   Weldon Pictures Corp.   B&W
Director: Edgar G. Ulmer, Story: Don Davis and Edgar G. Ulmer, Dialogue: Don Davis, Cinematog-

raphy: Al Siegler, Editor: Otto Meyer, Sound: Glenn Rominger, Clinical Supervision: Dr. Gordon Bates.
With Diane Sinclair, Lyman Williams, Murray Kinnell, Harry Myers, George Irving, Almeda Fowler, Charlotte Merriam, Jason Robards (Sr.), Marceline Day, Bobby Burns, Harrison Greene, Victor Potel.

Plot synopsis: In the classic VD plotline, a young man contracts a disease and passes it on to his unsuspecting wife. She attempts suicide but he discovers her before she is suffocated by the gas. Together they seek medical treatment and attempt to continue their lives together.

DELINQUENT DAUGHTERS
1944   PRC Pictures Inc.   B&W
Producer: Donald C. McKean and Albert Herman for American Productions Inc., Director: Albert Herman, Screenplay: Arthur St. Claire, Assistant Director: Lou Perlof, Cinematography: Ira Morgan, Editor: George Merrick, Sound: Arthur B. Smith, Musical Director: Lee Zahler.
With June Carlson, Fifi D'Orsay, Teala Loring, Mary Bovard.

Plot synopsis: *Mom and Dad*'s June Carlson stars as a wayward schoolgirl in this Poverty Row picture disguised as an exploitation film.

DEMENTIA (aka DAUGHTER OF HORROR)
Exploitation Productions, Inc.   B&W
An H.K.F. Production   Producer, Screenplay and Director: John Parker, Cinematography: William C. Thompson, Technical Production Associates: Everett Baker, Albert Duval, Editor: Joseph Gluck A.C.E., Special Photographic Effects: Albert Simpson, Prod. Design: Ben Roseman, Sound: Buddy Myers, Musical Director: Ernest Gold, Featured Voice: Marni Nixon, New Concepts in Modern Sound: Shorty Rogers and His Giants, Associate Producer: Bruno De Sota and Ben Roseman, Music: George Antheil.
With Adrienne Barrett, Bruno De Sota, Ben Roseman.

Synopsis: Sort of a beatnik *Maniac*, *Dementia* is a low-budget experiment in surrealism in which a woman's sexual psychoses are dramatized, backed by jazz instrumentation. A narration track (spoken by Ed McMahon) was later added when the title was changed to *Daughter of Horror* in 1955.

DEVIL'S HARVEST
1942   Consolidated Pictures, Inc.   B&W
Producer: Ralph Cushman, Director: Ray Test, Cinematography: Phil Cantonwine, Story: Edward Clark, Sound: Corey Cook.
With June Doyle, Leo Anthony, George Graham, Ben Barlow, Ed Murray, Floyd Hermann, Charles Davis, John Clayton, Tom Leffing, Sally Barton, Lloyd Reed, Claire Richards.

Plot synopsis: Following the well-established formula of the drug scare film, *Devil's Harvest* follows a group of high schoolers who are coaxed to sample marijuana at a wild party... which ends in one of their deaths and brings about a movement to clean up the dope ring.

THE DEVIL'S SLEEP
1949   Screen Classics   B&W
Producer: George Weiss, Director & Editor: W. Merle Connell, Screenplay: Danny Arnold and Richard S. McMahan, Assistant Director: Danny Arnold, Cinematography: William C. Thompson, Sound: Fred McAlpin, Musical Director: Sanford H. Dickinson, Tech Director: Dr. A. Manek.
With: Lita Grey Chaplin, William Thomason, Timothy Farrell, Laura Travers, John Mitchum, George Eiferman.

Plot synopsis: A detective, at the urging of a local judge, uses his high school nephew to find out about a drug ring that supplies high school parties and also a health club for obese women with pills and drugs.

ELYSIA (VALLEY OF THE NUDE)
1934   Foy Productions, Ltd.   B&W
Producer: Bryan Foy, Supervisor: Hobart Glassey, Ph.D., Cinematography: William Sullivan.

Plot synopsis: A reporter is assigned to investigate a nudist colony outside Los Angeles, and is given an education in the healthful benefits of nudism.

ENLIGHTEN THY DAUGHTER
1934   Exploitation Pictures, Inc.   B&W
Supervised by Louis Weiss, Director: John Varley, Screenplay: Arthur Hoerl, From the Story by Ivan Abramson, Additional Dialogue: Bob Lively and Betty Laidlaw, Cinematography: William E. Miller and Nicholas J. Rogalli, Editor: Patricia Rooney, Art Director: Anthony Continer, Music: Lou Herscher

(Played by Paul Vincent and his New Yorkers).
With Herbert Rawlinson, Beth Barton, Charles Eaton, Claire Whitney, Edmund MacDonald, Russell Hicks, Ara Gerald, Miriam Battista, Jack Arnold, Eunice Reed, Wesley Barry, Audrey Maple, Lillian Walker, Robert Emmett Keane.

Plot synopsis: Parental neglect is the familiar theme of this sex-education drama. Lillian Stevens returns home from school and is soon left alone by her father (who publicly lectures about how to be a better parent) and mother (who flirts with gentlemen at a bridge party). Lillian ends up pregnant and commits suicide.

THE EXPOSE OF THE NUDIST RACKET
1938   Roadshow Attractions Co.   B&W   (short)
Producer: Louis Sonney and Dwain Esper. Narrated by Wedgwood Nowell.

Synopsis: This documentary short recycles footage that constitutes several other nudist shorts, adding fresh titles and a soundtrack of witty narration.

FIT TO WIN
1919   American Social Hygiene Assn., Inc.
Screenplay: Edward H. Griffith.

Banned in New York State, 1919.

FORBIDDEN ADVENTURE (aka ANGKOR)
1937   Warner-Allender Roadshows   B&W
Producer and Story: Henry Warner and Roy Purdon, Director: George M. Merrick, Screenplay: Armine Von Tempski and Minnie F. Shrope, Assistant Director: Harry P. Crist, Editor: Grace McKee, Music: Dominic McBride, Research: Gladys McConnell, Effects: Ray Smallwood. Introduced and Narrated by Wilfred Lucas.

Plot synopsis: A pair of explorers venture into southeast Asia to find the missing kingdom of Angkor, and discover a perplexing relationship between wild gorillas and the topless women who have been hired to carry the explorer's baggage.

FREAKS (aka NATURE'S MISTAKES)
1932   Metro-Goldwyn-Mayer   B&W
Director: Tod Browning, Screenplay: Willis Goldbeck and Leon Gordon, Based on the Story "Spurs" by Tod Robbins, Additional Dialogue: Edgar Allan Woolf and Al Boasberg, Cinematography: Merritt B. Gerstad, Editor: Basil Wrangell.
With Harry Earles, Wallace Ford, Leila Hyams, Olga Baclanova, Roscoe Ates, Henry Victor, Daisy Earles, Rose Dione, Daisy and Violet Hilton, Johnny Eck, Frances O'Connor, Matt McHugh, Edward Brophy.

Synopsis: Though not produced as an exploitation film, this major-studio picture was acquired by Dwain Esper in the mid-1940s and roadshown as if it were. Esper added the long title scroll at the beginning of the film (which remains on circulating prints and videos today) and often sold the film from a sexually suggestive angle. The film was often toured with sideshow performers in attendance, so the freak show extended from the screen into the auditorium, lobby and theatrefront, which Esper blanketed with sawdust for a suitably circus-like atmosphere.

GAMBLING WITH SOULS
1936   Jay Dee Kay Productions   B&W
Producer: J.D. Kendis, Supervisor: Louis Mosher, Director: Elmer Clifton, Story: J.D. Kendis, Cinematography: James R. Diamond, Editor: Carl Turner, Sound: Clifford Ruberg.
With Martha Chapin, Wheeler Oakman, Bryant Washburn, Gay Sheridan.

Plot synopsis: Accused of killing gambler "Lucky" Wilder, Mae recounts in court how she came to be involved in the gambling and prostitution rackets.

GIRL GANG
1950   Screen Classics   B&W
Producer: George Weiss, Director: Robert C. Derteno.
With Timothy Farrell, Joanne Arnold, Harry Keatan.

Synopsis: In this borderline film that illustrates the transition from traditional exploitation film to '50s juvenile delinquency thriller, a group of drug-fueled girls (supervised by Farrell and Arnold) terrorize the suburbs of Los Angeles. Features relatively explicit scenes of drug use.

GLEN OR GLENDA? (aka I CHANGED MY SEX, I LED TWO LIVES, GLENN OR GLENDA?)
1953   Screen Classics   B&W
Producer: George Weiss, Director & Screenplay: Edward D. Wood, Jr., Cinematography: William C. Thompson, Sound: Ben Winkler, Musical Director:

205

Sanford H. Dickinson, Med. Advisor: Dr. Nathan Bailey.
With Bela Lugosi, Daniel Davis (Wood), Dolores Fuller, Lyle Talbot, Timothy Farrell.

Plot synopsis: This semi-documentary analysis of transvestitism uses surreal imagery and incoherent commentary by Bela Lugosi to explore cross-dressing and sex-changes, focusing primarily on one man, Glen, who is having difficulty confessing his dark secret to his new bride.

GOW
1933   States Rights   B&W
Producer: Captain E.A. Salisbury, Narrator: William Peck.

Plot synopsis: The exploitable elements of this anthropological documentary of life in the South Seas include a scene in which women are bartered for pigs, a cannibal dance ceremony and the display of human skulls taken as trophies by the tribal chieftain Gow.

GUILTY PARENTS
1934   Jay Dee Kay Pictures   B&W
Producer: J.D. Kendis, Supervisor: Nat H. Spitzer, Director & Screenplay: Jack Townley, Cinematography: Robert Doran, Editor: Ethel Davey.
With John St. Polis, Jean Lacy, Gertrude Astor, Robert Frazer, Elen Aristi, Lynton Brent, Donald Keith.

Plot synopsis: A lack of sex education leads high school girl Helen into a drinking party, pregnancy, robbery, prostitution and suicide, while her friend Betty experiences alcohol, abortion and a death of her own.

HIGH SCHOOL GIRL
1934 Foy Productions   B&W
Director: Crane Wilbur, Producer: Bryan Foy, Screenplay: Wallace Thurman.
With Helen MacKellar, Mahlon Hamilton, Cecelia Parker, Carlyle Moore Jr., Noel Warwick, Treva Scott, Crane Wilbur, Mildred Gover.

Variety: "*High School Girl* is a tiresome preachment on the facts of life and parental neglect. The kids, at whom it is aimed, may snicker at it... Story picks out a young boy and girl who are forced to sneak their dates, parties, etc. The inevitable occurs, the girl's folks too late realizing their neglect. A biologist who blasts himself out of a school job because he dared to start wising up his young flock, figures as the trail-breaker for modern enlightenment. In order that a happy finish be provided he is reinstated. The boy offers a marriage promise as soon as the girl is out of the hospital for another finishing touch." (March 20, 1935)

HIGHWAY HELL (aka HONKY TONK GIRL, GOING MY WAY, MR.?, HITCHHIKE TO HELL)
1937 B&W
Exec Producer: William L. O'Hearn, Director: Patrick Carlyle, Screenplay: Gil Patrick, Cinematography: J. Rey Palmer, Editor: Holbrook N. Todd, Sound: Benjamin Winkler and Arthur B. Smith.
With Charles Maurice, Diane Winthrop, Don Hirsch, Julian Harris.

Plot synopsis: An old tavern owner with a young son, Bob, watches the workings of a local ring of prostitutes who ply their trade to passing motorists. His son, rejecting a nice local girl, Barbara, becomes involved with one of the prostitutes. The girls' pimp blackmails Barbara with nude pictures he has taken after spiking her drink. The ring is broken up and the prostitutes go home.

HITLER'S STRANGE LOVE LIFE (aka CONFORM OR DIE, THE LOVE LIFE OF ADOLF HITLER)
ca. 1948 B&W
Producer: Dwain Esper.

Synopsis: Composed of seized Nazi footage and material shot by the U.S. Army Signal Corps, this feature explores (in graphic detail) the war crimes of Hitler, Mussolini and (in a revised version) Stalin. At the time of his death, Esper was again revising the film (which had already assumed many different forms) under the title *Day of the Despot*.

HOLLYWOOD BURLESQUE
1949   Continental Pictures, Inc.   B&W
Producer: J.D. Kendis, Director: Duke Goldstone, Associate Producer: James R. Palmer, Cinematography: Len Powers, Costumes: Ann Henry, Music: Howard G. Mathis.
With Joy Damon, Honey Hayes, Bobby Roberts, Marie Duran, Dyann Torry, Hilary Dawn, Jenne, Mary King, Robert Ross, Legrand Torry, Charles Vaughn, Eddie Ware.

Synopsis: One of the mavericks of exploitation, J.D. Kendis, began the transition to nudie movies with this fairly tame burlesque feature (a full five years before Irving Klaw produced the better-known *Varietease* and *Teaserama*).

HOW TO UNDRESS (aka HOW TO UNDRESS IN FRONT OF YOUR HUSBAND)
1937 Hollywood Producers and Distributors B&W (short)
Director: Dwain Esper, Story and Adaptation: Hildagarde Stadie (Esper), Cinematography: Roland Price, Sound: Herb Eicke, Narrator: Albert Van Antwerp.
With Elaine Barrie Barrymore, Trixie Friganza, Hal Richardson.

Synopsis: After a brief introduction discussing the modern plague of voyeurism, a lesson is given on how to and how not to undress before bed. Elaine Barrie Barrymore provides the favorable example, while former burlesque star Trixie Friganza demonstrates the improper approach.

THE LASH OF THE PENITENTES
1936 Harry Revier Productions B&W
Presented by: Parke J. Levinson, Producer: Harry Revier, Director & Screenplay: Zelma Carroll, Story & Cinematography: Roland C. Price, Music Supervisor: Lee Zahler.
With Marie DeForest, William Marcos, Victor Justi, Joseph Swickard.

Plot synopsis: A newspaper reporter, George Mack, travels to New Mexico to investigate tales of a religious cult called The Penitente Brotherhood, which practices flagellation and crucifixion. Mack becomes involved with a village girl, who is branded a witch and stripped and whipped. The Penitentes command Mack's houseboy, Chico, to shoot the writer. He is later captured and persuaded to confess.

THE LAWTON STORY (aka THE PRINCE OF PEACE)
1949 Hallmark Productions 101 min. Cinecolor
Producer: Kroger Babb, J.S. Jossey and Neil E. Bogan, Director: William Beaudine and Harold Daniels, Screenplay: Scott Darling, Treatment: Milton Raison, Story: Mildred A. Horn, Original Pageant Story: Rev. A. Mark Wallock, Narrator: DeVallon Scott, Cinematography: Henry Sharp, Editor: Dick Currier, Special Songs: Lee "Lasses" White, Steven Edwards and Andy Page, Vachel Lindsey.
With Ginger Prince, Forrest Taylor, Millard Coody, Ferris Taylor, Maude Eburne, Gwyn Shipman, Darlene Bridges, Willa Pearl Curtis, Ray Largay, W.A.S. Fisher, Hazel Lee Becker, Lee "Lasses" White.

Variety: "The annual 'Prince of Peace' Easter pageant, at Lawton, Okla., has been put on film by Hallmark Productions for theatre distribution. It would have been a finer picture had not producers seen fit to drag in a crass, commercial showcasing of a precocious moppet, apparently in an attempt to strike a broader popular market.

"Film serves as an introduction for Ginger Prince, six-year-old and around her precociousness has been fashioned a banal yarn, full of hokum and schmaltz, that permits the youngster to display her ability to read lines, act cute and sing. Her debut would have been more effective if she had not been called upon to carry the entire story load in this fictional framework. The expected results from the hokum are achieved by William Beaudine's direction." (April 6, 1949)

MAD YOUTH
1939 Real Life Dramas B&W
Pres and Story: Willis Kent, Director: Melville Shyer, Assistant Director: Charles Wasserman, Cinematography: Marcel Le Picard and Harvey Gould, Editor: Robert Jahns, Sound: Carson Jowett.
With Mary Ainslee, Betty Compson, Willy Castello, Betty Atkinson, Tommy Wonder.

Plot synopsis: A mother, Mrs. Morgan, and her young daughter, Marian, are both engaged in a fast-paced lifestyle, the mother hiring paid gigolos for her upper-class functions, and the daughter having strip-poker and drinking parties for her friends. Marian begins a relationship with a sophisticated European escort, Count De Koven, hired by her mother. One of Marian's friends, Helen, is discovered staying out all night and decides to run away to another town where she has been corresponding with a suitor through a mail-order matchmaking service. When Mrs. Morgan discovers her daughter's affair with the Count, Marian decides to spend some time away from her mother with Helen. But upon arrival in the new town, Marian discovers that the matchmaking ad is a front for a white slavery brothel, where Helen is being kept prisoner. The Count and Mrs. Morgan find the girl's address and the Count goes to the brothel where he rescues Helen and Marian.

MANIAC (aka SEX MANIAC)
1934   Hollywood Producers and Distributors   B&W
Producer: Louis Sonney. Director: Dwain Esper, Screenplay: Hildagarde Stadie, Assistant Director: J. Stuart Blackton, Jr., Cinematography: William Thompson, Editor: William Austin.
With Bill Woods, Horace Carpenter, Ted Edwards, Phyllis Diller, Theo Ramsey, Jenny Dark, Marvel Andre, Celia McCann, J.P. Wade, Marion Blackton. Incorporates footage from the Italian film *Maciste in Hell*.

Plot synopsis: This schizophrenic mad scientist film incorporating elements of Edgar Allan Poe's "Murders in the Rue Morgue" and "The Black Cat" concerns a scientist who reanimates corpses, and whose identity is then assumed by his assistant, Maxwell.

MARCH OF CRIME, THE
1937   Roadshow Attractions Co.   B&W
Producer: Louis Sonney, Director: Dwain Esper. Written and Narrated by Wedgwood Nowell.

Synopsis: Originally released as a feature, later re-edited as a pair of short films, this cornucopia of crime is cobbled together from old newsreel footage, still photos and reenactments.

MARIHUANA: WEED WITH ROOTS IN HELL
1936   Roadshow Attractions Co.   B&W
Director: Dwain Esper, Story: Hildagarde Stadie (Esper), Continuity: Rex Elgin, Cinematography: Roland Price, Editor: Carl Himm, Dialogue Director: Alexander Leftwich.
With Harley Wood (Burma Roberts), Patrick Carlyle (Tony Santello), Hugh McArthur, Paul Ellis, Dorothy Dehn, Richard Erskine, Juanita Crosland, Hal Taggart, Gloria Brown.

Plot synopsis: A crowd of high school kids involved in late-night drinking and roadhouse hopping hook up with a pair of older sophisticates who introduce the gang to marihuana at a house party where one girl drowns and the central character, Burma, becomes pregnant while under the effects of marihuana. Burma's boyfriend takes a job drug trafficking with the men to support his expecting girlfriend but dies in a gunfight with police. Burma gives her child up for adoption at the urging of the two men and becomes their drug dealer, and a drug addict herself. She devises a plan to kidnap her sister's child (Burma harbors an intense jealousy of her sister, who has married well and caused her mother to neglect Burma) and hold her for ransom but is ultimately caught, along with the two men, by police, and dies of a drug overdose.

MATED: An Illustrated Lecture on Film (aka MIS-MATED)
1951   Federated Film Productions   B&W
Writer, Supervisor, Cinematographer and Editor: Gordon Schindler. Sound: Glen Glenn. Medical Consultant: John R. Peters, M.D.

Synopsis: This documentary-style film is non-narrative, with a voice-over narrator explaining sex roles, philosophy, biology, accompanied by stock footage of nudes in illustrations, medical footage and film.

MODERN MOTHERHOOD
1934   Hollywood Producers and Distributors   B&W
Producer: Louis Sonney, Director: Dwain Esper, Screenplay: Gardner Bradford.

Plot synopsis: A fast-living couple decides theirs is a modern marriage, where children have no place. That is, until Molly discovers she is pregnant and has a change of heart. Film is distinguished by an actual face-lift operation and a V.D. film-within-a-film called *Sins of Love*, which helps Molly decide to take a more traditional marital route.

MOM AND DAD
1944   Hygienic Productions   B&W
Producer: J.S. Jossey and Kroger Babb, Under Personal Supervision of Barney A. Sarecky, Director: William Beaudine, Screenplay: Mildred A. Horn, Cinematography: Marcel Le Picard, Music Director: Eddie Kay, Editor: Lloyd Friedgen, Assistant Director: Arthur Hamburger, Special Effects: Ray Mercer, Makeup: Ted Edlin, Executive Assistant: Betty Sinclair.
With Hardie Albright, June Carlson, Lois Austin, George Eldredge, Jimmy Clark, Bob Lowell, Wheeler Oakman, Francis Ford, Jimmy Zanes, Jane Isbell, Virginia Vane, Willa Pearl Curtis, Forrest Taylor, John Hamilton, Jack Roper, Betty Sinclair, Kay Renard, Lucille Vance, The Liphams.

Plot synopsis: Without proper sex education in the schools or at home, an innocent young girl whose mother is indicted for failing to educate her daughter, becomes pregnant. Her boyfriend dies in a tragic accident, leaving her alone and forced to tell her parents. In a parallel storyline, a popular high school teacher crusades for sex education being taught in the schools and is fired for his outspoken views. Midpoint in the film, medical footage of venereal disease and childbirth is used to illustrate the need for sex education for young people. Meanwhile, the girl is sent away to have the child and returns home.

THE NAKED TRUTH (aka T.N.T.)
1924 Public Welfare Pictures B&W
Producer: Samuel Cummins, Screenplay: George D. Walters.
With Jack Mulhall, Helene Chadwick, Leo Pierson, Charles Spere, Irene Davis, Emmett King.

Synopsis: The importance of sexual education is illustrated as three young men encounter adulthood head on. The educated one adjusts normally, while another contracts a disease and is victimized by a quack doctor, and the third ignores the disease and becomes a homicidal maniac.

NARCOTIC (aka NARCOTIC RACKET)
1933 Hollywood Producers and Distributors B&W
As Interpreted by Dwain Esper, Producer: Hildagarde Esper, Director: Vival Sodar't, Story: A.J. Karnopp, Prod Manager: Bob Farfan.
With Harry Cording, Joan Dix, Patricia Farley, Jean Lacey, J. Stuart Blackton, Jr., Paul Panzer, Miami Alvarez. Charles Bennett.

Plot synopsis: A promising medical student becomes addicted to drugs and spirals on a downward path to degeneracy that ends in suicide.

NATION AFLAME
1937 Treasure Pictures Corp.
Producer: Edward Halperin, Director: Victor Halperin, Screenplay: Oliver Drake and Rex Hale, Story: Thomas Dixon in collaboration with Oliver Drake, Additional Dialogue: William Lively, Assistant Director: Paul Hughes, Cinematography: Arthur Martinelli, Editor: Holbrook Todd, Sound: J.S. Westmoreland, Musical Director: Edward Kilenyi.
With Noel Madison, Norma Trelvar, Lila Lee, Snub Pollard, Douglas Walton, Lee Shumway, Roger Williams.

The New York Times: "It's another expose of the Black Legion, this time calling them the Avenging Angels. Also attempts to bring in the organization as a strike power and a political machine on a national scale similar to the Klux days." (April 7, 1937)

NO GREATER SIN
1941 University Film Productions B&W
Director: William Nigh, Story: Mary Ransone, Screenplay: Michel Jacoby, Production Manager: Melville Shyer, Cinematography: Harry Neumann, Editor: Robert Golden, Sound: Karl Zint, Art Director: Frank Sylos, Music Director: Eddie Kay, Medical Consultant: H.M. Elliott, M.D.
With Leon Ames, Luana Walters, Adele Pearce, George Taggart, Guy Usher, Bodil Rosing, John Gallaudet.

Plot synopsis: The Owl's Nest roadhouse operates as a front for prostitutes who are infecting local soldiers with venereal disease. A crusading health commissioner and newspaperwoman team up to expose the health hazards but not before the reporter's sister is infected.

ONE TOO MANY: THE IMPORTANT STORY OF ALCOHOLISM
1951 Hallmark B&W
Producer: Kroger Babb, Director: Erle C. Kenton, Assistant Director: Mack V. Wright, Assoc. Producer: William Stephens, Story: Kroger Babb, Treatment: Mildred A. Horne, Screenplay: Malcolm Stuart Boylan, Cinematography: Carl Berger, Editor: Edward Mann, Sound: John Carter, Music Supervisor: David Chudnow, Makeup Supervisor: Ern Westmore, Sets: Martin Obzina. Technical Advisors: Margaret ("Bobbe") Burger, Dr. David L. Olinger.
With Ruth Warrick, Richard Travis, Ginger Prince, William Tracy, Rhys Williams, Thurston Hall, Onslow Stevens, Mary Young, Larry J. Blake, "The Harmonaires."

Plot synopsis: A friendly and knowledgeable bartender helps the members of a small community learn about the dangers of alcoholism and delivers a series of lectures encouraging involvement in Alcoholics Anonymous.

THE PACE THAT KILLS
1928   True-Life Photoplays   B&W
Presented by: Willis Kent, Director: Norton S. Parker and William A. O'Connor, Titles: Ruth Todd, Cinematography: Ernest Laszlo, Editor: Edith Wakeling.
With Owen Gorin, Thelma Daniels, Florence Turner, Florence Dudley, Harry Todd, Arnold Dallas, Virginia Roye.

THE PACE THAT KILLS (aka COCAINE FIENDS, COCAINE MADNESS)
1936   Willis Kent Productions   B&W
President: Willis Kent, Director: William A. O'Connor, Assistant Director: Louis Gemomprez, Cinematography: Jack Greenhalgh, Editor: Holbrook N. Todd, Sound: T.T. Triplett.
With Lois January, Noel Madison, Sheila Manners, Dean Benton.

Plot synopsis: A naïve country girl, Jane, hooks up with a cocaine dealer and mobster and follows him to the city where she becomes a drug addict and prostitute. Her brother also goes to the city to find her and becomes a cocaine addict whose drug habit is supported by his prostitute girlfriend who eventually commits suicide. A beautiful girl from a rich family, Dorothy, is dissatisfied with her slow-paced life and seeks excitement at seedy clubs. She is abducted at one such club by white slavers but ultimately saved when Jane calls the police, who find Dorothy's father, revealed to have been an underworld figure, about to meet the "new girl," Dorothy. Ends with Dorothy and boyfriend, an undercover narc, about to begin life together.

POLYGAMY (aka ILLEGAL WIVES)
1937 Continental Pictures Inc.   B&W
Director: Patrick Carlyle, Based on the Novel *I Am a Polygamist* by Peter Salia, Cinematography: Irving Akers, Editor: Earl Turner, Sound: John Eilers, Musical Director: Lew Porter.
With Charles Maurice, Ann Marien, Bruce Wyndham, Slim Simms, Robert Stevenson.
Also released by Unusual Pictures, Ted Toddy, President. Later acquired by Jay Dee Kay (George C. Kendis, Cleveland, Ohio).

Reviewed by the PCA September 15, 1936: "This purports to be a true story of a group who practiced polygamy at Short Creek, Arizona."

PROBATION
1937   Chesterfield   B&W
President: George C. Batcheller, Director: Richard Thorpe, Screenplay: Edward T. Lowe, Assistant Director: Melville Shyer, Cinematography: M.A. Anderson, Editor: Vera Wade.
With Sally Blane, John Darrow, J. Farrell MacDonald, Clara Kimball Young, Betty Grable.

Plot synopsis: Allen is two-timing fiancee Janet with an underage sweetie, Ruth. Ruth's protective older brother Nick savagely beats Allen after discovering their liaison. Janet's uncle, Judge Holman, hires Nick as Janet's chauffeur to save him from jail for beating Allen. Nick looks past his dislike for Janet's upper-crust lifestyle and falls in love with his employer.

RACE SUICIDE (aka VICTIMS OF PASSION, WHAT PRICE, PASSION?)
1937   Real Life Dramas   B&W
Producer: Willis Kent, Director: S. Roy Luby, Assistant Director: Charles Wasserman, Cinematography: Marcel LePicard and Harvey Gould, Editor: Robert Jahn, Music: Milton Royce, Sound: Hans Weeren.
With Willy Castello, Lona Andre, Erma Deen, Carleton Young.

Plot synopsis: Concerns an illegal abortion practice run by Von Hersten and a secretary who dies at its hands before a crusading district attorney's assistant goes undercover to smash the ring. The subject, abortion, is only implied and never spoken of directly in the film.

RECKLESS DECISION (aka SUSPICIOUS MOTHERS, PROTECT YOUR DAUGHTER)
1933   High-Art Pictures Corp.   B&W
Adapted by John Noble from *Protect Your Daughter*. Cinematography: Frank Zukor, Music & Effects: Eugene Roder.
With Doris Eaton, Adele Riggs, Donald Thompson.

Plot synopsis: A mother worries that her daughter is running wild and one night learns she is spending the night with her boyfriend at a strange farmhouse after their car breaks down. This same night, a visitor to the family's home tells the girl's mother and father a tragic tale of her own reckless youth and how her strict minister father's rigid upbringing caused her to lash out in promiscuity and drinking, a fate she warns the mother not to repeat with her own daughter. The story within a story flashback ends with the father and daughter's reconciliation and the daughter (in the bracketing story) marrying her boyfriend.

REEFER MADNESS (aka TELL YOUR CHILDREN, THE BURNING QUESTION)
1936   G&H Productions   B&W
Producer: George A. Hirliman, Director: Louis Gasnier, Screenplay: Arthur Hoerl, from a story by Lawrence Meade, Additional Dialogue: Paul Franklin, Cinematography: Jack Greenhalgh, Assistant Director: Ray Nazarro, Assoc Producer: Sam Diege, Editor: Carl Pierson, Sound: Hans Weeren, Musical Director: Abe Meyer.
With Dorothy Short, Kenneth Craig, Lillian Miles, Dave O'Brien, Thelma White.

Plot synopsis: A group of naïve high school students becomes involved with older dope peddlers, who operate out of Mae Coleman's apartment. Mary's brother, Jimmy, kills a pedestrian while driving under the influence of reefer. Meanwhile, Mary's boyfriend Bill is seduced by a reefer moll, Blanche. Looking for her brother at Mae's, Mary is sexually assaulted by hophead Ralph. Ralph and Bill struggle and Mary is killed. During Bill's trial, the crazed Ralph murders Mae's right-hand man, Jack, leading to the arrest of Ralph, Mae and Blanche. Bill is eventually cleared of responsibility for Mary's death. Blanche commits suicide at the courthouse by leaping from a window and Ralph is placed in an institution for the criminally insane.

THE ROAD TO RUIN
1928   True Life Photoplays   B&W
Presented by Willis Kent, Producer: Cliff Broughton, Director: Norton S. Parker, Assistant Director: David Hampton, Cinematography: Henry Cronjager, Editor: Edith Wakeling.
With Helen Foster, Virginia Roye, Grant Withers, Tom Carr, Don Rader, Florence Tucker, Charles Miller.

THE ROAD TO RUIN
1934   True Life Photoplays   B&W
Producer: Willis Kent, Director: Mrs. Wallace Reid and Melville Shyer, Story: Mrs. Wallace Reid, Assistant. Director: George Curtner, Cinematography: James Diamond, Editor: S. Roy Luby, Sound: Homer Ackerman.
With Helen Foster, Nell O'Day, Glen Boles, Bobby Quirk.

Plot synopsis: Two young girls, Anne and Eve, make out, drink and dance with their boyfriends and eventually meet two older sophisticates at a nightclub, who lead them even further down the road to ruin. Anne is arrested, along with Eve, at a skinny-dipping party and is taken to juvenile girls' court, where both are declared "sexual delinquents" and Eve is tested positive for syphilis. When they are released, Anne learns she is pregnant, is given an abortion by her older lover's friend, and dies from infection.

SCARLET FLOWER, THE (aka MAN'S WAY WITH WOMEN)
1938   (Swedish film originally titled "Sangen om den Eldroda Blomman")

Letter from Dr. Irwin Esmond, Director, State of New York Education Dept. to Dr. James Wingate, April 29, 1938
"*The Scarlet Flower* is the story of the love life of an oversexed man who was said to have inherited his propensities from his father. The father is first shown in the picture (while the boy is yet a baby) sleeping with a servant girl and when this affair is interfered with by the wife, he throws a hatchet at her. When the boy grows to manhood he becomes interested in various women. With one he is shown swimming in the nude. On separate occasions he is shown sleeping with others. These are definitely portrayed as innocent young girls whom he has seduced. One of them commits suicide when the young man finally marries. All is forgiven by the wife of his choice and they are supposed to live happily ever after. I cannot think this is a decent story to put on the screen. While the picture has been cut somewhat, it is not materially different from the picture the Commissioner of Education reviewed on appeal and turned down in the Swedish version two years ago."

SECRETS OF A MODEL
1940   Continental Pictures, Inc.   B&W
Producer: J.D. Kendis, Director: Sam Newfield. Screenplay: Sherman Lowe and Arthur St. Clare, Cinematography: Jack Greenhalgh, Editor: George Merrick, Sound: Hans Weeren.
With Sharon Lee, Harold Daniels, Julian Madison, Phyllis Barry.

Motion Picture Herald: "The story of *Secrets of a Model* is a familiar theme, that of a small town girl who goes to Hollywood to seek a career but becomes in[volved in] sordid complications. It is a slow-moving production... The girl detours from the narrow path to get money for a sick mother back home. A man with 'influence' gets her a job modeling for his artist friend. At a party he gets her intoxicated and she awakens the next morning alone... The afternoon audience was not enthusiastic over the pace or the plot." (April 27, 1940)

SECRETS OF BEAUTY (aka THE MARRIAGE BED, WHY MEN LEAVE HOME, REDHEADS AND BLONDES, MAN AND WIFE)
1951 Hallmark Productions Color
Producer: Kroger Babb, Director: Erle C. Kenton. With Julie Bishop, Richard Denning, Ginger Prince, Myrna Dell, Larry J. Blake, Ern Westmore, Arthur Lee Simpkins.

Plot synopsis: In this flimsy film designed to sell deluxe packages of makeup, a woman discovers that her appearance is the key to saving her marriage.

THE SEVENTH COMMANDMENT
1932   Hollywood Producers and Distributors B&W
Producer: Dwain Esper, Director: James P. Hogan. With Stuart James, Victoria Vinton.

Plot synopsis: A country boy travels to the city where he falls in with a crowd of ne'er-do-wells, including some who dress in drag and participate in orgies. The young man decides to return to the simple hometown life and marry his sweetheart whom he unfortunately infects with the syphilis he contracted in the big city. After childbirth, their baby dies of the disease, but the boy eventually finds medical salvation.

SEX MADNESS (aka HUMAN WRECKAGE: THEY MUST BE TOLD)
1938 Cinema Service Corp. B&W
Screenplay: Joseph Seiden and Vincent Valentini. With Vivian McGill, Rose Tapley, Al Rigeli, Stanley Barton, Linda Lee Hill.

Plot synopsis: The various vices of city life—wild parties, burlesque revues—are examined through one small-town girl's fall from grace. She is a chorus girl seduced by a show-biz producer who contracts syphilis. A doctor, using medical footage, illustrates to the girl the dangers of the disease if left untreated and advises her to seek proper medical care. The girl returns to her small-town home, where she delays marrying her longtime sweetheart in order to be cured of the disease. But a quack gives her a fake cure and she eventually infects her new husband and their baby. A parallel storyline tells of a crusading venereal disease doctor's son who has also contracted syphilis in the city and comes out to a conference of medical experts about his mistake. In a last-minute rescue, the syphilitic showgirl receives a call from a fellow chorine who has also had syphilis and been cured which persuades her not to commit suicide and to get herself and her husband a real cure.

SINISTER MENACE (aka THE NARCOTIC STORY, DOPE DENS OF THE ORIENT)
1948   Dwain Esper Productions   B&W (short)

Synopsis: This dry documentary short examines the Mid-East drug trade, and consists of footage presented by Harry Anslinger.

SINNER-AMA CUTIES
1954 Screen Classics Productions B&W
Director, Screenplay & Editor: Lawrence Raimond, Executive Secretary: Elinor Stocks; Executive Producer: Allen F. Stewart.
With George Eiferman and an otherwise anonymous cast. Narrated by Carl Princi.

Synopsis: This short film, made by the producers of *Glen or Glenda*. *The Devil's Sleep* and *Test Tube Babies* is a non-narrative exploration of the human form and hints at the naughty nudity that would soon take over the screen in sexploitation.

SINS OF LOVE
Produced in Mexico (Originally titled PECADOS DE AMOR) B&W
Director: David Kirkland.
With Beatriz Ramos, Angel T. Sola, Joaquin Coss, J.L. Jiminez, Matilde Carell, Luis C. Bareiro.

"This melodramatic account of the troubles of a fairly attractive stenographer, whose employer, a bank manager, is much less villainous in his conduct toward the girl he has betrayed than the usual run of such characters, is reminiscent of a type of motion picture pretty well passé north of the Rio

Grande... The photography and sound reproduction leave much to be desired." (*The New York Times*, April 24, 1934)

SLAVES IN BONDAGE
1937   Jay Dee Kay Productions   B&W
Producer: J.D. Kendis, Director: Elmer Clifton, Assistant Director: Mell DeLay, Screenplay: Robert A. Dillon, Cinematography: Eddie Linden, Editor: Earl Turner, Sound: Corson Jowett.
With Lona Andre, Donald Reed, Wheeler Oakman, Florence Dudley, John Merton, Louise Small.

Plot synopsis: Mary Lou is a manicurist who discovers her workplace is a front used to channel pretty young girls to the Berrywood roadhouse, a house of prostitution. With the help of an ambitious newspaperman and boyfriend, Mary Lou exposes the prostitution ring.

SMASHING THE VICE TRUST (aka CONFESSIONS OF A VICE BARON)
1937   Real Life Dramas   B&W
Producer: Willis Kent. Director: John Melville, Assistant Director: Lionel Backus, Screenplay: Marion Candler, Cinematography: Robert Cline, Editor: Fred Bain, Sound: Carson Jowett.
With Willy Castello, Vyola Vonn, Augusta Anderson, John Belmont.

Plot synopsis: Gangster "Lucky" Lombardo is the head of a ring of thugs who kidnap young girls to staff his bordellos. Lois is one of the naïve girls lured to the city with an offer to work in a beauty shop. "Lucky" takes a shine to Lois but she falls in love with an honorable young doctor. "Lucky" is enraged by the news of their marriage and attempts to rape Lois but the police arrive just in time to arrest "Lucky" and release his brothel full of sex slaves.

SOULS IN PAWN
1940   Real Life Dramas   B&W
Director: John Melville.
With Ginger Britton, Beatrice Curtis, Richard Beach, Lloyd Ingraham, Symona Boniface, Evelyn Mulhall, Patti Lacey, Sammy White, Donald Kerr, Richard Lee Spitz.

Plot synopsis: "Secretly married to a college student, a young woman discovers that she is pregnant. When her husband offers no support, she enters a crooked maternity home where she delivers her baby. The child is adopted as a publicity stunt by a burlesque queen, but all ends happily when the burlesque queen returns the child to its rightful mother and the young woman returns to her old employer and a happy life." (The American Film Institute Catalog)

THE STORY OF BOB AND SALLY
1948   Social Guidance Enterprises, Inc. B&W
Director: Erle C. Kenton, Producer: J.G. Sanford, Story: Margarite Buell Wilder, Cinematography: Ellis Carter, Editor: Paul Landres.

Plot synopsis: The benevolent Dr. Carey enlightens the troubled teens in a small town through explicit venereal disease films and a birth reel.

STREET CORNER
1950   Jay Dee Kay Productions B&W
Director: Albert H. Kelley, Producer: George McCall, Assoc Producer: William Collins, Screenplay: Edwin Roth, Story: Jack Jungmeyer, Albert H. Kelley, Cinematography: Virgil Miller, Production Design: Frank Dexter, Editor: John Faure, Music: Bernard Katz.
With Joseph Crehan, Marcia Mae Jones, John Treul, Billie Jean Eberhart, Gretl Dupont, Johnny Duncan, Jean Fenwick, Jan Sutton, Jean Andren, Sam Ash, Luella Bickmore, Don Brodie, Eddie Gribbon, Stuart Holmes, Wendell Niles, Milton Ross, Dale Van Sickel.

Plot synopsis: A well-made little melodrama clearly patterned after Kroger Babb's *Mom and Dad*, *Street Corner* observes as a pair of parents ignore the urging of the family doctor to educate their daughter on the subject of sexual hygiene. They do not and she soon finds herself pregnant and... after the sudden death of her boyfriend... alone. She borrows money from a waitress with a similar background and visits an abortionist. Her failing health draws attention to the matter and the abortionist is put on trial. The doctor shakes his head wearily, knowing that other parents and children will make the same mistake.

TEENAGE (aka TEENAGE JUNGLE)
1941   Jay Dee Kay Pictures   B&W
Producer: J.D. Kendis, Director: Dick L'Estrange, Screenplay: Elmer Clifton, Cinematography: Eddie Kull, Assistant Director: Clark Paylow, Editor: Fred

Bain, Sound: Corson Jowett, Supervisor: Edward E. Kaye.
With Herbert Heyes, Wheeler Oakman, Johnny Duncan, Fred Towns.

Plot synopsis: Ex-con Jim Murray finds his son has fallen in with a gang of criminals involved in murder.

TEN NIGHTS IN A BAR ROOM
1931   Roadshow Production, Inc.   B&W
Producer: Willis Kent, Presented by Howard G. Underwood, Director: William O'Connor, Screenplay: Norton S. Parker, Based on the Novel by Timothy Shay Arthur, Cinematography: Verne L. Walker, Assistant Director: A.L. Schaefer, Sound: Ernest W. Rovere.
With William Farnum, Thomas Santschi, Patty Lou Lynd, Robert Frazer, Phyllis Barrington, Rosemary Theby, Thomas Jefferson, Lionel Belmore.

Synopsis: Timothy Shay Arthur's legendary temperance novel is given relatively respectful treatment in this Willis Kent production. The plot follows the influence of alcohol upon the patrons and passersby of the Sickle and Sheaf Hotel in 1910 Cedarville.

TEST TUBE BABIES
1948   Screen Classics   B&W
Producer: George Weiss, Director: W. Merle Connell, Screenplay: Richard S. McMahan, Research: Roy M. Frisen, Technical Director: Dr. A. Maneck.
With Dorothy Dube, William Thomason, Timothy Farrell, John Michael.

Plot synopsis: A newly married couple living the fast life decide they want to escape the drinking/sex scene and start a family but find out they can't have children. A knowledgeable, caring doctor tells them about the miracle of artificial insemination through which they conceive two children.

THEY WEAR NO CLOTHES
1956   Social Service Pictures   B&W   (short)

THIS NUDE WORLD (aka THIS NAKED AGE, THE NUDIST WORLD)
1933   Crown Pictures   B&W
Producer & Director: Michael Mindlin, Story: Jan Gay, Cinematography: William Steiner, George O'Messerly, A.G. Weitzenberg and Andre D'Melier,
Editor: Max Rothstein, Music Supervisor: Irving Talbot, Narrator: Leo Donnelly.

Synopsis: An historical survey of nudism through the ages beginning with the Greeks, moving to modern New York City, documenting the nudist phenomenon.

TOMORROW'S CHILDREN
1934   Foy Productions, Ltd.   B&W
Producer: Bryan Foy, Director: Crane Wilbur, Screenplay: Wallace Thurman and Crane Wilbur, Story: Wallace Thurman, Cinematography: William Thompson.
With Diane Sinclair, Don Douglas, John Preston, Carlyle Moore, Jr., Sterling Holloway, Lewis Gambart, Crane Wilbur.

Plot synopsis: A family of drunks and halfwits, which has spawned several degenerate children, is forcibly sterilized by local health officials. Their one normal child, a daughter, has been supporting the family and taking care of the children, preparing to marry her fiancé, but is targeted for sterilization nevertheless, because she is related to the degenerates. As she lies on the operating table awaiting sterilization, her fiance, a compassionate doctor and a friendly minister rush to save her, discovering from her mother that she is actually adopted. They petition the judge who has ordered the sterilization to spare her and just barely save her before the scalpel descends.

UNASHAMEDITOR: A ROMANCE
1938   Cine-Grand Films, Inc.   B&W
Presented by & Director: Allen Stuart, Story: P.C. Prescott-Richardson, Screenplay: William Lively, Cinematography: George Sergeant, Editor: Holbrook Todd, Music: Frederic Chapin, Sound: Glen Glenn.
With Rae Kidd, Robert Stanley, Lucille Shearer, Emily Todd.

Plot synopsis: Secretary Rae's sickly boss Robert is encouraged by his doctor to convalesce at a nudist camp, Olympic Fields, where the girl is also a member. There, he falls in love with Rae, until his attentions are stolen away by socialite Lucille. Distraught over witnessing the pair making love, Rae throws herself off a cliff.

THE VANISHING GANGSTER
Texas Roadshow Co. B&W

Synopsis: This typical crime documentary focuses on the legendary figures of the Great Depression: Bonnie and Clyde, John Dillinger, "Pretty Boy" Floyd, etc.

THE VIRGIN OF SARAWAK (aka FORBIDDEN ADVENTURE, JUNGLE VIRGIN, INYAAH THE JUNGLE GODDESS)
1938 Ace Productions, Inc. B&W
Director: J.C. "Doc" Cook, Editor: Grace McKee. Narrator: Gayne Whitman.

Plot synopsis: Two explorers in Borneo discover a white goddess among the tribes. She reveals that she was the daughter of a rubber plantation owner. She and her mother were kidnapped, escaped into the jungle, learned to communicate with the animals, and exact a revenge upon the man who kidnapped them.

THE WAGES OF SIN (aka SKID ROW)
1938 Real Life Dramas B&W
Produced by Willis Kent, Director: Herman E. Webber, Assistant Director: Charles Wasserman, Cinematography: Harvey Gould, Editor: Robert Jahns, Sound: Hans Weeren.
With Constance Worth, Willy Costello, Blanche Mehaffey, Clara Kimball Young.

Plot synopsis: Marjorie works in a large laundry to support her family of deadbeats, until girlfriend Florence introduces her to the high life and gangster Tony Kilonis, who in turn introduces her to a career as a hotel call-girl. When Marjorie kills Tony and brothel madame "Fat Pearl," she is brought to trial and the court's decision is left up to exploitation film audiences in an epilogue which reads, "The jury is still out. What will the verdict be? What would YOUR verdict be? $100 in cash prizes will be given for the best answer—contest open to all. Win a prize. Mail your opinion in not over 300 words to Real Life Dramas, 4376 Sunset Drive, Hollywood California."

WHAT PRICE INNOCENCE?
1933 Columbia Pictures B&W
Director: Willard Mack, Story: Willard Mack, Cinematography: Joseph A. Valentine, Editor: Arthur Hilton, Technical Director: W.A. Vogel.
With Willard Mack, Minna Gombell, Jean Parker, Betty Grable, Bryant Washburn, Ben Alexander, Beatrice Banyard, Louise Beavers.

Plot synopsis: A kindly doctor encourages mother Amy to educate her daughter Ruth about the facts of life. But left ignorant, Ruth goes to bed with boyfriend Tommy and becomes pregnant. Abandoned by Tommy and shamed, Ruth drowns herself.

WILD WEED (aka SHE SHOULDA SAID 'NO'!, THE DEVIL'S WEED)
1949 Hallmark Productions B&W
Presented by J.S. Jossey and Kroger Babb, Producer: Richard Kay, Director: Sherman Scott, Story: Arthur Hoerl, Screenplay & Dialogue Director: Richard H. Landau, Cinematography: Jack Greenhalgh, Editor: Richard Currier and Seth Larsen, Art Director: Eugene Lourie, Set Decorator: Joseph Kish, Music: Raoul Kraushaar, Piano Soloist: Rudolph Friml, Jr., Ballet Staged by Alicia Adams, Theremin Effects: Dr. Samuel Hoffman, Sound: William Randall, Makeup: David Newell, Hair: Irene Beshon. Narrated by Knox Manning.
With Alan Baxter, Lyle Talbot, Lila Leeds, Michael Whelan, Mary Ellen Popel, Doug Blackley, David Holt, Don Harvey, David Gorcey, Jack Elam, Dick Cogan.

Plot synopsis: Lila Leeds, the aspiring starlet arrested in a 1948 marijuana bust with Robert Mitchum, stars in this melodrama on the pitfalls of pot.

WONDROUS STORY OF BIRTH (aka NO GREATER SIN: THE WONDERS OF BIRTH)
1963 Alexander Enterprises Color (Short)

YOUTH AFLAME (aka HOODLUM GIRLS)
1941 Jay Dee Kay Pictures B&W
Producer: J.D. Kendis, Director & Screenplay: Elmer Clifton, Story: Helen Kiely, Cinematography: Jack Greenhalgh, Editor: George Merrick, Assistant Director: Mel DeLay, Musical Director: Frank Sanucci.
With Joy Reese, Warren Burr, Kay Morley, Michael Owen, Rod Rogers, Edwin Brian, Julie Duncan, Sheila Roberts, Edward Cassidy, Mary Alden, Duke Johnson.

Plot synopsis: Told in flashback from the hospital bed of a dying teen, the film follows the downward path of two daughters whose widowed father is too busy working to help ready them for womanhood.

ACKNOWLEDGMENTS

Many who experienced the exploitation phenomenon firsthand generously shared their memories of the movement, and a debt of gratitude is owed them: Millicent Esper, David F. Friedman, August Helms, Kit Parker, Shan Sayles, Dan Sonney, Chuck Teitel and Mark Woods, Jr.

For their constructive ideas and reactions, we would also like to thank Tim Lucas, David Pierce, Eric Schaefer and Mike Vraney, as well as the staffs of the Margaret Herrick Library (Academy of Motion Picture Arts and Sciences), the Library of Congress, the Museum of Modern Art, the Performing Arts Library at Lincoln Center (New York Public Library) and the UCLA Film and Television Archives.

Without Gary and Susan Svehla this book would certainly not have been possible. Their confidence and support are evidenced not only in the physical pages before you, but the spirit of the words inhabiting them. Other important supports include Donald Krim and the Kino International family, Matthew Fisher and the designers and programmers at Night Kitchen Media, and Bruce Goldstein and company of Film Forum.

INDEX

Abbott, Bud 26
Affair of Honor, An 45
African Frenzy 164
Ake, Doris 181
Akers, Irving 32
Allan, Dr. Benjamin A. 108
Allen, Frederick Lewis 75
American Gang Busters 160
American Mutoscope and Biograph Co. 44, 45
American Society of Clinical Pathologists 139
American Vitagraph Company 46
America's Most Wanted 197
Ames, Leon *131*
And God Created Woman 193
Andersson, Harriet 192
Andre, Lola 74
Andrus, Rocky and Betty 108
Apres le Bal - le Tub 42
Arbus, Diane 196
Are You Fit to Marry? 51
Aristi, Ellen 37
Arthur, Timothy Shay **44**
Assassin of Youth 20, 36, 64, **98**, 187
Astaire, Fred 11
Automobile Thieves, The 46
Awakening of John Bond, The 48
Babb, Howard Kroger 24, 25, 36, 73, *79*, 79, 83, **107**, 108-115, 118, *126*, 132, 145, 164, 168
Baby Face 37, 86
Bardot, Brigitte 192, 193
Barnum, P.T. 97, 109, 124, 125
Barrias, Louis Ernest 183
Barrie, Elaine 32, 184
Barrow, Clyde 150, 151, **159**-160
Barrow, Mrs. Henry 151
Barrymore, John 32
Beaudine, William **25**-26, 109
Beasts of the Jungle 164
Because of Eve **19**, 20, 33, **94**, 108, 190, **191**
Beheading a Chinese Prisoner 45
Behind the Mask of Innocence 74
Benton, Thomas Hart 75
Bergman, Andrew 84
Beware, My Husband Comes 46
Beyond Bengal 164
Big Knife, The 26
Bigamist, The 46
Billboard 154

Biograph Studios (see American Mutoscope and Biograph Co.) 44-45
Biography 197
Birth Control 49-50
Birth of a Baby, The 64, 92, 142, 143
Birth of a Nation, The 26
"Black Cat, The" 102
Black Cat, The 117, 118
Blackton, J. Stuart 171
Blackton, J. Stuart Jr. 171
Blackton, Marion 171
Blair, Harry 103
Blood Feast 190
Blue Velvet 195
Body Beautiful, The 51
Bogdan, Robert 130, 131, 138
Boheme, La 176
Bo-ru the Ape Boy 13, 144
Boop, Betty 12
Bostwick, Barry 195
Bowanga! Bowanga! 164
Brady, Mathew 196
Breen, Joseph 62-63, 66-67, 79
Brent, Lyndon 37
Bretherton, Howard **94**
Breuer, Marcel 77
Bride and the Beast, The 163
Bride of the Monster 120
Brieux, Eugene 53, 118
Brind, Charles A. 67
Briskin, Irving 62-63
Brookhart, Smith W. 57, 59, 84
Browning, Tod **128**-**129**, 141
Brownlow, Kevin 74
B.S. Moss Motion Picture Corp. 50
Bullets or Ballots 60
Bundy, Ted 150
Burning Question, The (see *Reefer Madness*)
Burns, Stanley B. 77, 197
Burstyn v. Wilson 193
Burton, Tim 195
Cagney, James 60
Camp, Enoch 45
Canadian Social Health Council 62, 118
Cannibal Island 164
Capra, Frank 62
Carlson, June 61
Carlyle, Patrick 31, **32**, 32, 36, **63**, **95**, **104**, 120

Carnegie, Dale 80
Carroll, Zelma 165-166
Castello, Willy **31**
Castle, William 195
Chained for Life **127**
Chang 164
Chaplin, Lita Grey 33
Cherlov, Mrs. 67
Child Bride 23, 32, 33, 39, 40, 63, 127, 132, 175-176, **176**, 177
Child Bride (Columbia) 62
Child Conservation Conference 142
Child Wives 63
Child Robbers 46
Chute, David 190
Citizen Kane 33
Civilisation a travers les ages, La 45
Classic Pictures, Inc. 145
Classical Hollywood Cinema (CHC) 28, 34-35, 37-38
Clifton, Elmer **26**
Cocaine 180
Cocaine Fiends (see *The Pace That Kills*, 1933)
Cocaine Traffic, The 50
Cohn, Harry 118
Cohn, Jack 118
Columbia Pictures 23, **61**-62, 117, 118, 195
Compson, Betty 33
Confessions of a Vice Baron **27**
Conform or Die 168
Congo Pictures, Ltd. 160
Connell, Merle 25
Cooper, Courtney Ryley 89
Cooper, Merian C. 144, 164
Cording, Harry **70**, **185**
Cortez, Stanley 32
Costello, Lou 26
Costiello y Puentes, Jose 157
Couney, Martin Arthur 130
Country Stud Horse, A 173
Craig, Kenneth **18**
Crehan, Joseph **94**
Crime Does Not Pay Show, The 152
Croce, Arlene 75
Cry of the World **155**
Cummins, Samuel 167
Curse of the Ubangi, The 155, 161-162
Cuvier, Georges 139-140

217

Czolgosz, Leon 45
Daily Courier (Alamosa, CO) 94
Damaged Goods 20, 32, 34, 36, 51, 53, 74, 103, 106, 118, 174
Damaged Lives 20, 35, 36, 62, 118, 130, 131, **174**, 178, **179**, 180
Dame aux camelias, La 22
Dancing Darkies 43
Day, Marceline 33
Day of the Despot 117, 168
de Cordoba, Pedro 32
Dead March, The 168
Dealers in Death (gangster documentary) 159-160
Dealers in Death (war documentary) 168
Dean, James 194
Death in Paradise 197
Death Parade, The 167
Death Scenes 197
Delinquent Daughters **28**, *61*
Deliverance 40, 171
Dennis, James M. 77
de Mille, Cecil B. 37
Dermody, Frank M. 67-69, 147
Dern, Laura 195
Detour 118
Devil's Harvest, The 20
Devil's Killer, The 151
Devil's Sleep, The 20, 31, 33, 39, 119
Dieterle, William 118
Dillinger, John 150, 156, 158-**159**, 160
Dillinger, John Wilson 151
Dion, A.F. 160
Dope Dens of the Orient 149
Doris Ake Presenting Her Pearl Harbor Hula 181
Dracula 33, 128
Dudley, Florence 183
Duffy, John 93
Dumas, Alexandre 22
Dunn, Harry 45
Dust to Dust 79
Dye, Nancy Schrom 93
Ed Wood 32
Edison, Thomas (Edison Film Manufacturing Co.) 26, 41, 43, 44-46, 48
Educational Films 23
Edward Hickman, the Fox 150-151, 155
Edwards, Ted **170**
Electrocuting an Elephant 45

Elephant Man, The 195
Ellis, Havelock 174
Elysia 15, 23, 40, 65, 104, 117, 131
End of the Road, The 51
Enlighten Thy Daughter 22, 51, 74, *75*, 84, 106
Escort Girl **36**, 39, 105
Esmond, Irwin 67-69
Esper, Dwain 13, 15, 17, 20, 24, 25, **30**, 35, 36, 67, **70**-72, 82, **90**, 92, *93*, 95, **100**, **102**, 115-**116**, 117, 120, 122-123, 127-**128**, 129, 134, 149, **153**-**154**, 155, 161-162, 163, 167, 168, **169**-172, **184**-**185**
Esper, Dwain Jr. *116*
Esper, Hildagarde 12, 13, 92, 102, 115-116, *116*, 127, 128, 149, 171, 184
Esper, Millicent *116*, 149, 155, 161
Evening Graphic, The 157
E.V.I. Complex 25
Evidence 197
Execution of a Spy 45
Execution of Mary, Queen of Scots 45
Execution of the Spanish Spy 45
Expose of the Nudist Racket, The 146, 155
Extraordinary Films 165
Faces of Death 197
Falling Down 73
False Shame 51, 131
Farrell, Timothy 17, 24, 26, 33
Fate of the Artist's Model 45
Film Boards of Trade 63
First Division 165
Fit to Fight 51
Fit to Win 49, 50, 51, 74
Flaherty, Robert **144**
Flaubert, Gustave 22
Floyd, Charles Arthur "Pretty Boy" 160
Forbes, Elliot **54**, 107-108, 130
Forbidden Adventure 13, 67-**68**, 69, 144, **146**-149, **162**-**163**, 168
Forbidden Desire (see *Damaged Goods*)
Ford, Francis 33
Ford, Henry 120
Ford, John 33, 86, 120
Ford, Wallace **141**

Foster, Helen 54, **91**
Foucault, Michel 80
Found Guilty 155
Fox, Richard K. 45
Fox-Hearst Corporation 151
Foy, Bryan **58**, 65, 104, 117, **138**
Freaks **127**-128, **129**, **137**, *141*-142
Free Ride, A 173
Freeman, J.F. 67, 69
Friedgen, Raymond 63
Friedman, David F. 14, 24, 56, 105, 106, 108, 110, 118, **119**, 151, 152, 154, 173, 190, 191, 193
Friganza, Trixie 33
Gable, Clark 24
Gaieties of Divorce, The 46
Gallaher, Lillian 151
Gambling With Souls 34, **180**
Gardner, Roy 152, 155
Garland, Judy 175-176
General Service Studios 118
Gifford, Denis 168
Gilliam, Terry 73
Glen or Glenda? 32, 33, 119-120, **121**
Glendon, Bobby 56-57
G-Men 60, 158
Goldberg, Jack 168
Golden, Howard "Pappy" 118
Gone With the Wind 9, 110
Good Old Days of Burlesk, The 181
Goodrich, Ward 151
Gordon, Marshall 163
Gosling, F.G. 94
Gow, the Killer 144, 146, 164
Grable, Betty 26
Grand Canyon 73
Grant, Madison 84
Grapes of Wrath, The 39
Grass 144, 164
Grass Sandwich, A 173
Grey, Rudolph 32, 195
Griffith, D.W. (David Wark) 25-**26**, 44, 74
Guilty Parents 34, 37, 39, 91, 101, 179, 180, 187
Halfway to Hell 115, 168
Hall, Scott and Evy 127
Hand That Rocks the Cradle, The 50, 61
Hard Copy 197
Hardcore 73
Hardy, Thomas 22
Harrison, P.S. 52

218

Harrison's Reports 52, 84
Hayes, Curtis **54**, **97**, 108
Hays, Will (Hays Office) **49**, 52, 58, 59-60, 65, 77
Hayward, Susan 194
Helms, August 188
Henry, Portrait of a Serial Killer 159
Here's to Crime 89
Hickman, Edward 150-151
High-Art Pictures Corp. 36
High School Girl **58**
Highway Hell 31, 76, 102, **130**, 132-133, 178-179
Hills Have Eyes, The 40
Hilton, Daisy and Violet **127**-128
History of Human Atrocities, The 45
Hitler, Adolf 151
Hitler's Reign of Terror 167
Hitler's Strange Love Life 117, **167**-168
Holloway, Sterling 32, **139**
Hollywood Burlesque 182
Hollywood Producers and Distributors 24
Hollywood Rat Race 191-192
Honky Tonk Girl (see *Highway Hell*)
Hoodlum Girls 62
Hoover, J. Edgar 67, 150
Hope, Bob 115
Hopped Up (see *The Devil's Sleep*)
Hopper, Dennis 195
Horn, Mildred A. 109, 111, 114
Horrors of War 167
Hottentot Venus 136, 139-140
House of Wax 117
House of Women 117
How to Undress 13, 32, 116, 134-136, 163, 184-185
How to Win Friends and Influence People 80
Hughes, Howard 109
Human Wreckage 74
Hygienic Productions 24, 107
I Want to Live! 194
I Was a Communist for the F.B.I. 117
Illegal Wives (see *Polygamy*)
Immortal Mr. Teas, The 190
Ingagi **65**-**66**, 160-161, 163
Inside of the White Slave Traffic, The **47**
Inside the Walls of Folsom Prison 117

Intercontinent Film Corporation 165
Intolerance **26**
"Introduction to *Forbidden Desire*" 34
Invasion of the Body Snatchers 174-175
Inyaah the Jungle Goddess **164**
Is Your Daughter Safe? 52, 89, 119
Island of Lost Souls 26
It Happened One Night 62
It's a Mad, Mad, Mad, Mad World 26
Jack Miles Studios 25
Jacobs, Lea 87
Jailbait 120
Jaws of the Jungle 164
Jay-Dee-Kay Productions 24
Johnson, H.M. 58
Jossey, J.S. "Jack" 109
Journal of Social History 94
Juggs 185
Karamoja 144, 164
Karloff, Boris **117**
Katzman, Sam 63
Keighley, William 158
Kendis, J.D. **24**, **26**, 62, 129, **172**
Kendrick, Walter 173
Kent, Willis **22**, 24, 25, 26, **31**, 36, **44**, 53, 54, 56, 66, 101, 120, **189**
Kenton, Erle C. 26
Killers All 151, **158**
King Kong 164
King, Rodney 159
Kinnell, Murray 131
Kipling's Women 164
Ku Klux Klan 23
Laemmle, Carl 48
LaGuardia, Fiorello 82
Lang, Fritz 118
Laqueur, Thomas 80, 183
Lash of the Penitentes, The **23**, 40, 164-**165**, 166
Lasky, Art 26
Laszlo, Ernest 26
Latham, Gray, Otway and Woodville 41, 43
Laughton, Charles 32
Lawton Story, The 111-**113**, **114**
Lee, Lila 33
Leeds, Alexander **54**, 108, 130
Leeds, Lila 33
Leg Show 185
Legion of Decency 60, 79, 103, 104, 158

Lemmon, Jack 194
Leopold, Nathan 150
Lesy, Michael 30, 197
Levinson, Mike J. 166
Lewis, Arthur 136-137
Lewis, Herschell Gordon 118, 190
Lights of New York 117
Lincoln Productions 168
Lindbergh, Charles 157
Lindbergh, Charles Jr. 151, 157
Lindsay, Lee 113
Little Annie Rooney **25**
Little Egypt 136
Loeb, Richard 150
Looking at Death 197
Looram, Mrs. James 103
Lord, Daniel A. 59
Loren, Sophia 192
Lorentz, Pare 59
Lucas, Wilfred 162
Lugosi, Bela 33
Lumière, Auguste and Louis 42, 160
Lynch, David 195
Mad Youth 22, 34, 36, **38**-39, 73, 84, 86, 127
Madame Bovary 22
Madame Satan 37
Man With the Golden Arm, The 194
Manhandled 86
Maniac **30**-31, 38, 40, 82, **102**, 121, 152, 155, 169-**170**, 172, 184-185, 190
Mannix, Daniel P. 136
Mapel, Ed 67, 123, 167
March of Crime, The 145, 152-**153**, 155-156, 160
Marden, Leo W. 133
Marihunana: Weed With Roots in Hell **13**, 20, **37**, 39, **88**-89, **90**-91, **95**, 101, 122-123, 149, 155, 180
Married Love **52**, **54**, *108*
Martin, Olga J. 79
Mascot Pictures 23
Mated (aka *Mismated*) 20
Mau Mau 164
McCollum, Warren **83**
McCurdy, Elmer 154-155
McKay, Wanda **94**, **191**
McKinley, William 45, 156
MacLachlen, Kyle 195
McNaughton, John 159
Méliès, Georges **42**, 45
Menendez, Lyle and Eric 157

Merrick, John 141, 181
Metropolitan Motion Picture Co. 151
Meyer, Russ 11, 190
M-G-M (Metro-Goldwyn-Mayer) 27, 52, 57, 61, 128, **137**
Mildred and Bow: The Quality Sisters in Boogie Woogie 181
Miles, Lillian **18**, 87
Miles, Roger T. 108
Millard, S.S. 52, 119
Mills, Shirley 39
Miracle, The 193
Mitchum, John 33
Mitchum, Robert 33, 194
Modern Motherhood 10, 13, 35, 92-**93**, 155
Mom and Dad 9, 10, 20, **25**-26, 38, 39, 49, 57, 61, 64, 74, **79**, 83, 93, 106-**107**, 108, 109, 110-111, 113-115, 125, **143**, 168, 187, 190
Mondor, Card and Donna 127
Monogram Studios 23, **36**
Motherhood: Life's Greatest Miracle 51
Motion Picture Herald 84, 158
Motion Picture Producers and Distributors of America (MPPDA) 52, 58, 59, 67
Motion Picture Theatre Owners of America 53
Moving Picture World 46
MPI Home Video 159
Mullins, Moon 12
Murders in the Rue Morgue 164
Murnau, F.W. 118
Musmanno, Michael 80
Mussolini Speaks 168
Musser, Charles 46
Muybridge, Eadweard 41, 42, 106
Nanook of the North **144**
Narcotic 13, **20**, 35, **39**, **70**-**71**, 72, 84, 93, 127, 149, **169**, 178, **185**
Nation, The 125, 139
Nation Aflame 23
National Board of Review 48, 50
National Enquirer 197
National Organization for the Reform of Marihuana Laws (NORML) 17
National Police Gazette 44- 45
Nature se devoilant devant la science, La 183

Nelson, George "Baby Face" 157-158
New Age, The 73
New Line Cinema 17, 20
New York State Censor Board 31, 63, 67-69, 145, 147, 162-163, 193
New York Times, The 103
Nichols, A.W. 65
Nigh, William 29
Night of the Ghouls 120
Night of the Hunter, The 32
Nightmare of Ecstasy 32, 195
Nizer, Louis 145
No Greater Sin **29**, 76, **80**, **131**, *142*, 178, 187
Noble, John 36
Noguchi, Thomas 155
Nowell, Wedgwood 155-156
Nudists at Play 146
Oakman, Wheeler 33
O'Brien, Dave **18**, 87
O'Connor, Flannery 146
O'Day, Nell **34**
O'Dell, "Digger" 109
One Too Many 26, 33, 113-115, 132
Open Your Eyes 51
Orchids and Ermine 86
Orgy of the Dead 120, **192**
Ormond, June 99, 108
Ouanga 164
Pace That Kills, The (1928) 26, 54, 73, 75, 84, 101, 185
Pace That Kills (1936) (aka *Cocaine Fiends*) 17, 20, 34, 56, 64, 73, 84, 86, 88, 179
Page, Bettie (Betty) 23
Palmer, J. Rey 31
Paramount Studios 57, 61
Paris Slums 46
Parker, Bonnie 150-151, 159-160
Parker, Emma 151
Parker, John **191**
Parker, Marion 150, 156
Paroled from the Big House 62
Payne Fund 83, 87, 89-90
Pearce, Adele **29**
Pettijohn, C.C. 63-64
Phono-Kinema Studios 116
Pickford, Mary 25
Pierce, David 123
Pink Flamingos 194
Pitfalls of Passion, The 52
Plan 9 from Outer Space 120
Please Don't Touch Me 108
Poe, Edgar Allen 102

Police Gazette (see *National Police Gazette*)
"Police Pictures: The Photograph as Evidence" 196
Polygamy 23, **32**, **63**, **104**-105, 132
Pollard, Bud 168
Polyester 195
Popeye 12
Possessed 86
Poverty Row 23, 25, 33
PRC Studios 23, **28**, **36**, 61-62
Preisler, Doris 157
Presley, Elvis 109
Price, Roland 163, 164-165
Prince, Ginger **112**-113, 114
Prince of Peace (see *The Lawton Story*)
Probation 26
Production Code (Production Code Administration, Production Code Authority) 19, 37, 59, 60, 62-**68**, 77-78, 84, 87, 104, 158, 187, 193-194
Progressivism 73-75
Protect Your Daughter 36, 92
Purdon, Roy 162
Quigley, Martin 59, 84, 158
Race Suicide 23, 39, 74, 80, 85, 182-183
Ralph Like's International Studios 25
Ramsay, Terry 158
Ramsey, Theo **170**
Rapture, The 73
Ray, Joyce M. 94
Real Life Productions 24
Reckless Decision 22, 36, 92
Red Cross Seal, The 48
Red-Headed Woman 86
Reefer Madness **16**-17, **18**, 18, 20, 23, 37, 40, 82-**83**, 86-**87**, 134, 140, 178
Reformers, The 74
Reid, Roy 123, 127, 162-163
Reinhardt, Max 117
Republic Studios 23
Rescue 911 197
Revier, Harry J. 63, 165-**166**
Rich, S.H. 58
Ripley, Robert 109
RKO (Radio Keith Orpheum) 17
Road to Ruin, The (1928) 53, *54*, *133*, *168*, 195
Road to Ruin, The (1933) 12, 22, **34**, 36, 39, 53, 64, **76**, 84, 88, **91**-92, **175**, 177, **186**-187

Roadshow Attractions, Inc. 24, 102, 155, 162
Robinson, Edward G. 60
Rockefeller, John D. 48
Rocky Horror Picture Show, The 20, 195-**196**
Roeber, Ernest 45
Rogers, Ginger 11
Rogers, Will 38
Roosevelt, Franklin D. 80
Rose, Conrad F. 160
Ross, Duncan C. 45
Ross, Mary 89
Rossellini, Roberto 193
Rossitto, Angelo 32, 127
Rothafel, S.L. 8
Rule, Albert L. 167-168
"Russell's Penitentiary Portrayal" 151
Sadler, William S. 102
Salisbury, Edward A. 164
Salomé 38, 183
Samurai 82, 167
Sandow, Eugene 43
Sanger, Margaret 49-50, 52, 61
Sante, Luc 197
Sartorius, C.H. 58
Sayles, Shan 17
Scarlet Flower 67
Scarlet Youth 119
Schaller, Michael 82
Schenck, Harry 164
Schoedsack, Ernest B. 144, 164
Screen Classics 24, 119
Secret Museum: Pornography in Modern Culture, The 173
Secrets of a Model 172
Secrets of Beauty, The 113-114
Secrets of Life **51**
Seidenbaum, Art 8
Seminary Girls 44
Sennett, Mack 26
Seven Year Itch, The 43
Seventh Commandment, The **15**, 116, **154**-155
Sex 119
Sex and Buttered Popcorn 105
Sex Madness (aka *They Must Be Told*) 15, 17, 22, 33, 64, 73, 84-**85**, 88, 134, 141, 174
Sex Maniac (see *Maniac*)
Shame of a Nation 168
Shatner, William 197
Shaw, George Bernard 118
She Goes to War 167
She Shoulda Said 'No'! (see *Wild Weed*)

Sherman Anti-Trust Act 193
Showalter, Elaine 183
Shurlock, Geoffrey 66
Simpson, O.J. 157
Sinatra, Frank 194
Sinclair, Diane **138**, **174**
Sinister Urge, The 120
Sinner-ama Cuties 119
Sins of Love 100, 125, **188**
Six-Milliion-Dollar Man, The 155
Slaves in Bondage 22, 34, 74, 84-86, 129, 176-**177**, 183, 186, 195
Smashing the Vice Trust (see *Confessions of a Vice Baron*)
Social Guidance Enterprises, Inc. 97
Solomon, J. 56
Sonney, Dan 55-56, 106, 116, 119, 152, 154-155
Sonney, Edward 55
Sonney, Louis 24, 25, 55, 102, 152-**153**, **154**-155, 160
Sparks, Henry 57
Sparring Contest at Can-astoda 44
Sparrows 25
Special Agent 149
Spicy Detective 176
Spreading Evil, The 51
Sprouls, Joseph 157
Stack, Robert 197
Stalag 17 26
Stalin, Joseph 168
Star Is Born, A 33
Starkwearther, Charles 150
Stavsky, Alexandre 157
Stevenson, Robert Louis 20
Stolen Paradise 166
Story of Birth, The 9, **142**
Story of Bob and Sally, The 20-**21**, 26, 97, 108
Story of Temple Drake, The 37
Street Corner (aka *Main Street Girl*) 24, **56**, **96**, 108
Streets of Forgotten Women 51
Suffer Little Children... 48
Survey, The 89, 152
Suspicious Mothers (see *Reckless Decision*)
Swayne, Daniel 161
Talbot, Lyle 32
Tallis, George 26
Taylor, Carl 165-166
Taylor, M. Sayle **54**, 108
Teenage 34
Teenage Jungle 62

Telepictures 166
Tell Me Why 51
Tell Your Children (see *Reefer Madness*)
Temple, Shirley 112, 175-176
Ten Nights in a Bar-Room (1903) **44**
Ten Nights in a Bar-Room (1931) **44**
Tess of the D'Urbervilles 22
Test Tube Babies 33, 39, 40, 119, 190
Texas Chain Saw Massacre, The 40
Texas Roadshow Co. 159
Thalberg, Irving 27
They Must Be Told (see *Sex Madness*)
They Wear No Clothes 146
This Nude World 145
Thompson, William C. (Bill) 26, 120
Tijuana bibles 12
Time 110
Times Pictures 160
T-Men 117
T.N.T. (The Naked Truth) 51
Toddy, Ted 106, 151, **158**
Tomorrow's Children 23, 32, 36, 64, 74, 80, 84, 117, 131, **138-139**, 142-143, 177
Trade Practice Code 57
Traffic in Souls **47-48**, **60**-61, 74
Traviata, La 176
Tucker, George Loane 48, 61
20th Century-Fox 57, 117
Twin Peaks 195
Twin Peaks: Fire Walk With Me 195
UFA Studios 117-118
Ulmer, Edgar G. 35, 36, **117**-118, 130, **174**, 180
Unashamed 23, 40
United States Public Health Service 49
Universal Studios 48, **60**-61, 117, 157, 168
University Film Productions 29
Unknown Soldier Speaks, The 168
Unmarried Mother, The **49**
Unsolved Mysteries 197
Untamed Mistress 99, 146
van der Rohe, Mies 77
Vanishing Gangster, The 159-160
Variety 50, 56, 59, 119, 142, 160

221

Victims of Passion (see *Race Suicide*)
Victory Pictures 63
Virgin With the Hot Pants, The 183
Vision Pictures, Inc. 145
Vitagraph Company (see American Vitagraph Company)
Wages of Sin, The **22**, *31*, *33*, *34*, **189**
Walters, Luana **29**
War Is a Racket 167
Ware, Betty 181
Warner Bros. 57, 149
Warner, Henry 162
Warrick, Ruth 33
War's End 168
Watermelon Contest 43
Waters, John 11, **194**-195
Weber, Lois 50
Weegee 31, 196
Weinberg, Bill and Ella 108
Weird Tales 176
Weiss, Adrian 163
Weiss, George 24, 119
West, Mae 12
Westmore, Ern 113
What Happened to Tom in the Ladies Gym 181
What Price Innocence? **14**, ***61***-62
When Germany Surrendered 167
Where Are My Children? 50
White, Thelma 17-**18**, **87**
Whitford, Annabelle 43
Why Nudism 146
Wild Oats 51
Wild Weed (She Shoulda Said 'No'!) 20, 33, 64, 80, 115
Wilkes, George 45
Williams, Lyman **174**
Williams, Rhys 132
Windy Corner, A 43
Wingate, James 67
Winnie the Pooh **139**
Winstead, Hubert 161
Wisconsin Death Trip 30, 197
Wise Blood 146
Wizard of Oz, The 175
Wood, Edward D. Jr. 32, 36, 119-**120**, **121**, 163, 191-192, 192
Wood, Grant 75, 76-77
Wood, Harley **37**, **90**, **95**
Woodin, Harry 67-69
Woods, Bill **183**
Woods, Mark 128-129
World in Revolt 167
Worth, Constance **22**, **31**
You Can't Beat the Rap! 152, 155

Young, Carleton **18**, **83**
Young, Clara Kimball 33
Your Show of Shows 115
Youth in Babylon, A 118, 191
Zane, Rita 181
Zimmerman, Charles and Ruth 108

Authors

Bret Wood is the producer/director of two silent film documentaries, *Kingdom of Shadows: The Rise of the Horror Film* and *Lon Chaney: Behind the Mask*, the author of *Marihuana, Motherhood and Madness: Three Screenplays from the Exploitation Cinema of Dwain Esper* and *Orson Welles: A Bio-Bibliography*. Wood's work has appeared in *Film Comment*, *Sight and Sound* and *Video Watchdog*.

Felicia Feaster is a contributing writer for Playboy Online and film critic for the Atlanta alternative weekly *Creative Loafing* whose writing has also appeared in *Film Quarterly*, *Art in America*, *ARTnews*, *Film History* and *The Atlanta Journal-Constitution*.

If you enjoyed this title you may enjoy these other books from
Midnight Marquee Press, Inc.

Midnight Marquee Actors Series
Bela Lugosi $20.00
Boris Karloff $20.00
Lon Chaney, Jr. $20.00
Vincent Price $20.00
Coming October 1999–Peter Lorre

Horror Film Titles
Dracula: The First Hundred Years $20.00
We Belong Dead: Frankenstein on Film $20.00
Guilty Pleasures of the Horror Film $20.00
Son of Guilty Pleasures of the Horror Film $20.00
Cinematic Hauntings $20.00
Drums of Terror: Voodoo in the Cinema by Bryan Senn $20.00
Psychos, Sickos and Sequels: Horror Films of the 1980s by John Stell $20.00
The Rise and Fall of the Horror Film by Dr. David Soren $15.00
Hollywood's Maddest Doctors by Gregory Mank $20.00
Bitches, Bimbos and Virgins: Women of the Horror Film $20.00
Coming in 1999
Forgotten Horrors by George E. Turner and Michael H. Price (May)
Tall, Dark and Gruesome: Christopher Lee (August)
Peter Cushing: An Autobiography (August)
Michael Ripper Unmasked by Derek Pyckett (August)
The Serials of Karloff, Lugosi and Chaney by Leonard Kohl (October)

Other Film Titles
Boris Karloff: A Gentleman's Life
Dwight Frye's Last Laugh by Gregory Mank and Jim Coughlin $20.00
It's Christmas Time at the Movies

For more information about Midnight Marquee titles write
Midnight Marquee Press, Inc.
9721 Britinay Lane
Baltimore, MD 21234
410-665.1198
or visit our website at www.Midmar.com